BUSINESS CYCLES IN YUGOSLAVIA

BRANKO HORVAT

BUSINESS CYCLES IN YUGOSLAVIA

Translated by
Helen M. Kramer

International Arts and Sciences Press, Inc., White Plains, N.Y.

Originally published as *Privredni ciklusi u Jugoslaviji*
by Institut ekonomskih nauka, Belgrade, 1969

Library of Congress Catalog Card Number LC 72-105544

© 1971 by International Arts and Sciences Press, Inc.
901 North Broadway, White Plains, New York 10603

Printed in the United States of America

CONTENTS

Preface to the American Edition   vii

Preface to the Yugoslav Edition   ix

Chapter 1. Fluctuations in Production and the
Quantitative Effects of Those Fluctuations in Yugoslavia   1

Chapter 2. Summary Review of Empirical Research
on Business Cycles in the World   8

Chapter 3. Inherent Instability of the Economy   17

3.1. A Yugoslav Model of Inventory Fluctuations   17
3.2. Cumulative Random Disturbances as a
Source of Cyclical Fluctuations   20
3.3. Autoregression Model, Linear Oscillator,
and Servomechanism as Possible Models   23

Chapter 4. Methodological Foundation for Empirical
Research on Cyclical Fluctuations of the
Yugoslav Economy   30

4.1. Introductory Considerations   30
4.2. Characteristics of the Model Selected   34

Chapter 5. Cyclical Fluctuations of Production and
Investment   43

5.1. Cycles of Industrial Production   43
5.2. Measured Characteristics of Business Cycles   48
5.3. Investment Cycles   61

Chapter 6. Agricultural Cycles and the Influence of
Agriculture   67

Chapter 7. Regional Cycles   73

Chapter 8. Regularities in the Trend of Labor
Productivity   80

Chapter 9. Inventory Cycles   91

9.1. Some Characteristics of Inventory Formation
in the Yugoslav Economy   91
9.2. Cycles of Components of Industrial Inventories   96
9.3. Cycles of Total Industrial Inventories   107

Chapter 10. Monetary-Credit Factors and Prices   119

10.1. Fluctuations in the Aggregate Values of
Industry and the Economy as a Whole   119
10.2. The Volume of Transactions, Money, and
Indebtedness   131
10.3. Price Movements   136

Chapter 11. Cycles of Exports and Imports and the
Influence of International Trade   152

11.1. Introductory Theoretical Considerations   152
11.2. Basic Empirical Findings   155
11.3. Intermediate Goods Imports and Other
Questions   166

Chapter 12. Administrative Cycles and the Influence
of Administrative Interventions   170

12.1. Cycles of Legal Regulation   170
12.2. Institutional Content of Business Cycles   178
12.3. Frequency of Legal Regulations and the
Rate of Economic Growth   187

Chapter 13. International Comparisons   193

Chapter 14. Long Cycles   206

14.1. Correlogram   206
14.2. Periodogram   210
14.3. Autoregression Scheme   215
14.4. Moving Averages   220

Chapter 15. Conclusions: The Mechanism of Movements in the Yugoslav Economy   227

Mathematical Appendix   237

Glossary   242

Tables   243

Graphs   245

Index   247

PREFACE
TO AMERICAN EDITION

It is well known that capitalist or market economies are unstable and that they have been plagued by business cycles. It has
been widely held that socialist or planned economies are stable,
or at least are not subject to cyclical fluctuations. If there are no
business cycles, there is no sense in studying them, which is why
business cycles have not been studied in socialist economies.

If the rate of growth is high, say around 9-10% a year, cyclical
fluctuations, even if they exist, do not matter very much. But
when the rate of growth is retarded, as happened in Yugoslavia
after 1960, instability becomes a serious economic problem.

Research undertaken at the Institute of Economic Studies
showed that there were very strong systematic components in the
fluctuations of the Yugoslav economy. The study of these components led to research on business cycles in a socialist economy.
In a rapidly growing economy like that of Yugoslavia, cycles manifest themselves in systematic changes in the rates of growth.
And the institutional framework — workers' management — is responsible for certain novel features of business cycles not found
elsewhere.

I might add that this is the first comprehensive study of business cycles in a socialist economy.

BRANKO HORVAT

Belgrade, April 1971

PREFACE
TO YUGOSLAV EDITION

The relatively great instability of the Yugoslav economy and
the intensification of instability from 1960 on stimulated the Yugoslav Institute of Economic Studies to undertake an examination of
this phenomenon in its research program. It appeared that in a
certain sense society had begun to lose control over economic
movements, and it was necessary to examine the causes. There
were indications that in our economy, in spite of planning, there
were business cycles, which are considered characteristic only
of capitalist economies. It was necessary to determine whether
this was true and, if cycles did indeed exist, to find out how the
cyclical mechanism functioned. All these questions were obviously of more than academic significance: they were exceptionally
urgent from a practical political point of view. Long-term policy
for stabilization and growth can be scientifically substantiated
and efficient only if it is known beforehand how, in fact, a de-
centralized market economy of the Yugoslav type functions. The
task of this study is to increase our knowledge in that area and
thus to contribute to a solution of the serious and complicated
problems with which our economic policy is today confronted.

The study was begun as early as 1965. After several months
of research, the funds of the Institute were exhausted, and all attempts to interest federal governmental and economic agencies
in the work and in offering financial support were unsuccessful.
This being the case, the initial results of the research were prepared for publication (Ekonomist, 1966, Nos. 1-4; Economic
Science and the National Economy [Ekonomska nauka i narodna

privreda], Zagreb, Naprijed), but further work was interrupted for an indefinite period. At the beginning of 1967, the Economic Chamber of Belgrade became interested in the work of the Institute. An agreement was reached on long-term arrangements for mutual collaboration, within the framework of which the entire investigation of business cycles in Yugoslavia was assured and financed. Thus it became possible to finish this study and present it for the use of our economy and the scientific community.

The interruption of the work and the postponement of its completion have resulted in a certain lack of statistical uniformity in the text. In the majority of cases the latest available data for 1966 or 1967 are included in the tables, graphs, and analyses. However, in a certain number of cases, when it was a question of complicated and expensive calculations whose revision would not only increase the cost of the work but delay completion of the research, I have retained the calculations from the first phase of the study. This is why the data used sometimes do not go beyond 1964 or 1965.

The relatively rapid completion of the work, which demanded numerous special investigations, construction and reconstruction of statistical series, and complicated statistical calculations, was made possible by the exceptional collaboration I have had at the Institute. The chapter on inventories is based on Ljubomir Madžar's comprehensive research; the chapter on regional cycles, on Marta Bazler's research. The last two sections of the mathematical appendix and the calculations in connection with it were prepared by M. Bogdanović. My assistants Zvonimir Marović and Milena Jovičic prepared the bulk of the statistical material; and statistical calculations were performed by the Institute's statisticians, Mirosinka Dinkić and Nada Brakus. D. Jarić prepared all the graphs in the text. T. Rakić did all the calculations at the Institute's Electronic Calculating Center. The results of individual phases of the research were discussed by the research staff of the Institute, and those discussions resulted in many improvements in the original version of the text. If, despite the conscientious and high-quality work of my collaborators and the critical comments of other members of the Institute, there are still unnecessary gaps and erroneous conclusions in the completed text, the responsibility for these inadequacies naturally can be solely mine.

BRANKO HORVAT

Belgrade, January 1968

BUSINESS CYCLES
IN YUGOSLAVIA

Chapter 1

FLUCTUATIONS IN PRODUCTION AND THE QUANTITATIVE EFFECTS OF THOSE FLUCTUATIONS IN YUGOSLAVIA

A quarter of a century has already passed since the Liberation. That is a sufficiently long period for definite regularities in economic development and the functioning of the economic system to manifest themselves. One of the facts with which one is immediately confronted is the frequent changes in general business organization. In this connection, one gets the impression that the economy is in a state of some kind of chronic instability. Is this an objective consequence of building and perfecting a new economic system, or is there something that until now has been neither known nor perceived? To what degree has economic policy in particular situations been adequate? Could economic development and, along with it, the rate of raising the standard of living objectively have been even faster? The task of this study is to examine the feasibility of answering these and similar questions, to make possible the perception of some basic characteristics of the functioning of our economic mechanism, and thus to contribute to its further development.

Everyone who uses the publications of the Federal Statistical Bureau or simply reads the daily press knows that in certain years the Yugoslav economy grows rapidly, while in others it grows slowly or not at all. Fluctuations are therefore evident. These fluctuations are considered in government offices and political forums — and even in professional circles — as something that life itself entails and that essentially cannot be rectified. They are regarded almost in the same manner as are fluctuations in the harvest, conditioned by hazards of the weather. Moreover,

the quantitative effects of these fluctuations are unknown and un-
derestimated. (1) In fact, if these effects were not significant,
this entire study would have only an academic character. For
this reason, quantification of the production lost through economic fluctuations represents a convenient introduction to — and social justification for — the investigation that follows.

Insofar as an enterprise for some reason does not utilize its
capacity, production is less than it might be and, correspondingly,
the income of the collective is also less. Accordingly, the cost of
unutilized capacity can be measured by the amount of lost income.
A similar calculation can also be applied to the economy as a
whole. In so doing it is necessary to exclude agricultural production, since it depends to a great extent on weather conditions. We
shall make use of Federal Statistical Bureau data for the social
product (excluding agriculture) in constant 1960 prices for the period 1952-1965. We shall extend that series to 1966 and 1967 with
the aid of the index of nonagricultural physical production (industry, including mining and electric power, forestry, and construction) for 1966 and the first seven months of 1967. Unfortunately,
the Federal Statistical Bureau still has not calculated quarterly
figures for the social product; and so we must use annual data,
which make a more precise periodic profile of the cycles impossible. The calculated results are shown in Graph 1.1, which we
shall subject to a short analysis.

The lower solid line shows the trend of the social product,
while the higher indicates the potential trend; the difference between them represents the losses due to retarded growth of production. These losses consist of two parts: losses due to the uneven trend of production, and losses due to retardation in growth.
This is what is in question.

When, in the course of the cycle, the line of the rate of growth
turns downward, the path of achieved social product exhibits con-
vexity to the right. It can be seen that the troughs of the cycles
were reached in 1953, 1956, 1962, and 1967. If we connect the
peaks of the cycles by straight lines, we obtain a continuous line,
with the shaded area A lying between it and the broken line representing achieved social product. The shaded area A represents
the social product lost because of the uneven trend of production.

Because of the production lost through successive retardation,
the average rate of growth was also reduced. By how much?
That, naturally, we do not know exactly; but we can calculate it on

the basis of several assumptions. We shall assume that the possible rates of growth are somewhere in the middle between the average rate of growth in the course of the cycles and the rate of growth in the phases of the cyclical upturns. That means, in other words, that we are assuming that the high rate of growth in the phase of cyclical upturn only partially reflects the long-run developmental possibilities of the economy, and that the remaining part is the result of unutilized capacity and accumulated inventories. Thus, for example, for the cycle 1957-1960, the average rate of growth amounted to 11.6%, and the rate of growth in the upturn phase (1958-1960), to 12.5%; then we use as the possible rate of growth $\frac{11.6 + 12.5}{2} = 12.1\%$. Final results of these calculations are presented in Table 1.1.

Table 1.1

Social Product Lost Due to Business Cycles
(1960 prices, in billions of old dinars)

	1952-60	1960-64	1964-67	1952-67
Losses due to uneven growth	246	625	1,376	2,247
Losses due to retardation	761	1,711	3,830	6,302
Total lost social product	1,007	2,336	5,206	8,549
Achieved social product	13,316	10,998	10,384	34,698
Losses as % of achieved social product	7.6%	21.2%	50.2%	24.6%

The more developed the economy, the more complicated and thus more sensitive it is to every disturbance. Moreover, the same percentage losses mean an ever-greater total of lost production, and the losses due to retardation are accumulated from period to period. Insofar as all these factors are not taken sufficiently into account, the losses can attain surprising amounts. Thus, it is shown on the graph that the period 1952-1960 passed on to the succeeding period a difference between actual and potential social product of 214 billion dinars. By the end of 1964 that difference increased to 659 billion dinars, and with that deficit the reform was begun. The deficit multiplied in the course of the re-

3

form, so that for the last three years the lost social product amounted to half the achieved social product. And that is precisely the measure of retardation and stagnation that we wished to establish.

We can now take one further step in the analysis. It is obvious that fluctuations in the economy cannot be completely eliminated. Therefore, part of the established losses could not be avoided. Which part? It is probably indisputable that the management of the economy in the period 1952-1960 was not ideal. If, therefore, we take the proportion of losses from that period (7.6%) as the unavoidable minimum, then the difference of 42.6% for the last three years surely is not an exaggerated figure for the loss that could have been avoided if from 1960 on an adequate economic policy had been followed. When the loss of 4,420 billion dinars thus obtained is valued at 1966 prices by use of the index of wholesale prices (for lack of better data) — which, according to data of the Statistical Yearbook of Yugoslavia [Statistički Godišnjak S.F.R.J.], for 1967 gives a valorization factor of 1.63 — we obtain an amount of 7,200 billion dinars. The economic meaning of those masses of resources is seen from the following few illustrations.

The social product of the Yugoslav economy (excluding agriculture) amounted to 7,200 billion dinars in 1966. Accordingly, the entire production of the country for one year was lost. Total expenditures for education, science, and culture amounted to 453 billion dinars in 1965. A comparison of these funds with the lost social product leads to the conclusion that all the pressing material problems in the above-mentioned areas could have been solved, and that significant amounts would still have remained for other needs. It is known that we have already struggled with the housing problem for a quarter of a century. Total housing and communal investment in 1966 amounted to 444 billion dinars. This means that with the above-mentioned funds even the housing problem could have been eliminated. Also, several hundred thousand new workers could have been employed, thereby liquidating the currently recorded unemployment. These examples, naturally, do not imply the conclusion that these are the only things that must be done. They merely demonstrate in a concrete way the huge potential economic power hidden in higher rates of growth.

It is obvious from the calculations in Table 1.1 that the estimated size of losses depends to a great extent on the assumptions on which the estimate is based. A small change in the assumptions

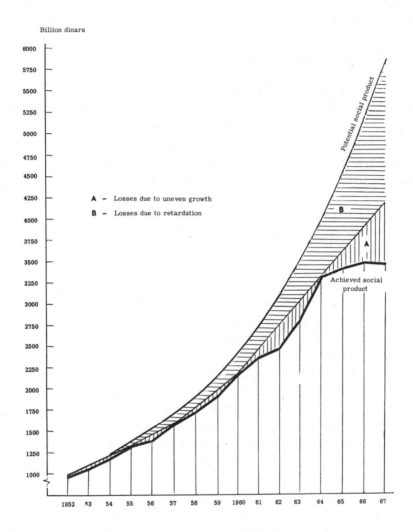

Billion dinars

A — Losses due to uneven growth
B — Losses due to retardation

Potential social product

Achieved social
product

Graph 1.1   Achieved and Potential Social Product
(Excluding Agriculture, at 1960 Prices)

5

can change the absolute amounts significantly. For this reason the amounts cited must be treated as the order of magnitude, not as precise data.

Similar calculations of losses are made in other market economies, and it will undoubtedly be of interest for us to cite just one of those calculations. Thus, the Woytinskys estimated that in the United States in the period 1947-1958, approximately $413 billion were lost (almost half a trillion old dinars), of which $113 billion represent the direct loss and $300 billion are related to the loss due to retarded growth. (2) It is interesting that the ratio of the first to the second loss is similar to the ratio in our calculation (27:73 for the USA, 26:74 for Yugoslavia). It is very important to notice that the losses due to retarded growth are two-and-a-half times greater than the losses due to uneven growth, which are, in fact, the only ones directly observable.

The Woytinskys made their calculations on the assumption that the production growth achieved in the last year before the downward turn of the cycle could be maintained. They therefore extrapolated that growth until it came again to a cyclical upturn, and from that point on, the line of potential product is parallel to the line of actual production. If this method of estimation is adopted, then the extrapolation of production from the last year before the peak of the cycle can be made in two ways: by extrapolation of the absolute growth of production, or by extrapolation of the rate of growth. In an economy of relatively slow growth, such as the U.S. economy, there is no great difference between the two variants; in fact, the Woytinskys accepted the first, more elementary variant. In a rapidly growing economy, such as that of Yugoslavia, the difference can be very great. In that case the first variant represents a fairly conservative calculation. Its interpretation is as follows: even if the economy cannot attain the same relative growth, it can increase production in the future by at least as much as the absolute increase in production in the preceding year. When the losses of the Yugoslav economy are thus calculated for the above-mentioned three periods — 1952-1960, 1960-1964, and 1964-1967 — they amount to 941, 1,560, and 4,025 billion old dinars — in all, 6,526. The total is 23% less than that in the table. The actual difference is, in fact, smaller because we reduced the figures from the table by 7.6%, leaving a final difference of about 15%, which for calculations of this type is a more than satisfactory result. Accordingly, we might say that in the period 1952-

6

1967 the Yugoslav economy, because of uneven growth and departure from the average line of economic expansion, lost somewhere between 6,500 and 7,500 billion dinars, at 1960 prices. Of this sum, 61% was lost in the last three years (1964-1967).

The calculations presented depend upon the assumptions made. What is the meaning of those assumptions? Are they scientifically founded? Are they justified? Or did the Woytinskys, I, and other economists who carry out similar calculations play around with statistical data and arithmetic? Needless to say, the justification for the assumptions does not derive from them, but from the theory on which they are based. That theory may or may not be in harmony with reality. Consequently, the task of this investigation is to introduce a certain order into the statistically recorded confusion of economic movements, not just to describe those movements, but to explain them theoretically in a consistent way.

Time and again in this introduction we have used expressions such as "cyclical movements," "turning of the cycle," and the like, that, strictly speaking, now only represent still unproved hypotheses. All that is seen directly in Graph 1.1 are certain deviations of production from some trend. There is not even a trace of some regular cyclical fluctuations. If they do exist, it is necessary only to reveal them. We shall proceed in the usual way by acquainting ourselves first with all relevant similar discoveries in other countries and by other economists. Then, treating the economy as one complex system, we shall attempt, on the basis of general knowledge, to determine the stability characteristics of that system. Thus prepared, we will be able to enter into an empirical analysis of economic trends in Yugoslavia.

Notes

1) For this reason, when the first quantification of these effects was published (B. Horvat, "Cijena usporenog rasta," Vjesnik u srijedu, November 8, 1967), the effect on the public was one of complete shock, as may be seen from the reaction of part of the press and the statements of certain individuals in some political bodies.

2) W. S. and E. S. Woytinsky, Lessons of the Recessions, Washington, D. C., Public Affairs Institute, 1959, p. 9.

Chapter 2

SUMMARY REVIEW OF EMPIRICAL RESEARCH ON BUSINESS CYCLES IN THE WORLD

Business cycles have been studied since Marx's time. In fact, periodic crises of overproduction are considered one of the basic characteristics of the capitalist method of production. In this connection, it has long been observed that there is more than one type of business cycle. There are several of them: some are general, some sectoral; they develop simultaneously and are superimposed one on the other, thus creating the irregular periodicity of general economic movements. Schumpeter proposed a tricyclical scheme: long cycles with waves of 54-60 years' duration, intermediate cycles of 9-10 years' duration, and short cycles of 40 months' duration. (1) These cycles were named for the economists who first described them — the terminology later also entering into the literature — and were linked so that the short cycles would be included in the longer: the long cycle (Kondratiev) contains six intermediate (Juglar) cycles; and these, in turn, each contain three short (Kitchin) cycles. Statistical research later revealed the existence of 20-year cycles, which were usually associated with a long-term swing in housing construction. Then there were also found to be shorter housing and construction cycles. An entire series of cycles — of the cobweb type — was established in agriculture: cycles of hogs and cattle, a coffee cycle, etc. It is necessary briefly to examine the empirical base of all these cycles, for the knowledge gained will be useful to us in interpreting our own cycles.

Kondratiev. Director of the Business Cycles Institute in Moscow, Nikolai Kondratiev, at the beginning of the 1920s, investigated statistical series of prices, rates of interest, deposits, wages, im-

8

ports, exports, and production and consumption of coal and iron in France, England, the United States, and Germany for the period 1789-1921. Kondratiev divided the annual data by the number of inhabitants, eliminated the trend, and smoothed deviations from the trend by use of nine-year moving averages, so that intermediate and short cycles and random deviations would be eliminated. As a result of this procedure, there appeared long waves in economic activity of about half a century's duration. (2) Kondratiev gave these data for his three cycles:

Cycle I: rise from 1780-1790 to 1810-1817
           fall from 1810-1817 to 1844-1851
Cycle II: rise from 1844-1851 to 1860-1875
           fall from 1870-1875 to 1890-1896
Cycle III: rise from 1890-1896 to 1914-1920
           fall from 1914-1920

Schumpeter, within the framework of his noted theory of innovations, attempted to give an entirely economically determined interpretation of these long waves of economic activity. Whereas Kondratiev measures the waves from trough to trough, Schumpeter measures them at the beginning of the prosperity phases. In his view, the first wave includes the period 1783-1842 and reflects the Industrial Revolution. The second wave, 1842-1897, represents an era of steel and steam and, particularly, of railroad building in the world. For the third wave, which begins with 1897, the application of electric power, the development of chemistry, and the use of automobiles are characteristic. Long cycles remain a subject of discussion in the learned literature. For our present research they are, naturally, not directly relevant; but it is necessary to bear them in mind, for they represent a definite framework for the analysis that follows.

Juglar. In earlier discussions of business cycles, the cycles normally thought of were of 7-11 years' duration. These are the classic ten-year cycles which manifested themselves throughout the entire nineteenth century, particularly in England, and whose duration Marx compared with the average lifetime of equipment in industry. (3) A century ago the former medical doctor Clément Juglar first described these periodic economic fluctuations systematically, analyzing statistical series of prices, rates of interest, and balances of the central bank. (4) If we measure the length of the cycle from peak to peak, then there were in England during Marx's lifetime — that is, in the period 1820-1870 — five cycles with crises, which means that the average duration of the cycles was ten years. That periodicity continued in the succeeding period, 1870-1914, when the next four cycles lasted nine, seven, ten, and seven years. And, finally, another two cycles with crises appeared in the period 1920-1938. (5) Accordingly, in a period of more than a century, England experienced crises at intervals of about ten years. This, however, does not hold for other countries. In the United States in the period 1854-1938, there was one cycle longer than six years. (6) And even the English data have been subjected by Matthews to a reinterpretation for the period after 1870. (7) Today there is a growing conviction among economists that it is necessary to stipulate as intermediate cycles those with a duration of about twenty years.

Kitchin. Following World War I, the English statistician Joseph Kitchin analyzed series of bank clearings, prices, and rates of interest in the USA and England for the period 1890-1922 and discovered short cycles of three-and-a-half years' (40 months') duration. Kitchin considered these cycles psychologically conditioned. (8) Later it was established that these short cycles arose from the accumulation and depletion of inventories. In five interwar cycles in the USA, accumulating inventories absorbed 23% of the average expansion; in three postwar contractions, depletion of inventories accounted for 50-100% of the decrease in social product. (9) And whereas ten-year cycles are characteristic of the English economy, three- or four-year cycles prevail in the United States. In the period 1854-1961 in the USA, there were 26 cycles, of which 17, or two-thirds of the total number, were three or four years in length. (10) In the period 1854-1958 the duration of such cycles varied between 27 and 99 months, with an average of 50 months, of which 30 months fell within the expansion and 20 months within the contraction. After World War II the expansive phase was prolonged by one-third, and the contractions were shortened by 42%, so that the rate of growth of the U.S. economy markedly increased. These cycles have been empirically investigated very systematically. Thus, it has been established that some economic series always come first in the phase (changes in inventories, 10 months; bankruptcies, 7; starts in housing construction, 6; equipment orders, 5; net profits, 2; etc.), some are simultaneous (personal income, unemployment, wholesale prices, etc.), and some

10

lag behind changes in social product (investment expenditures on equipment, 1 month; consumer credit, 4.5; interest rates on bank credits, 5. (11) This information is useful in forecasting upswings. Where amplitude is concerned, it is known that production and consumption of durable consumer and producer goods fluctuate significantly more than production of reproduction materials* and services, and inventories fluctuate most. Wholesale prices vary more than retail prices; prices of raw materials, much more than prices of semifinished and finished products. Industrial production fluctuates considerably more than the social product. (12) Finally, imports narrowly accommodate themselves to the business cycle, but exports do not. (13)

Yugoslavia's four-year cycles are similar in timing to the U.S. cycles, but their conditioning is, as we shall see, different. Further, the psychological stages of which Kitchin spoke also are not decisive. However, one should not ignore them completely. In view of the sequence of changes in our public life, the impression arises that every three or four years there is a buildup of impatience and dissatisfaction with existing conditions; the belief arises that something must be changed, various political bodies begin to carry out a reorganization, and individuals begin to change their places of employment. (14) If this impression is accurate, the respective phenomena represent a subject for study by sociologists or political scientists. Our research will bring us to the conclusion that a certain combination of exports and imports that has very accentuated cyclical behavior and great amplitudes plays the decisive role in Yugoslav cycles. Whether the Yugoslav economy also has cycles with a duration of more than four years, and what their natures are, cannot be established with certainty, for a period of two decades is too short for empirical analysis. There are certain indications. The quickening of growth in the decade 1952-1960 and the subsequent slowing down can develop into a 16-year or longer cycle if stabilization is achieved at the price of reducing the rate of growth. The acceleration of agricultural production before 1960 and the slowing down after that year, and the slowing down of industrial exports before 1961 and the acceleration after 1961, also point to longer cycles; but at this moment it is impossible to pre-

---

*"Reproduction materials" consist of resources consumed in current production, e.g., raw materials, fuel, grease, energy, packaging — Translator.

dict their duration. The waves of total gross investment also appear longer: one trough occurred in 1955-1956, and a second in 1965-1966, which points to ten-year periodicity.

Construction cycles. Twenty-year cycles were discovered first in construction, above all in housing construction in the USA, England, Germany, Sweden, and Canada. (15) The amplitudes of those cycles are fairly great. They are explained by the well-known relationship between total and marginal volumes: a slight percentage change of the total volume leads to enormous percentage changes of the marginal volume. Total housing space is a function, other things being equal, of total population; but housing construction is a function of the growth of population. (16) Accordingly, if in the course of time the growth rate of the urban population increases from 1% to 2% annually, housing construction in the cities must increase by 100%. The length of the cycle is explained by the slowness of population changes and the durability of buildings. It is also stated that in capitalist countries it is chiefly small contractors who carry on construction activity. When supply exceeds demand, they abandon their work with difficulty, the disequilibrium is increased, and the crisis is prolonged and aggravated. Later, when demand begins to grow rapidly, the shortage of skilled labor (which in construction is apprenticed a relatively long time) and the small scale of construction enterprises (which are not in a position to invest more capital and quickly expand the volume of production) prevent rapid adjustment of production to expenditures. For the period 1862-1933 in the USA, Gordon cites four construction cycles that, measured from trough to trough, lasted 15 to 22 years. (17) From what has been said it appears probable that there will also be short cycles in construction. Dauten cites, for the period 1879-1933 in the USA, an average length of 59 months in 11 construction cycles. (18) Guttentag established four housing cycles of 31-35 months' duration for the postwar period in the USA (1948-1959). These cycles were conditioned, in the first place, by the volume of mortgage credit, i.e., by the available funds for financing. As Graph 5.2 shows, the Yugoslav construction cycle is linked to the industrial cycle. It has a much greater amplitude, while being conditioned by available funds. As for the long construction cycle, it cannot normally develop while there is a chronic lack of housing space.

Twenty-year cycle. After the 20-year construction cycle was established, similar periodicity was discovered in other series as well. Abramovitz adduces that the rate of growth of production in the United States in the period 1814-1938/39 passed through cycles of 15-20 years' duration. Similar cycles were also noticed in prices, the growth of population, and movements of people and capital. (19) These cycles are linked with the construction cycles. Matthews noticed that great crises of general economic activity occur at 20-year intervals and correspond to the troughs of the construction cycles. (20) It is important to observe that the 20-year American and 10-year English cycles differ from short cycles in the intensity of the contraction that we call the crisis. The troughs of these crises correspond to the troughs of the construction cycles. R. A. Easterlin (21) writes that research on the 20-year cycle shows:

> that one of the mechanisms responsible for long swings in economic growth may involve interactions among aggregate demand, labor-market conditions, and household growth, with a feedback effect from the last to the first. An upswing in the growth of aggregate demand and the growing labor-market tightness induced thereby engenders accelerated marriage, migration, and household growth. These are critical decision-points in the life cycle, entailing spending commitments extending over several years as a new home is established and a family started or settled.... A bunching of such commitments serves to cushion the economy against the usual business cycle and becomes exhausted only gradually.

Agricultural cycles. These cycles are of a somewhat different nature than the others. They arise from the fact that the process of production is relatively long and the volume and costs of production depend on weather conditions. If the price of soybeans is low this year, farmers will reduce the area under soybeans and sow something else. The next year, supply will be less than demand, the price will increase, and the production decisions will be changed. Such two-year cycles are characteristic of one-year crops. In the production of hogs and in cattle-breeding generally, the process of production is prolonged by the time necessary for the production of fodder. Since 1900, U.S. hog cycles have lasted an average of five years; for cattle they are somewhat longer and less regular. With crops such as coffee, more years are necessary for maturation. "Coffee cycles" last, on the average, 15 years. (22) However, the cycles, or at least cyclical components, can be longer even for one-year crops because of climatic fluctuations and other causes. The well-known Beveridge periodogram of the index of grain prices in Western Europe through three centuries shows the strongest intensity for the cyclical component with a period of 15 1/4 years. (23) I do not know whether such cycles have been studied in the Yugoslav economy. In this study they are not included for, if they exist, they have only secondary significance in relation to the great fluctuations in agricultural production as a whole.

The various cycles established point to the possibility that an economy is inherently unstable, i.e., that an economy is an inherently unstable system. It is of interest to examine whether such an assumption is accurate.

Notes

1) J. A. Schumpeter, "The Analysis of Economic Change," Review of Economics and Statistics, 1935, No. 4, pp. 2-10; Business Cycles: A Theoretical, Historical and Statistical Analysis of the Capitalist Process (New York: McGraw-Hill, 1939).

2) The hypothesis was put forward in 1919-1921, was published for the first time in a study in Moscow in 1922, and finally was discussed in an article, "Bol'šie cykly konjunktury," Voprosy konjunktury, 1952, No. 1. Since the original was not accessible to me, I cite the English version, "The Long Waves in Economic Life," Review of Economics and Statistics, 1935, No. 6, pp. 105-115, and reprinted in J. J. Clark and M. Cohen, eds., Business Fluctuations, Growth and Economic Stabilization (New York: Random House, 1963).

3) Kapital, Vol. II (Zagreb: Kultura, 1947), p. 148. Marx's views on economic crises are discussed comprehensively in the study by Z. Baletića, Marksistička teorija ekonomske krize (Zagreb: Naprijed, 1965). Marx thought of an empirical treatment of business cycles. Of interest in this connection is his letter to Engels of May 31, 1873, in which he says: "You are acquainted with the tables which present the zig-zag up and down movement of prices, discount rates, etc., in the course of the year, etc. I have attempted several times — for the analysis of crises — to calculate these ups and downs as irregular curves and have thought (and still think that it is possible, with sufficiently refined material) of determining mathematically from that calculation the principal laws of crises. Moore ... maintains that in fact it is for now impracticable, and I decided to let it go for the time being" (Prepiska, IV, Belgrade: Kultura, p. 444).

4) C. Juglar, Les crises commerciales et leur retour périodique

en France, en Angleterre et aux Etats Unis, 1860.

5) R. C. O. Matthews, The Business Cycle (Chicago: University of Chicago Press, 1959), pp. 216-220.

6) C. A. Dauten, Business Cycles and Forecasting (Cincinnati: Southwestern Publishing Co., 1961), p. 246.

7) Loc. cit. Matthews considers that the ten-year periodicity in the second period is accidental and that it is the result of the existence of two unsynchronized waves — each approximately twice as long — in domestic and foreign investments. In the third period it is a question of structural changes.

8) J. Kitchin, "Cycles and Trends in Economic Factors," Review of Economics and Statistics, 1923, No. 1, pp. 10-16; reprinted in Clark and Cohen, op. cit.

9) Dauten, op. cit., p. 260.

10) Ibid., p. 246.

11) Ibid., pp. 255, 373.

12) E. C. Bratt, Business Cycles and Forecasting (Homewood, Illinois: Irwin, 1953).

13) A. F. Burns, "Mitchell on What Happens During Business Cycles," in Clark and Cohen, op. cit., p. 10.

14) For example, in the 14 years from 1951 to 1964, four governors of the National Bank of Yugoslavia were replaced, and in the Federal Economic Planning Bureau — four directors; in 13 years four systems of taxation had their turn (M. Hanžekvić, "Savremena porezna politika i oporezivanje privrednih organizacija," Ekonomski pregled, 1965, No. 11-12, p. 780), reelection of directors is fixed for every four years, the electoral period for political bodies is four years, etc.

15) Matthews, op. cit., p. 98.

16) A. F. Burns, "Long Cycles in Residential Construction," in Clark and Cohen, op. cit.

17) R. A. Gordon, Business Fluctuations (New York: Harper & Row, 1952), p. 210.

18) Op. cit., p. 287.

19) M. Abramovitz, "The Nature and Significance of Kuznets Cycles," Economic Development and Cultural Change, 1961, No. 3, p. 229. However, in statistical determination of the length of long cycles, it is right to be cautious, for some techniques of smoothing short cycles result in long cycles even where they do not exist in the original data. See R. C. Bird et al., "Kuznets Cycles in Growth Rates: The Meaning," International Economic Review, 1965, No. 2, pp. 229-239.

20) Matthews comments: "...the twenty-year cycle is the only systematic periodic element in the annals of fluctuations in the USA besides the short inventory cycle" (op. cit., p. 212).

21) Ibid., p. 209.

22) R. A. Easterlin, "Economic-Demographic Interactions and Long Swings in Economic Growth," American Economic Review, 1966, No. 5, p. 1092.

23) Dauten, op. cit., p. 294.

24) W. H. Beveridge, "Wheat Prices and Rainfall in Western Europe," J.R.S.S. (1922). The basic results of that work are discussed in M. G. Kendall, The Advanced Theory of Statistics (London: Griffen, 1959), pp. 423-435.

Chapter 3

INHERENT INSTABILITY OF THE ECONOMY

One often encounters the belief that the market can efficiently regulate the economic process. This layman's belief is, of course, entirely mistaken — and dangerous. A market economy is inherently unstable and must therefore be directed. That direction does not have to be administrative — in fact administrative direction is the most primitive form of direction — but in every case there must be direction if one wants to avoid cycles. What form that direction takes is not the subject of this study. What we wish to demonstrate here, with empirical parameters and using the Yugoslav economy, is how cycles necessarily arise in a pure market economy.

Marx demonstrated the inherent instability of a market economy a long time ago on the basis of the proportions postulated by his reproduction models and of the capitalist institutions that necessarily destroyed the required proportions. (1) However, besides the instability one can also demonstrate the cyclical nature of a market economy and show that those cycles are not dependent upon the institutional system. This can be done in various ways. (2) I shall use one of the economic models I constructed earlier. (3)

3.1 A Yugoslav Model of Inventory Fluctuations

Let us assume that investment in fixed capital and inventories in division I of social production are determined from without and that inventories of consumer goods are formed in proportion to expected consumption. Let us also assume that it is planned that consumption will increase from period to period by some factor a. We will take the planning period as one year, which is in fact an assumption of empirical behavior, although at first glance it does not appear to be. Therefore, planned inventories at the end of year t will amount to

$$\hat{H}_t = ha\ C_{t-1} \tag{3.1}$$

where $\underline{h}$ is the coefficient of inventory formation (the reciprocal of the number of turnovers) and C_{t-1} is consumption in the preceding period. Actual inventories (H_t) will differ from those planned $(\hat{H}_t)$ by as much as actual sales of consumer goods (C_t) differ from planned sales $(a\ C_{t-1})$. Accordingly,

$$H_t = h\ a\ C_{t-1} - (C_t - a\ C_{t-1}) \tag{3.2}$$

We will assume that actual consumption maintains a constant share of social product (Y_t) by the action of governmental bodies:

$$C_t = cY_t \tag{3.3}$$

It follows that the planned social product will be

$$Y_t = a\ C_{t-1} + (h\ a\ C_{t-1} - H_{t-1}) + I_t \tag{3.4}$$

where the expression in parentheses represents the planned increase in inventories of consumer goods and I_t is externally given investment expenditures. Substituting (3.2) and (3.3) into (3.4), we obtain:

$$Y_t - c\ [a\ (1+h) + 1]\ Y_{t-1} + a\ c\ (1+h)\ Y_{t-2} = I_t$$

For the sake of simplification, let $1 + h = \chi$,

$$Y_t - c\ (a\chi + 1)\ Y_{t-1} + a\ c\ \chi\ Y_{t-2} = I_t \tag{3.5}$$

We will assume for the sake of simplicity that investment expenditures expand by a factor a, $I_t = I_o a^t$. For the solution of the difference equation of the second degree (3.5), it is important whether the roots of its characteristic equation are real or not. It can be shown that the necessary condition for the roots to be real is

$$c > \frac{4\,a\,\chi}{(a\,\chi + 1)^2} \tag{3.6}$$

18

In the case of rapid growth (large $\underline{a}$) and generally large inventories, the product a_χ is relatively large. When a_χ grows, the expression on the right side of (3.6) decreases. Let us take extreme empirical values of the parameters in a situation of rapid growth: $a = 1.1$, $\chi = 1.7$, from which we obtain the most favorable case for satisfying relation (3.6). It follows that $\underline{c}$ must be greater than $\frac{7.5}{8.2} = 0.91$. This is unrealistic, for when there is rapid growth, parameter $\underline{c}$ is relatively small (in Yugoslavia, between 0.6 and 0.7). Accordingly, the roots of the characteristic equation are complex, and the solution of the difference equation runs

$$Y_t = Ap^t \cos(\theta t - \varphi) + \bar{Y}_0 \alpha^t \tag{3.7}$$

which means that the social product oscillates with an amplitude of A and with the phase φ. On the basis of the parameters of the Yugoslav economy, it follows that $\underline{p}$ is greater than one:

$$p = \sqrt{a c \chi} \qquad > 1$$

which means that the <u>oscillations in the social product are explosive</u>. We may still be able to find the period of oscillation. From

$$\theta = \frac{c(a\chi + 1)}{2\sqrt{ac\chi}} = \frac{0.6\,(1.08 \times 1.3 + 1)}{2\sqrt{1.08 \times 0.6 \times 1.3}} = \frac{1.44}{1.6} = 0.9$$

it follows that $\theta = 0.45$. According to this, the period of fluctuation amounts to

$$P = \frac{2\pi}{\theta} = \frac{6.28}{0.45} = 14 \text{ years}$$

which is a somewhat longer period than the classical business cycle.

It is worth observing how $\cos\theta$ grows with the growth of χ, because of which period P then also increases. It follows that larger inventories increase stability, and smaller inventories make the economy unstable. It appears, as we shall see later, that something of this holds true for the actual Yugoslav economy.

However, the model presented was not intended to be realistic. The point was only to show, from a few very simple economic relations that are, in addition, entirely plausible, how cycles are necessarily generated. The cycles in our case also appear even in the most favorable case, when investment regularly expands by some factor α. Intuition tells us that regular expansion of investment and planning of consumption are all that is necessary for a stable economy. But intuition in this case, as so often in economics, proves to be mistaken. Besides, investments can move altogether irregularly, with their own oscillations, as in fact happens in Yugoslavia (see Graph 5.5). In that case oscillations conditioned by inventories are superimposed on oscillations caused by investment. Insofar as the periods of oscillation are similar (and graphs 5.1, 5.2, 5.4, and 5.5 show that they are identical), there appears, as in physical systems, a resonance effect, i.e., greater and greater deviations. And in every case, the instability of the economy increases in the absence of control.

3.2 Cumulative Random Disturbances as a Source of Cyclical Fluctuations

What we have just established is not all we know today about the performance of economic systems. It would therefore be useful to consider the problem from still one more, at first glance very different, aspect. Forty years ago the Soviet econometrician and statistician E. E. Slutsky took a series of final figures from a table of Soviet lottery loans and calculated a second series of numbers from them by moving averages of every ten numbers. (4) When this second series was presented graphically, a picture was obtained of the English business cycles in the period 1855-1877 such as results from the indices of Dorothy Thomas from 1916. Slutsky then once more calculated ten-number moving averages from his second series, and the new curve showed an arrangement of fluctuation periods such as the American Mitchell found empirically for 93 cycles of 12 different countries. These results perhaps appear as some sort of black magic. Actually, they disclose, relatively simply, an explainable fact: that the accumulation of random disturbances leads to a cyclical process. Let us see what is involved.

Let us take four-number moving averages, which we often use in this study. Let the original data be random numbers — which means that they are mutually uncorrelated — and let us designate them by x_i. Instead of moving averages we shall calculate only moving sums — dividing by 4 to obtain averages is not necessary for investigating the effects that interest us — which we will designate by y_i. It follows:

$$\begin{aligned} y_1 &\quad x_1 + x_2 + x_3 + x_4 \\ y_2 &\qquad\quad x_2 + x_3 + x_4 + x_5 \\ y_3 &\qquad\qquad\quad x_3 + x_4 + x_5 + x_6 \end{aligned}$$

We observe immediately that the adjoining y's each have three common terms and are therefore, as distinguished from the x's, mutually <u>correlated</u>. Accordingly, the moving averages (sums) are no longer random numbers, but numbers that maintain some regularity; correlation is strongest for adjoining terms and falls toward zero with the increase in interval. In fact, the coefficients of serial correlation are easily obtained. Without limiting the generality of the results, let us use $E(x_i) = 0$, according to which $E(y_i) = 0$; then

$$E\left(y_i^2\right) = \sigma_{yi}^2 = n\sigma_{xi}^2$$

$$E(y_i \, y_{i+k}) = (n-k)\,\sigma_{xi}^2 \qquad\qquad (3.8)$$

$$\therefore \ r_k = \frac{n-k}{n}$$

In relation to our case in which $n = 4$, the serial coefficients amount to:

$$r_0 = 1, \ r_1 = r_{-1} = \frac{n-1}{n} = \frac{3}{4}, \ r_2 = r_{-2} = \frac{1}{2}$$

$$r_3 = r_{-3} = \frac{1}{4}, \ r_4 = r_{-4} = r_5 = r_{-5} = \ldots = 0$$

If two quantities are mutually positively correlated, as in this case, then there is a tendency for them both to move in the same direction. Therefore, if y_i increases, there will be a tendency for y_{i+1} also to increase — and similarly with decreases. However, neither increase nor decrease can be continued long. In the original series, for every x_i there exists the probability of $1/2$ that its value is above or below the given average (zero). The probability is $1/4$ that the following term, x_{i+1}, is found on the same side of the mean; the probability that the third term, x_{i+2}, will be on the same side is $1/8$; etc. Therefore, the probability that successive terms will be far below or above the line representing the average is very slight. And since the terms y_i consist of sums of x_i, this means that in the series, y_i must arrive at a reversal of direction and crossing of the line of the average. We thus come to this result: the moving sums will change, successively departing for some time from the average, then approaching the line of the average and cutting it from time to time. Except for the progress by steps and the existence of turning points and an average, these movements are rather irregular.

If we express the initial differences in our series of moving sums as

$$\Delta y_1 = y_2 - y_1 = x_3 - x_1$$
$$\Delta y_2 = y_3 - y_2 = x_6 - x_2$$

we notice that successive initial differences do not have common terms and therefore are uncorrelated. Hence there are also the irregular fluctuations, to which we drew attention in the preceding paragraph. If, however, we apply the procedure of moving sums also to the series y_i so that $z_i = \sum_{i=1}^{n} y_i$, then the initial differences will have common terms and will be correlated. Thus the fluctuations will be slightly straightened, and there will be a tendency for individual segments to appear straight. If we now apply, for the third time, the calculation of moving averages, the new series $w_i = \sum_{i=1}^{n} z_i$ will have correlated second differences as well, and therefore segments of the waves will appear as parabolic curves. The successive use of moving sums is nothing other than the change of the weights of terms in the original series. As there is no reason why these weights would be equal and, moreover, equal to one — which would imply simple moving averages — then in empirical series we can expect correlation of higher differences and, consequently, curvilinear segments in the fluctuations.

If segments of the waves are curvilinear and there are turning points and inflections (in the vicinity of the averages), does that not mean that perhaps there is also some tendency of the curves to be sinusoidal? This would then also imply greater regularity with regard to amplitude, phase, and periodicity. Let us consider a difference equation of the second order:

$$\Delta^2 y_t = -a y_{t+1} \tag{3.9}$$

22

For $0 < a < 4$ the solution of the equation is sinusoidal (see the mathematical appendix). Regression coefficient $\underline{a}$ always satisfies the necessary conditions for

$$-a = \frac{E\,(\Delta^2\,y_t x y_{t+1})}{\sigma^2 y} = \frac{E\,[(y_{t+2}-2\,y_{t+1}+y_t)(y_{t+1})]}{\sigma^2 y} = -2\,(1-r_1) \tag{3.10}$$

Applying the same judgment as in the preceding section, Slutsky concludes that a tendency toward sine wave movement will exist if there is negative correlation between the second differences and the terms y_{i+1}. For example, in our case of averaged indices of industrial production for the period from the middle of 1955 to the beginning of 1965, i.e., for the last three cycles, the corresponding coefficient of correlation $\underline{r}$ = -0.67; this coefficient is highly significant and shows the existence of strong cyclical components, which we shall discuss below. In his models Slutsky obtained relatively low coefficients of correlation (-0.3 to a maximum of -0.6), and concludes that it is probably an insufficient criterion, since equation (3.9) holds only for one sine curve, but actual movements can represent the sum of several sine waves of various lengths. Slutsky therefore used a difference equation of the fourth order, which represents the sum of two sine waves and gives satisfactory results. Finally, he also shows the conditions for obtaining a complete sinusoidal shape. (5)

3.3 Autoregression Model, Linear Oscillator, and Servomechanism as Possible Models

Slutsky's work is rarely quoted, probably because it is rather difficult; and when it is mentioned, its unreality is emphasized first of all, inasmuch as it purports to represent an explanation of business cycles. (6) Slutsky's hypothesis implies that economic movements are determined by the weighted sum of random disturbances in the course of the present and several previous periods. Such cumulative stochastic disturbances result in more or less regular cyclical fluctuations. In this form the theory does not have much meaning, for we know that in an economy there are both random disturbances and systematic relationships. For this reason economic movements are expressed much more realistically by an autoregression model of the type

$$y_t = f(y_{t-1}, y_{t-2}, \ldots y_{t-n}, \varepsilon_t) \tag{3.11}$$

where y_t represents present social product and ε_t is the disturbance factor. (7) Our model, expressed by equation (3.5), also belongs to this type, except that the stochastic element in it is not explicitly designated. It was therefore incomplete and it was necessary to consider Slutsky's results in more detail. In this context it is also useful to mention an interesting study by Irma Adelman. She departs from the Klein-Goldberger model (whose equations by themselves do not describe cycles), superimposes stochastic shocks on the model, and obtains a system that represents very well the cyclical fluctuations of the U.S. economy. (8) From these investigations we know that both systematic and random components and their combinations show tendencies toward cyclical fluctuation. Since we find both the first and the second component in an economy, we must conclude that an economy is inherently unstable.

It will be useful to mention here still one more possible approach to economic fluctuations. If we adapt from physics the concept of the spring that oscillates around some equilibrium point, as did Joseph Schumpeter under the influence of Ragnar Frisch (9), then economic equilibrium becomes a kind of attractive force that is stronger the greater the deviation from equilibrium. Schumpeter determines equilibrium by the points of inflection on the curve of economic indices. It can therefore be assumed that a change in the velocity of the system's movement from the equilibrium position is inversely proportional to the distance from that position, i.e.,

$$y'' = -ky \tag{3.12}$$

where $\underline{y}$ represents the deviation, for example, of social product from its equilibrium value, and $k > 0$ is a constant proportion. We notice immediately that it is a question of the familiar equation of the linear oscillator whose solution gives a sine wave. Besides the attractive force of the equilibrium position when the system departs from that position, there can also appear some brakes (bottlenecks, for example) that are proportional to the velocity of the system's movements. The new equation

24

$$y'' = -ky - ry'$$

(3.13)

represents the familiar equation of damped oscillation, in which
$r > 0$ is the braking factor. Insofar as it is desired to avoid regularity with respect to phase, periodicity, and amplitude — and
that regularity is lacking in a real economy — then the constant
coefficients in our differential equations can be replaced by functions of time, which in the simplest case means

$$y'' + f(t) y = 0$$

(3.14)

Finally, if the structure of the system is such that it spontaneously
fluctuates by damped oscillations and after some time subsides to
an equilibrium orbit, it will, however, not reach it; oscillations
will continue endlessly and will always be activated anew by external shocks that come from stochastic economic disturbances. (10)

It is interesting to note the similarity of equation (3.13) and (the
homogeneous part) of equation (3.5). The former is a differential
equation of the second order; the latter is a difference equation of
the second order. That one is a differential equation and the other
is a difference equation is not a fundamental distinction, for the
latter equation also can be constructed so that it is differential.
The point is that economic phenomena are often discrete in their
origin — for example, investment expenditures this year will yield
new production only next year, final income accounts [zavrseni
racuni] are calculated annually, not at every moment, etc. —
whereas physical phenomena are usually continuous — a force acts
on some body continuously so long as it still acts. Therefore, economic phenomena are often described by difference equations, and
physical phenomena — by differential equations. However, one essential difference is much more significant. When the physicist
speaks of a linear oscillator he describes the phenomenon by the
hypothesis that "the change in the velocity of movement of the system from the equilibrium position is inversely proportional to the
distance from that position." When the economist says that "producers attempt to maintain inventories in constant proportion to
expected sales," he explains a phenomenon. And since in both
cases it is a question of systems, the formal algebraic presenta-
tion will be the same.

The last described model is very clearly illustrated by Kendall's (11) position:

Imagine a motorcar proceeding along a horizontal road
with an irregular surface. The car is fitted with springs
which permit it to oscillate to some extent but are de-
signed to damp out the oscillations as soon as the com-
fort of the passengers will permit. If the car strikes a
bump or a pothole in the road the body will oscillate up
and down for a time but will soon come to rest.... If,
however, it proceeds over a continual succession of bumps,
there will be continual oscillation of varying amplitude
and distance between peaks. The oscillations are continually renewed by disturbances, though the distribution of the latter along the road may be quite random.
The regularity of the motion is determined by the internal structure of the car; but the existence of the motion
is determined by external impulses.

The value of this illustration is that it directly suggests a solution. If we wish to increase the velocity of the car and the com-
fort of the traveler and reduce the expenses of repair, then we
can achieve relatively little by improving and constantly changing the springs; the basic solution lies in constructing a smooth
and durable road that rain will not wash out and that will not be
repaired by piles of gravel. If we substitute the springs for the
instruments of economic policy and the durable road for the institutional conditions of business activity, then the whole example
has its macroeconomic interpretation.

Still another analogy is possible, this time with technical regulation. The economy can be thought of as a complex system with
a multitude of reciprocal links (for example, investment expenditures influence income, and income influences investment). In
fact, that is not just an analogy: the economy is, in essence, a
large servomechanism. A servomechanism functions well only if
all its parts and operations are precisely constructed so that they
exactly dovetail in the functioning of the system as a whole. Insofar as that is not the case, there will be disturbances, vibrations,
and oscillations that can be so strong as to result in a breakdown
of the mechanism. In this case the system "does not oscillate because of some lagged response; it oscillates because of its own
inherent dynamic contradictions." (12)

Let us now conclude this part of the analysis. We approached
the problem of economic stability in four different ways. These
approaches do not differ in essence; they represent variations of

a single approach with emphasis on various aspects of the problem. The autoregression model can be understood as a special case of the model of moving averages of random disturbances. On the other hand, that model represents systematically an explanation of the linear oscillator model. The servomechanism model can be understood as a broadening of the autoregression model in an area where explicit mathematical solutions become impossible and the solution is arrived at by simulation. However, although we began that way, we always unambiguously maintained that there was no reason whatever why the economy should in itself be stable, and that there are many reasons for its instability. Therefore, oscillatory, not equilibrium, movements must be considered the rule. The inherent instability of the economy demands very active regulation and control by way of adequately determined economic policy and adequately formed economic institutions that act as automatic stabilizers.

Notes

1) Paul Sweezy presented an interesting and simple formulization of a possible Marxian approach. See Teorija kapitalističkog razvitka (Zagreb: Naprijed, 1959), pp. 198, 201-204.

2) R. C. O. Matthews (The Business Cycle, University of Chicago Press, 1959, Chs. III and IV) provides an elementary survey of models of cyclical fluctuations. The simplest is the model of the interaction of the multiplier and the accelerator or of the multiplier and the adjustment of fixed capital. When a lag is introduced, these models with realistic values of the parameters always result in cycles. Nonlinear effects are achieved by the introduction of various restraints with respect to available resources, by which even usually exponential movements are transformed into periodic ones. Technical progress, renewal of fixed capital, and various external shocks can activate damped fluctuations which are abated, but which are otherwise inherent in the economic mechanism.

3) B. Horvat, "Dva modela efekta formiranja zaliha na kretanje društvenog proizvoda," Ekonomski pregled, 1964, No. 7; Yugoslav Institute of Economic Studies, Tearsheet 30.

4) E. E. Slutsky, "Solženie slučajnyh pričin kak istocnik cikliceskih procesov," Voprosy konjuktury, Vol. III, No. 1 (1927), and reprinted in Slutsky, Izbrannye trudy, USSR Academy of Sciences Publishing House, Moscow, 1960, pp. 99-132. That work was

entirely forgotten by economists until the author published it, with certain extensions, in the journal Econometrica, 1937, No. 2, pp. 105-146 ("The Summation of Random Causes as the Source of Cyclic Processes").

5) Op. cit., pp. 118-19. The series which satisfies those conditions represents the mth difference of the nth-fold two-term moving sums of random numbers when m and n tend to infinity and such that m/n = constant.

6) See Matthews, op. cit., p. 201.

7) However, here it is worthwhile also to observe that formally the autoregression model represents only a special case of accumulative random disturbances, as can be seen from the following. Let us take the difference equation of the first order

$$y_t = a\, y_{t-1} + \varepsilon_t$$

whose general solution consists of the sum of the solution of the homogeneous part and of the particular solution. For $a < 1$ we can ignore the solution of the homogeneous part, $y_o a^t$, for over time it tends to zero. Therefore, after a sufficiently long period the general solution is reduced to the particular solution with the precision we desire. And the particular solution can be carried out as follows:

$$y_t = \varepsilon_t + a\, y_{t-1} = \varepsilon_t + a\,(\varepsilon_{t-1} + a y_{t-2})$$
$$= \varepsilon_t + a\varepsilon_{t-1} + a^2\,(\varepsilon_{t-2} + a y_{t-3})$$
$$= \varepsilon_t + a\varepsilon_{t-1} + a^2\,\varepsilon_{t-2} + \ldots$$

Accordingly, the autoregressive series is equal to the series of moving averages of random elements with definite values of the weights and an infinite number of terms.

8) I. Adelman, "Business Cycles — Endogenous or Stochastic?" Economic Journal, 1960, pp. 783-796.

9) J. A. Schumpeter, Business Cycles (New York: McGraw-Hill, 1939), p. 210.

10) Ragnar Frisch first worked out such a model of business cycles in his work "Propagation Problems and Impulse Problems in Dynamic Economics," published in Economic Essays in Honour of Gustav Cassel (London, 1939). Frisch thus explained his conception: "The most important feature of the free oscillations consists of the length of the cycles and the damping tendency of certain characteristic values of the system which oscillates, whereas the intensity (amplitude) of the fluctuations is determined first of all by external impulses. An important consequence of that is that

more or less regular fluctuations can be called forth by a cause which acts irregularly" (p. 171).

11) M. G. Kendall, The Advanced Theory of Statistics, II (London: Griffen, 1959), p. 423.

12) R. M. Goodwin, "Econometrics in Business-Cycle Analysis," in A. Hansen, Business Cycles and National Income (New York: Norton, 1951), p. 453. See also R. G. D. Allen, Mathematical Economics (London: Macmillan, 1956), Ch. 9: "Economic Regulation: Closed-Loop Control System," pp. 281-313.

Chapter 4

METHODOLOGICAL FOUNDATION FOR EMPIRICAL RESEARCH ON CYCLICAL FLUCTUATIONS OF THE YUGOSLAV ECONOMY

4.1 Introductory Considerations

This study is confined to the analysis of a limited number of strategic factors. Such an approach does not imply a denial of the existence of other relevant factors. However, it is desirable to avoid complicating the analysis unnecessarily and to examine some key hypotheses with a minimum number of variables.

The statistical series on which the analysis is projected must satisfy the following conditions:

a) the series must be sufficiently disaggregated so that individual phenomena can be precisely located in time, even within a period of one year;

b) seasonal components must be excluded.

For the satisfaction of condition (a), annual data are insufficiently selective but monthly data contain an excessively large random component. Therefore, quarterly data were chosen. Condition (b) is usually satisfied by the use of moving averages. However, moving averages, precisely because they are averages, reduce deviations (i.e., besides the seasonal component, they to a large extent also eliminate the random component) and thus embellish the picture of the movements. Insofar as such a picture shows regularity even without moving averages, it can only be still more regular with them. The seasonal component was therefore eliminated in such a way that in calculating the rate of growth the same quarters of different years are placed in relation. Furthermore, by use of moving averages the series would be shortened by two quarters at the beginning and at the end of the period. In view of the fact that quarterly series exist only from 1952 or 1953, this would be a serious loss. The method used eliminates the loss. Finally, moving averages distort the oscillatory movements, which my method avoids. It will be useful to demonstrate immediately and formally the first and third characteristics of moving averages.

We assume that the terms of our series $y_t = f_1 + f_2 + f_3$ consist of three additive components, trend f_1 (t), oscillatory components f_2 (t), and random components f_3 (t). Let us calculate the terms of the trend by operation of the moving averages T:

$$Ty_t = Tf_1 + Tf_2 + Tf_3$$

We assume that in this way the trend is exactly calculated, and by its subtraction from the original series we obtain the deviations that contain only an oscillatory and a random component:

$$y_t - Ty_t = (f_2 - Tf_2) + (f_3 - Tf_3)$$

The terms Tf_2 and Tf_3 can distort the oscillatory component and introduce nonexistent oscillations into the random component. The latter, known as the Slutsky effect, has been examined in Section 3.2. Here we can only notice the reduction in variability of the random elements through the adoption of moving averages. If the variance of random elements equals $\underline{v}$, and the moving averages have $\underline{n}$ terms, then their variance is $\frac{v}{n}$. (1) Accordingly, <u>with averages of four terms the variance of random elements will be reduced to one-fourth its original value.</u> We assume that the oscillatory component has a sinusoidal shape:

$$f_2(t) = \sin(\alpha + \lambda t) \tag{4.1}$$

then

$$\sum_{t=1}^{n} \sin(\alpha + \lambda t) = \frac{\sin\frac{1}{2}n\lambda}{\sin\frac{1}{2}\lambda} \sin[\alpha + \frac{1}{2}(n+1)\lambda] \tag{4.2}$$

which means that the moving average will have the same period and phase, but its amplitude will be reduced by the factor $\dfrac{1}{n}\dfrac{\sin\frac{1}{2}n\lambda}{\sin\frac{1}{2}\lambda}$.

Here we can notice still another effect, which is intuitively obvious and which we will use in the analysis of long cycles. Namely, the term Tf_2, i.e., the distortion of the oscillation, will be small if n is large or if $\frac{1}{2}n\lambda$ is a multiple of π, i.e., the span of the moving average corresponds to the period of oscillation in f_2 (t). If the oscillation is slow, i.e., λ is small, and if $n\lambda$ is small, i.e., the span of the moving average is short, then the amplitude is slightly reduced and the term $f_2 - Tf_2$ therefore declines. This means that moving averages become a trend and eliminate a slow oscillation. If the span of the moving average is somewhat longer than the period of oscillating, $n > \frac{2\pi}{\lambda}$, the factor of distortion, can have a negative sign, as a result of which the oscillations will increase. (2) Consequently, moving averages can increase, decrease, or eliminate the oscillatory component, and therefore it is desirable that they be replaced by some other method.

In studying business cycles, two methods, having several variations, are used. The first consists of separating the trend from seasonally adjusted data, on the assumption that the former has an additive (as above) or multiplicative character, and then considering deviations from that trend. This method has great shortcomings. First of all, every interpolation is arbitrary. Second, if values for some usual mathematical curve are interpolated, the trend must be recalculated for every extension of the time series. If moving averages are adopted, they produce distortions, which we discussed above. In an expanding economy, especially if the rate of growth is high, absolute deviations do not have much meaning. And relative deviations, because of the arbitrariness of the trend, do not directly tell us anything. Therefore, the second method of measuring cycles attempts to avoid the previous elimination of trend. The best-known example of this second method comes from the U.S. National Bureau of Economic Research, and it is useful to be acquainted with this technique. (3) The Bureau proceeds from the assumption that cycles are a constant phenomenon in a capitalist economy, that they maintain the essential characteristics of the functioning of the mechanism of that economy and that, accordingly, there is no sense in choosing only one statistical aggregate for measuring general fluctuations. Therefore, on the basis of an analysis of some 800 different statistical series, a so-called reference cycle is determined, which represents the general fluctuation. One of the ways of determining the reference cycle is by using an index of diffusion. The index of diffusion shows which proportion of all the series considered are series that increase (or decrease) in definite months or quarters. It shows the turning point — that moment when, after a rise, the index of diffusion stops increasing and when, after a fall, it stops declining and begins to rise. In that way the initial trough, the peak, and the final trough of the reference cycle are determined. The subdivision of the cycle between the initial trough and the peak is divided into three equal parts, and the same thing is done with respect to the subdivision between the peak and the final trough. Thus nine reference points and eight reference segments of the cycle are obtained.

In the determination of specific cycles of individual economic series, seasonal influences are first eliminated from the empirical data, and then two troughs and the peak that correspond to the reference data are established. From seasonally adjusted data the average for the whole cycle, which represents the base of the cycle, is calculated; and quarterly or monthly data are expressed as percentage deviations from that base. Peaks and troughs are determined on the basis of three-monthly averages of seasonally refined data, so that random disturbances are eliminated. Then the specific cycle, like the reference cycle, is divided into eight segments. These segments are averaged for several cycles so that a typical cycle may be obtained for the period being studied. It is then possible to compare directly the typical specific and the typical reference cycles: differences in amplitude, period, and phase (lags and leads) in individual segments and variability of amplitude and duration of the cycles measured; and characteristic differences in retardation and acceleration in individual segments are established. Thus systematized knowledge of the empirical characteristics of economic movements can then be usefully employed in forecasting economic upswings.

The following remarks can be made with regard to the usefulness of the Bureau's technique for our analysis. This technique eliminates trend between cycles, but not within cycles. For the relatively slow-growing U.S. economy and relatively short cycles, this does not lead to any analytic difficulties. However, the Yugoslav economy expands 2.5 times faster than the American, and the intracyclical trend becomes a significant factor in the analysis. It would therefore be necessary to make modifications in the technique. Furthermore, such a technique makes sense when a larger number of cycles are analyzed. In our case it is a question, as we shall see later, of four cycles in all, of which the first is entirely atypical, so that a complicated technique would not lead to knowledge that was not attainable on the basis of a simpler method of analysis as well. And, finally, a special reference cycle does not appear necessary to me. Although it is true that cyclical tendencies are constantly present in the economy — about which there was some discussion in the preceding chapter — it is also true that planning must correct and level off these tendencies. The basic task of economic policy is the stabilization of production at a high rate of growth. Accordingly, our reference series would have to be a series on the social product. In the absence of that series, and taking into consideration the fact that in the Yugoslav economy industry* directly conditions the movements of all other economic sectors (except agriculture), we will use the series of industrial production as representative, and the industrial cycle as the reference cycle.

Along with the inadequacies mentioned, it is worth emphasizing also that the Bureau's method gives as the cycle the deviations from a base that is unknown beforehand. Therefore, a current forecast becomes difficult. That, as well as the majority of other inadequacies, can be removed if chain indices of economic movements are used for measuring cycles. That method is used in this study. Since chain indices and the rate of growth are not the same and do not change equally as absolute amounts, it is necessary to examine here the characteristics of that method, especially with regard to the possibility that it results in distorting amplitude, phase, and the period of cyclical movements.

4.2 Characteristics of the Model Selected

We assume that our economy follows some long-run trend at a constant rate of growth $(a - 1)$. Accordingly, the trend will be determined by the equation $y_t = a^t$. We assume, further, that in the short run the economy regularly oscillates about that trend along some cosine curve, but in such a way that the amplitude of deviations is proportional to the values of the trend at every moment, t. This is necessary because it is plausible to assume that with expansion of the economy, the movements also increase absolutely, but not relatively as well. The factor of proportionality, k, must

---

*Throughout this work, the term "industry" refers to manufacturing, mining, and the generation of electricity — Translator.

be less than one to avoid the absurd result of a rate of growth in some part of the cycle greater than 100%. The path by which the economy moves is given by the equation

$$y_t = ka^t \cos t + a^t \tag{4.3}$$

which in shape is identical to equation (3.7), to which we came by an entirely different route. Equation (3.7) thus represented the oscillatory movements of the social product:

$$Y_t = A\, p^t \cos(\theta t - \varphi) + \overline{Y}_0\, \alpha^t$$

Let us make the initial equilibrium product equal to one, $\overline{Y}_0 = 1$, which depends on the proper choice of the units of measurement. Then we arrange the measurement of time so that $\theta = 1, \varphi = 0$. Finally, we introduce one assumption that can be empirically tested, namely, that both components of the social product expand by the same factor $p = \alpha = a$. In that case equation (3.7), which was deduced from certain assumptions about the behavior of economic subjects and of empirical values of certain structural coefficients, is transformed into equation (4.3), which will serve as the statistical model for the investigations in this study.

$$y_t = k\, a^t \cos t + a^t$$

With the empirical values of the Yugoslav economy, y_t indeed oscillates, but constantly increases (see Graph 4.1). We will now compare the amplitude, phase, and period of that equation with the equations that result from applying the two methods discussed above. Let us examine, first, the movement of relative deviations, d_t, from the line of the trend:

$$\frac{d_t}{\bar{y}_t} = \frac{y_t - \bar{y}_t}{\bar{y}_t} = \frac{(ka^t \cos t + a^t) - a^t}{a^t} = k \cos t \tag{4.4}$$

The relative deviations also oscillate along a cosine curve of the same period and phase, but the amplitude of oscillations is naturally less, and in fact equal to the factor of proportionality. The case is somewhat more complex when, instead of relative deviations, we use chain indices. Since the indices represent the number 100 plus the rate of growth, it will be simpler for us to consider the oscillation of the rate of growth. In so doing we will use

Graph 4.1

ALTERNATIVE REPRESENTATIONS OF BUSINESS CYCLES

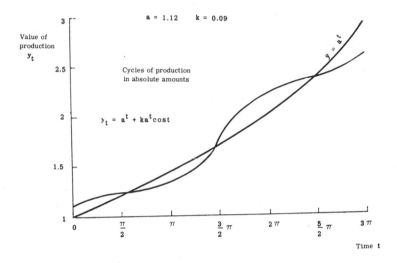

$a = 1.12 \qquad k = 0.09$

Value of production y_t

Cycles of production
in absolute amounts

$y_t = a^t + ka^t \cos t$

$\bar{y} = a^t$

Time t

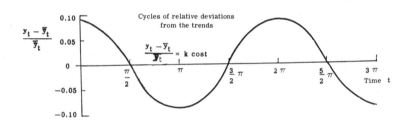

Cycles of relative deviations
from the trends

$\dfrac{y_t - \bar{y}_t}{\bar{y}_t} = k \cos t$

Time t

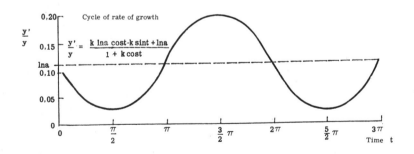

Cycle of rate of growth

$\dfrac{y'}{y} = \dfrac{k \ln a \cos t - k \sin t + \ln a}{1 + k \cos t}$

$\ln a$

Time t

instantaneous rates of growth, for they make possible a simpler mathematical analysis than the usual interval rates of growth. Accordingly,

$$\frac{dy}{dt}\frac{1}{y} = \frac{k \, \ln a \cos t - k \sin t + \ln a}{k \cos t + 1} \tag{4.5}$$

For characteristic values of t, the curve of the rate of growth assumes these values:

t	0	$\frac{\pi}{2}$	π	$\frac{3}{2}\pi$	2π
$\frac{y'}{y}$	$\ln a$	$\ln a - k$	$\ln a$	$\ln a + k$	$\ln a$

In order to get a conception of the order of magnitude of our constants, we can insert the empirical magnitudes that will most frequently appear in the analysis. We can use 12% annually as the average instantaneous rate of growth of industrial production, which gives $\ln a = 0.11$. One can see from the table that the highest cyclical rate of growth will be somewhere in the vicinity of $t = \frac{3}{2}\pi$. As empirical data show that the highest cyclical growth rate of industrial production is about 20%, that would amount to a proportionality factor of approximately $k = 0.20 - 0.11 = 0.09$. On the basis of those constants, curves are drawn on Graph 4.1. The extreme curves are given by the equation

$$\frac{d}{dt}\left(\frac{y'}{y}\right) = \frac{-k(k - \cos t)}{(1 - \cos t)^2} = 0 \tag{4.6}$$

$$\therefore \cos t = -k = -0,09$$

As $\cos t = -\cos(\pi \pm t)$, that is $180° \pm t = 84°50'$. At the minimum, $t_{min} = 180° - 84°50' = 95°10'$, at the maximum, $t_{max} = 180° + 84°50' = 264°50'$. The smaller the factor of proportionality, k — i.e., the smaller the deviations from the exponential path — the closer are the extremes to the points $\frac{\pi}{2}$ (for the minimum) and $\frac{3}{2}\pi$ (for the maximum).

When we insert the condition for the extreme (4.6) in the equation of the curve (4.5), we obtain as values of the extremes

$$\frac{y'}{y} = \ln a \pm \frac{k}{\sqrt{1-k^2}} \tag{4.7}$$

which means that the curve oscillates about $\ln a$. As a is near one, that means $\ln a \doteq a - 1$, which represents the rate of growth. Consequently, the <u>curve of the rate of growth oscillates about some average rate of growth</u>, which corresponds to the rate of growth from the trend, and that is intuitively obvious. The smaller the factor <u>k</u>, the closer are the extremes to the values $\ln a \pm k$, i.e., to the values given in the table above. For our value $k = 0.09$, the corrective factor is practically equal to one: $\dfrac{1}{\sqrt{1-k^2}} \doteq 1$.

We must still ascertain at which points the curve of the rate of growth cuts the line of the average growth rate about which it oscillates. In order to do that we subtract the values of the latter from the values of the former:

$$\frac{k \ln a \cos t - k \sin t + \ln a}{k \cos t + 1} - \ln a = -\frac{k \sin t}{1 + k \cos t} \qquad (4.8)$$

The expression obtained will be cancelled for all values for which $\sin t$ is cancelled, i.e., for $t = n\pi$, $n = 0, 1, 2, \ldots$.

Now we can resume the discussion of the characteristics of the curve of the growth rate (4.5). That curve oscillates about the average rate of growth given by the trend. It cuts the line of the average rate of growth — more precisely, the line $\dfrac{y'}{y} = \ln a$ — in regular intervals for $t = \pi$. Our curve resembles the cosine curve shifted toward the origin by $\dfrac{\pi}{2}$ (see Graph 4.1); however, that shift is valid precisely only for zero points, but not for the extremes. The extremes are found at the points $\dfrac{\pi}{2} \doteq \Delta t$ (minimum) and $\dfrac{3}{2}\pi - \Delta t$ (maximum), which means that the interval between the extremes is by $2\Delta t$ less than the interval between zero points, which amount to exactly π. That also means that individual phases of the cycle are not symmetrical. The retardation phase (recession and depression) is somewhat prolonged, and the acceleration phase (revival and boom) is somewhat shortened in relation to a regular cosine curve. As in real life, the retardation phase is usually shorter than the acceleration; in that way a spontaneous correction is carried out in the direction of symmetry of the empirical curve. Those "corrective" deviations are very small; in our case $\Delta t = \dfrac{1}{36}\pi$, and besides that $\Delta t \to 0$ when factor $k \rightarrow 0$. The amplitude of the curve of the growth rate is equal to $k \frac{1}{\sqrt{1-k^2}} \doteq k$ for small values of k, which appear in practice, which means that it is practically equal to the amplitude of relative deviations. We can therefore conclude that for all practical purposes the curve of the growth rate represents the curve of relative deviations from the trend shifted toward the origin by $\frac{\pi}{2}$. The shift of phases of $\frac{\pi}{2}$ or one-fourth of the length of the cycle in advance in relation to the remaining two cosine curves is obvious and intuitive. The rate of growth attains its extremes in the vicinity of the points of inflection of the original curve, and passes through zero in the vicinity of the maximum and minimum of the original cosine curve. In empirical work there appear further complications which will be discussed in the next chapter.

The noncorrespondence of the phases is the price that must be paid for the other advantages of our method. But that price is not too high. In an expanding economy, changes in the rates of growth are of primary importance. One of the cycle-producing mechanisms, the accelerator, reacts directly to changes in rates of growth, and not simply to absolute changes. It is necessary, however, to have constantly in mind the import of the phasal shift. It is only when the rate of growth just begins to fall that the deviation upwards from the trend begins; when the rate of growth decreases through the average, the deviation scarcely attains the maximum; when the rate of growth begins to increase again, the deviation just enters the negative quadrant. Insofar as we measure cycles of the growth rate — as we will do in this study — from the first inflection of the cosine curve, then to those cycles correspond cycles of relative and absolute deviations whose cosine curves are shifted so that they begin with the peak at the origin. In other words, measurement of cycles of growth rates from descending to descending inflections corresponds to measurement of cycles of deviations from peak to peak.

Thus we have arrived at the problem of determining the beginning and the end of the cycle. In physics, osciallations are measured from the ascending (descending) to the ascending (descending) inflections. The same approach was adopted by Schumpeter, for whom the points of inflection represent points of economic equilibrium from which outbursts of innovative impulses quickly push the system upward. That approach is now rare in the study of business cycles. The duration of cycles is determined almost always by time intervals from trough to trough or from peak to peak. The advantage of such a method of measuring is that peaks and troughs can be determined more precisely than other points and that a period of duration of the cycle, so determined, is then relatively invariant in relation to later occurrences or another analytic approach. Moreover, the length of the cycle is obtained as a simple number of expansive and contractive phases. I did not, however, decide upon that traditional mechanical approach, for I consider that the fundamental criterion in determining the cycles must be its economic interpretation. Later it will be seen that each of five of our postwar business cycles began with some significant economic reform. The beginnings of those reforms fall right at a time when the retardation part of the cycle cuts the trend line, i.e., they fall in the vicinity of the point of inflection. Since the duration of empirical cycles is different if they are measured by troughs rather than by peaks, and those differences are sometimes rather pronounced, measurement by points of inflection gives some kind of average duration and thus avoids extremes.

Determining cycles by points of inflection also emphasizes the heterogeneity of individual stages of the cycle, of which there are six and which we can designate as follows, according to the development of the cycle: (1) depression; (2) lower turning point or trough of the cycle; (3) revival; (4) boom; (5) upper turning point or peak of the cycle; and (6) recession. (4) The cycle begins with the depression — which is contrary to the usual approach in the analysis of cycles — for we determined the boundaries of the cycle at the points of inflection of the descending segments. The first three stages develop below the trend, the latter three above the trend. We shall call the ascending segment the accelerative phase, and the recession and depression the retardation phase of the cycle. The revival and boom form part of the accelerative phase, and the recession and depression are part of the retardation phase. The peaks and troughs, i.e., the turning points, shall be designated as separate stages of the cycle, for the reversal of economic movements represents a different phenomenon from their cumulative extension in the same direction and in fact represents a basic theoretical and practical problem in the sphere of business cycle analysis.

One more remark should be made in connection with terminological questions. In physics, vibrations and oscillations differ;

oscillatory movements are vibratory and also periodic. In the analysis of time series the English statistician Kendall proposes that the unsystematic components of residual fluctuations (after seasonal influences and trend are eliminated) be called stochastic movements, and the systematic components be called oscillatory; the oscillations may, but need not, also include a cyclical component that is a periodic function of time. (5) Economic fluctuations are never strictly periodic functions, but nevertheless it is usual to call them cycles. This terminology will be used in the present study. Fluctuations mean some kind of deviation from a uniform trend or a stationary level. Insofar as we discover in these deviations systematic elements (regularity in amplitudes, definite periodicity) we shall speak of cycles. We can use fluctuations and oscillations as alternative terms.

One additional introductory remark is necessary in connection with statistical series. Our statistics, unfortunately, do not elaborate quarterly series of the social product, as is the practice in more advanced statistical services. Quarterly indices are calculated of movements of industrial production and the sum of production of industry, forestry and construction (so-called production excluding agriculture). Earlier research in the Yugoslav Institute of Economic Studies showed that in the Yugoslav economy movements of all economic sectors (except agriculture) are narrowly correlated with industrial production. (6) Therefore we can probably use the quarterly indices of industry and production (excluding agriculture) of the Federal Statistical Bureau as indicators of the quarterly movement of the social product excluding agriculture. Further difficulty in the analysis stems from the fact that the Federal Statistical Bureau reports investments very incompletely. Here not only are quarterly data nonexistent, but there are no annual data in constant prices for investment in fixed capital or for growth of inventories. Therefore we shall have to use the other statistical series as substitutes.

Notes

1)
$$y_t = \frac{1}{n}(\varepsilon_1 + \varepsilon_2 + \cdots + \varepsilon_n)$$

$$E(\varepsilon_t \varepsilon_{t-1}) = 0, \quad E(\varepsilon_t) = E(y_t) = 0$$

$$E y_i^2 = \frac{1}{n^2} E(\varepsilon_1 + \cdots + \varepsilon_n)^2 = \frac{nv}{n^2} = \frac{v}{n}$$

2) M. G. Kendall, The Advanced Theory of Statistics, II (London: Griffen, 1959), pp. 378-380.

3) See C. A. Dauten, Business Cycles and Forecasting (Cincinnati: Southwestern Publishing Co., 1961), Ch. III, "Measurement of Economic Fluctuations."

4) The business cycle model can be ordered differently. For example, A. Spiethoff, in his well-known work of 1923, analyzes English and German cycles of the period 1822-1913 by this model: crash or depression (1 — recession, 2 — first revival); upswing (3 — second revival, 4 — boom, 5 — shortage of capital); crisis. We cite the version "Business Cycles," International Economic Papers, 3 (1953), 123.

5) Op. cit., p. 370.

6) B. Horvat, Pristupna kvalifikacija globalnog modela privrednog razvoja Jugoslavije za period od 1963 do 1970 godine, SZPP, Serija B, br. 20.

Chapter 5

CYCLICAL FLUCTUATIONS OF
PRODUCTION AND INVESTMENT

5.1 Cycles of Industrial Production

At one time it was imagined that in a socialist economy there
would be neither commodity-money relations nor business cycles.
In contrast to the former, the latter assumption is much more
justifiable, for planning ought to eliminate business cycles. However, study of economic movements shows that in the first twenty
years of socialist construction in Yugoslavia not even the latter
assumption was accurate (1): there are pronounced business cycles which recur at regular intervals. This discovery implies an
unpleasant consequence. What is disturbing is not the denial of a
false assumption, but the fact that economic policy is conducted as
though that assumption were accurate. In other words, those who
determine economic policy are unaware that they are acting in the
context of business cycles and that by their actions they are creating those cycles.

By way of illustration, the planning and implementation of three
successive annual plans of industrial production in the period 1960-
1963 can be mentioned (2):

	Rate of Growth	
	Plan	Achievement
1961	12.0	7.2
1962	12.6	7.0
1963	10.3	15.6

For 1961 the Federal Economic Planning Bureau essentially extrapolated the earlier high rate of growth. But as retardation had already begun in the middle of 1960, which remained unnoticed, the rate of growth achieved was 40% lower. That was considered accidental, and for 1962 a still higher rate of growth for industry was planned. (3) However, strengthened by inadequate economic measures, the retardation deepened and the actual rate was 45% lower. After personnel changes in the Planning Bureau, the principle of cautious planning was accepted, and for 1963 one of the lowest rates of industrial expansion for the entire decade was forecast. Meanwhile, a turning point had been reached, and the business cycle entered anew into the accelerative phase, so that the planned rate was exceeded by almost 50%. These errors contributed to the abandonment of two successive variants of the five-year plan worked out in that period, and in 1965 a third variant was worked out, with the period 1960-1965 remaining without a five-year plan. (4) As still more serious failures to hit the planned target occurred from 1965 on, even the third successive medium-term plan came into question and the need appeared for serious revisions or the construction of a fourth variant.

In the 16 years from 1949 to 1965 there were four industrial cycles. Except in 1951 and 1952, and then again in 1967, the rate of growth was never negative and that is the first significant characteristic which distinguishes Yugoslav cycles from the classical business cycles. Therefore we will not proceed in the analysis by way of study of absolute amounts, or of relative deviations, which are customary in the classical analysis of business cycles. We will, as was explained in the methodological survey, study changes in the rates of growth (5); instead of relations of absolute quantities and deviations, we shall analyze relations of growth rates. To avoid negative rates of growth, in the numerical analysis we will use indices which, as is known, represent the sum of 100 and the rate of growth.

Business cycles in Yugoslavia appear as fluctuations around a rising and rather steep trend. In Graph 5.1 that trend is shown by a horizontal line that represents the average rate of growth (12.3%) for the period 1952-1965, derived from actual empirical values for the beginning and final years of the period. Where that horizontal line cuts the broken line of the quarterly industrial indices, the boundaries of individual cycles are determined. The beginnings of the cycles are fixed at the descending phases. The economic significance of that decision will become clear later. Be-

44

sides the chain indices of the same quarters of successive years, the annual indices and indices on the basis of moving quarterly averages are given for the sake of comparison. As can be expected, these latter moderate random deviations of the direct quarterly indices, and in the last cycle give a picture of a true mathematical sine curve. It can be seen that taking either direct or average chain quarterly indices does not change the boundaries of the cycles. To avoid a mistaken interpretation it is desirable beforehand to call attention once again to the statistical content of all quarterly indices that are used in the graphs and tables of this study. These are not indices of successive quarters (not $\frac{\text{II quarter 1960}}{\text{I quarter 1960}}$), but indices of the same quarters of successive years (meaning: $\frac{\text{II quarter 1960}}{\text{II quarter 1959}}$). Such an index: (a) excludes seasonal components, for it compares the same parts of the year, and (b) reflects the annual and not the quarterly growth or decline, for it refers to successive years.

In the Yugoslav economy the accelerative and retardation phases correspond to the expansion and contraction phases of classical cycles. Those phases, as well as the dates of troughs and peaks, are presented for industrial cycles in Table 5.1. The data refer to the curve of the direct indices of the same quarters. The figures in parentheses present the dates and durations of the phases on the basis of the index of moving averages of the same quarters.

Table 5.1

Acceleration and Retardation Phases of Industrial Cycles

	Period	Duration in Quarters	
		Acceleration	Retardation
Trough	II/1951 (?)		
Peak	I/1955 (IV/1954)	15 (14)	
Trough	I/1956 (I/1956)		4 (5)
Peak	I/1957 (I/1957)	4 (4)	
Trough	III/1958 (IV/1958)		6 (7)
Peak	II/1960 (I/1960)	7 (5)	
Trough	I/1962 (I/1962)		7 (8)
Peak	I/1964 (IV/1963)	8 (7)	
Trough	III/1967 (?)		14

The figures in Table 5.1 require very careful analysis. First of all, a question mark designates my estimate for 1951, for quarterly data of the Federal Statistical Bureau do not exist for that year. The question mark for 1967 similarly represents my forecast. Great regularity is noticeable in the duration of individual phases of the cycles except for the first cycle, which is significantly longer than the others, and the last, which shows abnormal length of the retardation. Analysis of Graph 5.1 establishes that the first cycle is not entirely homogeneous, and that it consists of two sub-cycles; accordingly, a peak in the fourth quarter of 1953 and a trough in the first quarter of 1954 are interpolated. Insofar as we may thus break down that cycle, instead of an accelerative phase of 15 quarters we would obtain this picture:

		Duration in Quarters	
		Acceleration	Retardation
Trough	II/1952		
Peak	IV/1953	10	
Trough	I/1954		1
Peak	I/1955	4	

That picture agrees well with the one that follows from Table 5.1. However, I believe that breaking down the first cycle is not justified, and therefore that the retardation lasts one quarter altogether and is checked on a level which is higher than the other troughs. In addition, the curve on the basis of moving averages shows only one smaller jag. Accordingly, the first cycle is obviously not typical. Perhaps this interpretation is possible: as a result of freedom from the pressure of the economic blockade, emergence from the administrative stage of centralized planning, and orientation toward hurrying the completion of projects that were started in earlier years, economic movements had such an expansive force that the disturbance at the beginning of 1954 was quickly absorbed and the expansive phase was prolonged for nearly four years, which is twice as long as in later periods. In that prolonged acceleration, the great expansion of construction in 1952 and 1953 probably played a significant role (see Graph 5.2).

What strikes one in the remaining part of Table 5.1 is the relatively long duration and lengthening not only of the accelerative but also of the retardation phase. That indicates an inefficient and inadequate economic policy. The "boom" is insufficiently controlled, and subsequently the "recession" does not respond to the stimulus of the measures adopted, but as we shall see later, acts negatively. In the last two full cycles, the retardation and acceleration phases last 6-8 quarters. The entire industrial cycle, accordingly, lasted 12-16 quarters or 3-4 years, which is somewhat shorter than business cycles in other European countries. (6)

Here it will be of interest to determine the extent to which our introductory theoretical analysis of alternative accounts of business cycles is in accord with empirical data. In Graph 5.3 industrial cycles are shown on the basis of chain indices and of relative deviations from the exponential trend (in both cases the data are based on moving averages). A definite phasal shift is noticeable, but it is not complete (the turning points of the chain indices precede by 0-3 quarters; with regular oscillations about the exponential path with a period of one quarter, the lead would have to be $3\frac{1}{2}$ quarters). Much more important is a phenomenon which follows from the fact that the fluctuations do not unfold about a constant rate of growth, as is assumed in the theoretical model. Since up to 1960 the average rate of growth increased and later decreased, the oscillations of relative deviations deviate upwards from the trend in the first subperiod and deviate downwards in the second. In that respect the oscillations of the chain indices present a more regular picture. The amplitudes of those oscillations are also greater, which reflects the greater sensitivity of this method of measuring business cycles. Generally, as follows from the general theory of economic growth (7), the economy reacts functionally to changes in the rate of growth, and not to absolute changes. The average annual rate of growth for the period III/1952-II/1965 amounts to 12.2% for the trend of values and 12.25% on the basis of the beginning and the end of the empirical series. The arithmetic average of the rate of growth would have to be somewhat higher than the geometric average rate of growth. It is, but only in the second decimal place, and amounts to 12.28%. Accordingly, with sufficiently long series and to the extent that fluctuations are not too extreme, we can take the average of annual rates as the approximate trend of growth rates. If we add, moreover, that calculation of trend and of relative deviations from the trend is complicated and time-consuming work, while chain indices and their average are calculated directly from basic data, it follows that our method computationally is significantly simpler and analytically

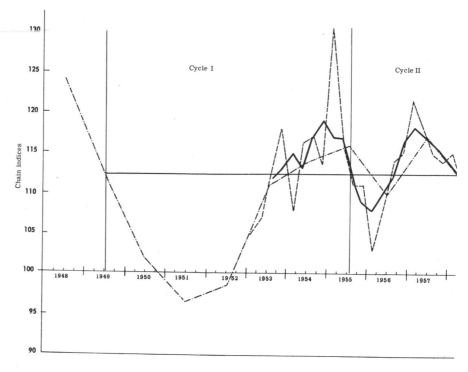

Graph 5.1 Industrial Cycle

more efficient. Meanwhile, even the asymmetry of the cycles of relative deviations from the trend have their significant informative value. It can be seen, as has already been emphasized, that before 1960 growth accelerated and later slowed down. Accordingly, there appeared accelerative and retardation phases of a longer cycle, which lasts at least 15 years. Later we will attempt to examine more fundamentally the origin of that longer cycle.

5.2 Measured Characteristics of Business Cycles

Since agriculture still accounts for about 26% of Yugoslavia's social product, and agricultural production is subject to large variations owing to weather conditions, that factor must be eliminated in studying business cycles. That may be done in such a way that the series of agricultural production is refined of sea-

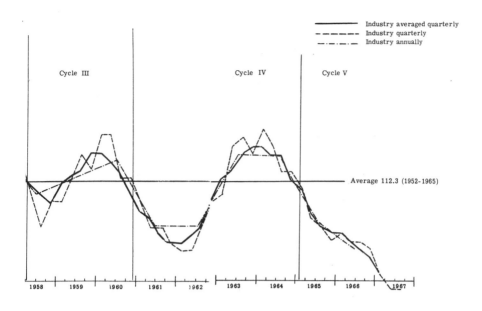

in Yugoslavia

sonal influences. However, as quarterly data for agricultural production do not exist, it is simpler merely to subtract agriculture and to consider movements of the economy without agriculture. As there are no quarterly data for that either, we will substitute, as was indicated, the aggregate of production of industry, forestry and construction (henceforth referred to as "IFC production").

That production, excluding agriculture, is shown in Graph 5.2. Two important facts are noticeable: (1) nearly all the troughs and peaks — of industrial and IFC production — coincide, and therefore the analysis carried out on the basis of Table 5.1 also holds for IFC production; (2) in relation to industrial production, the oscillations of IFC production are more pronounced. It is of interest to ascertain why those oscillations are greater. We establish easily that the oscillations of construction are huge, and that is precisely why IFC production fluctuates more than industrial.

49

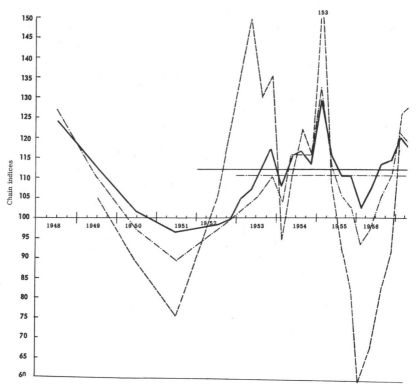

Graph 5.2   Business Cycles

Consequently, construction appears as one of the significant factors of instability of the Yugoslav economy. Owing to a series of
unresolved problems, and above all those involved in financing investment and housing construction, construction fluctuates with
huge amplitudes and in nearly every cycle experiences a classical depression with negative rates of growth. Therefore, and not
because of objective reasons in connection with the capacity of
construction operations, labor force, or the supply of raw materials (8), housing construction in Yugoslavia is half that in the Soviet Union or Sweden and is significantly less than in many other
European countries with much lower rates of growth. We are
forced to conclude that the standard of living of our working people
is unnecessarily below the productive potential of our economy.
In addition, the huge fluctuations in production prevent more ef-

50

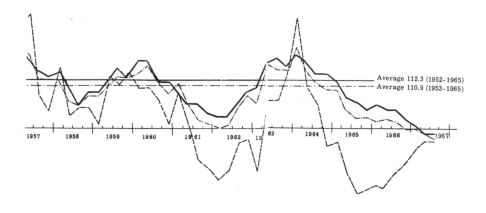

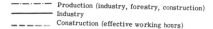
in Yugoslavia

ficient organization of construction enterprises: productivity is
low, quality poor, fluctuations of the labor force large, business
activity erratic, and services expensive. In the present depression once again an enterprise that at one time specialized in building roads is building apartment houses, and an enterprise special-
izing in housing construction is involved in bidding for roadwork
contracts. The repercussions for production are seen in the intensification of economic instability.

It remains for us to present the measured characteristics of
Graph 5.2 in tabular form. The boundaries of the cycles of IFC
production are determined in a manner similar for those of industry: by the intersecting of the horizontal line of average growth in
the period 1953-1965. The duration of the cycles of IFC production
is equal to that of industrial cycles, i.e., 3-4 years.

51

Table 5.2

Measured Characteristics of Production Cycles

Period	Duration in Quarters	Index of Annual Growth		
		Trough	Peak	Difference
Cycle I:				
industry production	III/1949-III/1955	24	97**	130	33
(exc. agr.)*	II/1949- II/1955	24	93**	133	40
construction			76**	149	73
Cycle II:				
industry production	III/1955- II/1958	11	103	121	18
(exc. agr.)*	II/1955- I/1958	11	94	122	28
construction			60	129	69
Cycle III:				
industry production	II/1958-IV/1960	10	107	118	11
(exc. agr.)*	I/1958-IV/1960	11	107	117	10
construction			102	115	13
Cycle IV:				
industry production	IV/1960- I/1965	17	104	119	15
(exc. agr.)*	IV/1960-IV/1964	15	101	121	20
construction			88	128	40

*Production excluding agriculture includes industry, construction and forestry.

**Quarterly data do not exist, and so the indices refer to the whole of 1951. Quarterly indices would be lower.

In the first three cycles there was a significant reduction of the difference between the maximum and minimum annual growth. That means that a tendency toward economic stabilization was at work. At the same time, the efficiency of investment was significantly improved and the rate of growth of the whole economy (excluding agriculture) increased. (9) Three conclusions are to a certain degree relevant to the discussion of centralization and decentralization. It was shown that decentralization entails both more efficient economic activity and a faster rate of growth, along with more stable expansion of production and, as will be seen later, more stable prices.

That positive trend underwent a reversal in the fourth cycle: the instability of the economy again began to increase, the rate of growth fell, and the increase of efficiency in investment slowed down or stopped. (10) Is this a matter of random phenomena? Before we attempt to answer that question we will consider in detail what happened to the rates of growth in the first four industrial cycles. Table 5.3 presents the data for analysis.

Table 5.3

Rate of Growth of Industrial Production by Cycles

	Indices of moving averages, base I/1952=100	Index of production growth within cycles	Duration of cycles in years	Annual rate of growth within cycles
Cycle I: III/1949	113*	100		
III/1955	163	144	6	6.3%
Cycle II: III/1955	163	100		
II/1958	224	138	2.75	12.3%
Cycle III: II/1958	224	100		
IV/1960	306	137	2.50	13.3%
Cycle IV: IV/1960	306	100		
I/1965	477	156	4.25	11.0%

*An annual index on the basis of the first quarter of 1952 = 100 is used; the average for 1952 is 111.

Source: Indeks, 1952-1965, monthly indices.

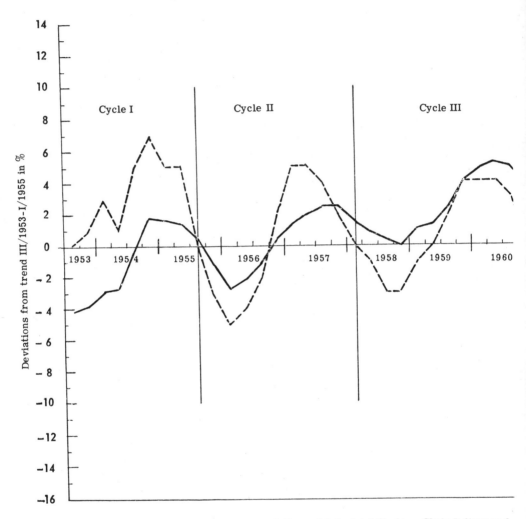

Graph 5.3   Alternative Representations of Industrial Cycles: Chain Indices and

(Data on the Basis of

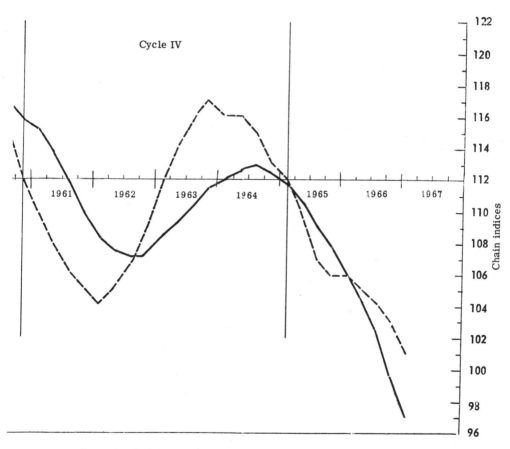

- - - - - - - Chain indices
———————— Relative deviations from trend $y = a \cdot 1.029^{t}$

Cycle IV

Relative Deviations of Industrial Production from the Exponential Trend

Moving Averages)

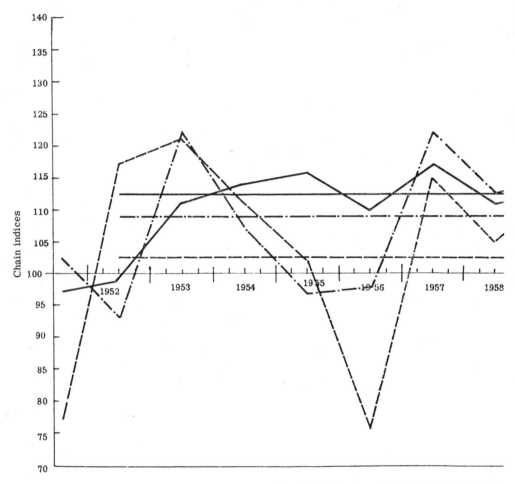

Graph 5.4   Cycles of Production of Industry,

56

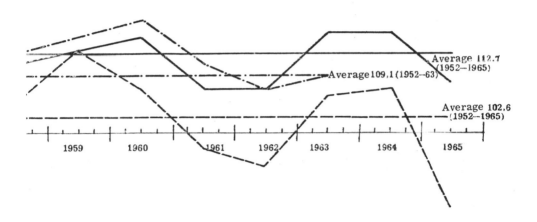

Legend:
- Industry
- Construction (effective working hours)
- Gross investment

Average 112.7 (1952—1965)

Average 109.1 (1952—63)

Average 102.6 (1952—1965)

1959   1960   1961   1962   1963   1964   1965

Construction, and Gross Investment

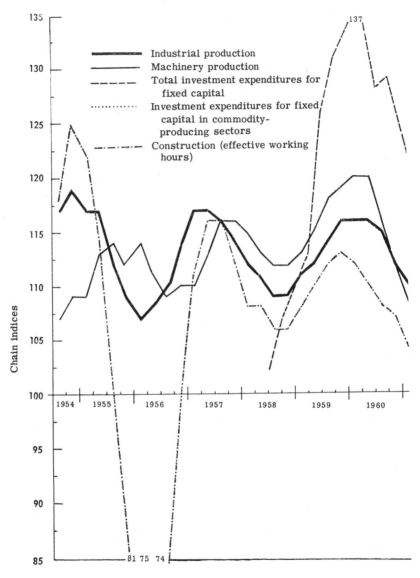

Graph 5.5 Cycles of Industrial Production, Machinery Production,

(Chain Indices on the Basis

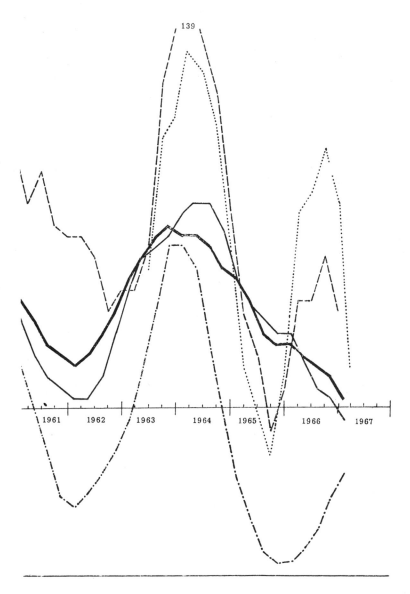

Construction, and Investment Expenditures for Fixed Capital

of Moving Averages)

In order to eliminate seasonal influences, the indices are calculated on the basis of 4-quarter moving averages centered on the
beginning and end of the cycle. It is notable, first of all, that production within cycles increases in rather narrow intervals, between 37% and 56%. That means that in the last 15 years we had
discontinuous development in segments of 50% increase in each.
If that tendency continues, then we shall have the next cycle when
current production increases by 50%. The rate of growth will determine when that happens. Longer cycles attain greater growth
of production within cycles, but along with a lower rate of growth.
This agrees with our general knowledge of the empirical characteristics of the economy, and therefore we can consider that phenomenon to be an expression of economic laws.

There is one more regularity that emerges. It is not probable
that the rate of growth in the present, fifth cycle will be greater
than that in the preceding one. Subsequent analysis will indicate
the possibility — insofar as the stabilization of the economy at a
low rate of growth continues — that the fifth cycle will be longer,
and will have a lower rate of growth, than the fourth cycle. If that
happens, and we then connect on the graph the average growth
rates through the cycles with one line, we shall obtain a longer
wave that may last about 16 years or longer.

What has been said is possible but not necessary. I believe that
in a planned economy there cannot be erratic necessities and that
when once a correct diagnosis is drawn up, there always exists in
principle the possibility of conscious correction and control. By
the same token it is improbable that the slowing down in the fourth
cycle is the product of chance. In fact, that slowing down of the
economy as a whole is still greater than is shown by the data for
industry, for in the same period there was an abrupt deceleration
of agricultural expansion. On the basis of the available information, the following hypothesis may be posited: the complexity of
the Yugoslav economy outgrew the framework of practical and administratively encumbered techniques that guided it. Economic
theory, general economic organization, and the preparedness of
the administrative apparatus appear to lag behind the needs of our
economic development. Insofar as this hypothesis is correct, and
we will have to return to it again, then it is clear that conclusions
follow concerning the actions that must be taken to avoid huge economic losses in the future. It is worthwhile to have in mind that
the social product (excluding agriculture) now amounts to about

7,200 billion old dinars annually. Every lost percent of increase of the social product represents a value of 72 billion. If the difference between the maximum and minimum annual growth rates increases by 10, as is the case in the fourth cycle in relation to the third, that means that the losses in unattained production have increased by 720 billion dinars annually. In comparison with that sum, all the savings in government budgets, however desirable — in the reduction of costs of administration, but not in the organization of cultural, educational, scientific and medical development to which, by the logic of circumstances, it is often related — appear to have rather second-order significance. The main reserves of the Yugoslav economy probably lie in another sector. (11)

5.3 Investment Cycles

Investment plays a significant role in theoretical explanations of the functioning of the cyclical mechanism. Unfortunately, our statistical service does not follow real investment quarterly, and does not even have reliable estimates of investment in constant prices for the preceding year. The available data on total annual real gross investment are juxtaposed in Graph 5.4 with the analogous data for construction and industrial production. It is evident that the movements of gross investment and construction correspond well, and also that gross investment fluctuates with much greater amplitudes than industrial production. These findings are not surprising when one bears in mind that construction activity comprises the greater share of investment. However, as the investment and production cycles correspond, investment policy — or its absence — represents one of the significant factors of instability in the Yugoslav economy.

Further information on investment cycles is presented in Graph 5.5, in which investment in equipment is approximated by production of machines, and investment in construction by effective working hours in construction. Money expenditures for investment in fixed capital are also drawn on the graph. It can be seen that the turning points of those expenditures correspond with total investment and investment in machinery and construction. All indices are calculated on the basis of 4-quarter moving averages, and all the movements turn out to be rather regular. Table 5.4 gives the basic data for comparative analysis.

First of all, it can be seen that the turning points of machinery

Table 5.4

Measured Characteristics of Cycles in Industry, Machinery Industry, and Construction
(on the basis of moving averages)

	Turning Points			Indices at Turning Points			Amplitudes		
	Industry	Machinery Industry	Con-struction	Industry	Machinery Industry	Con-struction	Industry	Machinery Industry	Con-struction
Peak	IV/1954	III/1955	IV/1954	119	114	125	–	–	–
Trough	I/1956	III/1956	II/1956	107	109	74	12	5	51
Peak	I/1957	III/1957	II/1957	117	116	116	10	7	42
Trough	III/1958	III/1958	III/1958	109	112	106	8	4	10
Peak	II/1960	II/1960	IV/1959	116	120	113	7	8	7
Trough	I/1962	I/1962	I/1962	104	101	91	12	19	22
Peak	IV/1963	II/1964	I/1964	117	119	115	13	18	24
Trough	..	..	I/1966	..	..	86	..	..	29

Average Lag (+) or Lead (–) in Relation to Industrial Production, in Quarters

Peak	–	+1.8	+0.0
Trough	–	+0.7	+0.3

production lag, especially at the peaks, whereas construction activity corresponds with the turning points of industry. Therefore, the rather useful conclusion can be drawn that <u>investment does not interrupt the flow of production; on the contrary, acceleration or retardation in production leads to interruption of investment activity.</u> That is a very important finding, for it shows that the usual theory of the accelerator is not applicable to the Yugoslav economy. On the average, almost two entire quarters after retardation of industrial expansion has begun, the machinery industry further accelerates the growth of its production. Accordingly, machinery production has <u>until now</u> acted as a stabilizing factor, contrary to the experience of other market economies, where it is a marked destabilizer. That phenomenon can be explained by the chronic hunger for investment in an economy in which there is complete faith in rapid and long-term economic expansion.

The synchronization of construction cycles with the others is suddenly interrupted in 1966, when an upward turning point is reached in construction long before the turning point is attained in industry or machinery production. That unexpected leap in construction might be accidental, but we can explain it. This is one of the possible explanations. Since in all other cases the downturn in construction and industry is synchronized, the turning point of the construction path in 1966 signalled that the time had also arrived for the turning point in industrial production. That conclusion is strengthened by the fact that at the same time there was a sharp increase of investment expenditures for fixed capital in the economy as a whole and in the commodity-producing sector. That the turning point in industry did not arrive, however, is explained by some new factors — factors of economic policy — which were not present in earlier cycles. Because of these factors, a year later there was again a reduction of investment expenditures. In the present phase of our research it is not yet possible to verify this hypothesis. But since it is a very important question, it will be necessary to work it out more fundamentally later.

The indices at the turning points and the line on Graph 5.5 show that industry and machinery production expand at approximately the same tempo, while construction develops more slowly. But construction has significantly greater amplitudes than the other two activities. Construction is, as we have already emphasized, a marked factor of instability in our economy. In the first two cycles the amplitudes of the activities concerned were reduced, and after that they increased. The instability of machinery production, whose amplitudes at first were less and later were greater than those of industry, especially increased. All this corresponds to the earlier observation that the acceleration of growth before 1960 was accompanied by a decrease in the instability of our economy, and that instability increased with the retardation of growth after that year. Since, as we shall later see, the instability of the economy is positively correlated with the rate of growth, the observed phenomenon can by no means be considered normal or regular.

The hypothesis may be posited that the discontinuity in 1960 came because of changes in institutional factors or, perhaps more precisely, because of unsatisfactory and inadequate changes in institutional factors. Investigation of this hypothesis is beyond the framework of this study. Therefore we shall content ourselves with an impression that was stated earlier, and which is deduced from the following. After workers' self-management was instituted in 1950-1952, there was an exceptionally rapid economic expansion in the period 1952-1960 — in fact, the fastest in the world at that time. In those eight years total production doubled and industrial production almost tripled. If we extend the relevant period another four years — to 1964 — then total production tripled and industrial production increased by more than four times. In the increase of the volume of production in that short period was compressed several decades of earlier development. However, the institutional foundation did not develop at the rate required by the overflowing of productive power, and this led to a gap between the needs of the economy and social organization (the knowledge and preparedness of social organizations to satisfy those needs). Almost overnight we found ourselves in a relatively developed economy, but with the organization, knowledge, mentality, and habits of a backward economy. The neglect of scientific work, the unwillingness of the state apparatus to rely upon scientific research, and the disregard of political bodies for the creation of conditions for scientific research are some of the reasons why the inherent possibilities of our society have not been utilized. The consequence is that the accurate prediction of economic movements is rapidly reduced and the economy evades conscious social control. That is especially pronounced in industry, where deviations from planning forecasts in the period 1961-1964 already increased two-and-a-half times in relation to the period 1957-1960. (12) And thus we had a long-term retardation of growth after 1960 and a failure of two reforms that were undertaken at the time precisely in order to adjust the institutional superstructure to the material base.

Notes

1) It is of interest to note that in this case the first methodological doubt was expressed in a creative period of Soviet economic theory that was terminated at the end of the 1920s by the brutal repressions of Stalin. Thus, E. A. Preobrazhensky wrote in 1924 about the economic crises in the NEP period (see Z. Baletić, Marksistička teorija ekonomskih kriza [Zagreb: Naprijed, 1965], p. 216). However, contemporary Soviet economists, for example, S. Khavina, consider that business cycles in socialist countries are a figment of bourgeois ideology, for "socialism does not know of antagonistic contradictions." Khavina then presents data on annual growth rates of Soviet industry, from which it may be seen that before World War II the cycles were five-year periods, and after the war, from 1952 on, the tempo of industrial expansion continually slowed down. Instead of analysis, these data drew the comment that it is a matter of "concrete historical conditions of economic development" ("Izmišljotine o 'krizama' i 'ciklusima' u socialističkoj privredi," Ekonomičeskie nauki, 1967, No. 2, pp. 65-67).

2) Total production is more difficult to forecast because of externally conditioned fluctuations of agricultural production, which still accounts for more than one-fourth of the total social product.

3) For the economy as a whole, the highest growth of the decade was planned (16.2%), but a rate of 4.3% was attained, or three-and-a-half times lower. See B. Horvat et al., Uzroci i karakteristike privrednih kretanja u 1961. i 1962. godine. SZPP, DAM (Belgrade, 1962), pp. 29-32.

4) It is of interest to note that the same Planning Bureau at that time rejected the proposal of a scientific institute that it investigate and analyze the implementation of plans in Yugoslavia. The Bureau explained in writing that it "considers that the study would not be able to show anything of great importance that is not already known."

5) In mathematical jargon it may be said that the new phenomena demand that instead of functions their (logarithmic) derivations be studied.

6) Postwar business cycles in ten European countries and the USA have durations extending from 16 quarters in Belgium to 21 quarters in Austria, with an arithmetic average of 18.3 quarters or 4-1/2 years for all eleven countries (see A. Maddison, Economic Growth in the West [New York: The Twentieth Century Fund, 1964], p. 48).

7) See "Optimalna stopa investiranja," in B. Horvat, Ekonomska teorija planske privrede (Belgrade: Kultura, 1961).

8) It is necessary, however, to mention that in planning there existed a systematic tendency to neglect the development of production of construction materials.

9) This question is emphasized in the so-called "Yellow Book" (see Uzorci i karakteristike, op. cit., pp. 1-9).

10) We shall measure the efficiency of investment by production coefficients (the social product in the course of the year in relation to fixed capital at the beginning of the year). The production coefficient of the economy, excluding agriculture, increased from 0.11 in 1952 to 0.18 in 1960, or by 64%. In the following three years, for which data exist, the efficiency of investment stagnated with coefficients of 0.18, 0.18, and 0.19. The data are from the study by P. Sicherl, Osnovna sredstva kao faktor privrednog rasta i planiranja, Yugoslav Institute of Economic Studies.

11) Anticipating a comparative analysis in a later chapter, here we can caution that business cycles are not specific to Yugoslavia, but appear in all socialist countries. The Czechoslovak economist Jozef Goldmann studied economic movements in Czechoslovakia, East Germany, Poland and Hungary on the basis of annual data for the period 1950-1964, and he established industrial production and investment oscillations with a duration of 7-9 years. "Fluctuations in the rate of growth," reasoned Goldmann, "differ in principle from cyclical development in capitalism ... the business cycle follows necessarily from the very essence of the capitalist system and can be reduced only by state intervention. On the other hand, fluctuations in the rate of growth are not inherent in the socialist system, but those fluctuations occur because of insufficient knowledge of the economic laws of socialism and inadequacies in their application." See "Fluctuations and Trend in the Rate of Economic Growth in Some Socialist Countries," Economics of Planning, 1964, No. 2, pp. 89-90, 94.

12) M. Ostraćanin, "Analiza izvršavanja društvenih planova," internal paper of the Yugoslav Institute of Economic Studies.

Chapter 6

AGRICULTURAL CYCLES AND THE
INFLUENCE OF AGRICULTURE

In addition to construction (and investment as a whole), agriculture is another sector with extreme oscillations and thus represents an exceptionally serious factor of economic instability. Let us consider the measured characteristics of agricultural cycles.

Table 6.1

Agricultural Cycles 1948-1964

	Year	Annual Index of Change		Difference
		Trough	Peak	
Cycle I	1950	75		
	1951		143	68
Cycle II	1952	69		
	1953		144	75
Cycle III	1954	89		
	1955		125	36
Cycle IV	1956	83		
	1957		145	62
Cycle V	1958	89		
	1959		131	42
Cycle VI	1960	90		
	1963		110	20
Cycle VII	1965	91		
	1966		116	25

Table 6.1 will be very interesting for astrologers and useful for
the student who must remember the data: the troughs of agricultural cycles fall in even years and the peaks in uneven years. The
first five cycles were uniformly two-year cycles. In the sixth
there was a great change: the length of the cycle doubled. Is that
a random phenomenon? Probably not. The sixth cycle is different
not only in the length of the cycle but in amplitude, which is significantly less. At the beginning of the period in productive years
agricultural production happened to be one-and-a-half times greater than in bad years. However, these differences show a tendency
to decrease, especially in the last two cycles. The modernization
of agricultural production (contemporary technology and orientation toward stock-raising) probably contributed to that, at least

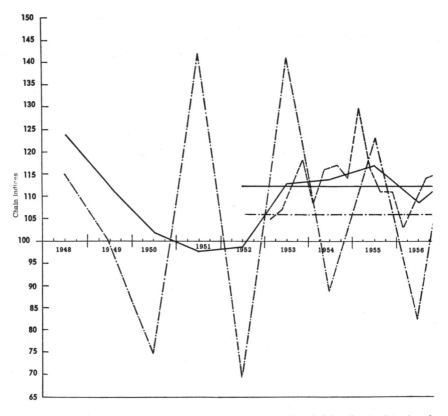

Graph 6.1   Agricultural and

partially. Moreover, the share of agriculture in national income (in current prices) fell from 35% in the first cycle to 26% in the sixth. Taking both facts into consideration, it follows that, in the future, economic policy can count on a strong factor of instability having been brought under control. However, it is also necessary to bear in mind that the troughs of the cycles were raised less than the peaks were lowered, which means that there had been a retardation of the growth of agricultural production.

Since in the period 1949-1965 there were six agricultural cycles and a total of four industrial cycles, they are obviously not synchronized. Accordingly, the influence of agriculture on the industrial cycle is neither decisive nor entirely simple. Agriculture can influence economic movements in three ways: (1) by the supply

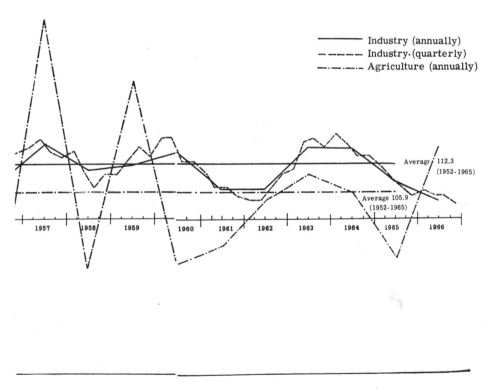

Industrial Cycles

of raw materials for other sectors; (2) by changes in the purchasing power of farmers; and (3) by the effect on the external balance of trade. Where the first effect is concerned, about 90% of all consignments of agricultural raw materials are absorbed by four industries: textiles, leather and footwear, food processing, and tobacco manufacturing. (1) Those four industries created about one-fourth of the social product of industry in the last ten years. However, the textile and leather industries can also produce with imported raw materials. There remain the food processing and tobacco industries, which are mainly oriented toward domestic raw materials and produce about 10% of the industrial social product. Therefore, the direct influence of agricultural fluctuations on industry will be relatively small and they do not contribute much to the explanation of the industrial fluctuations on Graph 6.1.

Prices move in reverse to agricultural production (Graph 10.4), offsetting fluctuations in the purchasing power of farmers. Remaining fluctuations are transmitted first of all to the production and prices of consumer goods and services. Growing (falling) demand leads to an expansion (contraction) of production, and the latter again to an increase (decrease) of imports and decrease (increase) of exports. Thus we have arrived at the external market effects which, it appears, are the most significant. It is worthwhile to survey certain compensatory movements. A good harvest reduces imports of food, but at the same time it increases raw materials and final goods imports for satisfaction of the increased purchasing power of farmers. The reverse is true when the harvest is poor. But even in spite of those compensations, the net effect on the balance of payments is great and must be analyzed.

It appears most natural to assume that a bad harvest in one year will lead to large net imports of agricultural products in the succeeding year and, along with that, an increase in the balance of payments deficit. Similarly, good harvests will eliminate net imports of agricultural products and contribute to a reduction in the balance of payments deficit. Table 6.2 shows that this assumption is correct only for the first three agricultural cycles, when the maxima and minima of the balance of payments deficit correspond with the peaks and troughs of agricultural fluctuations with a natural lag of one year. However, in the last three cycles that relationship does not exist. The discontinuity begins in 1958. (2) Unproductive years come nearer to productive ones. Agricultural production increased so much that it covers domestic needs, and

70

Table 6.2

Fluctuations of Agricultural Production and the
Balance of Payments Deficit

Year*	Annual Index of Agricultural Production	Share of Agricultural Production in Total		Deficit in Balance of Payments	Net Imports of Agricultural Products
		Imports %	Exports %	(billion dinars, $1= 300 d.)	
Peaks of Agricultural Cycles					
1951/1952	143	24	38	37	− 1
1953/1954	144	28	30	32	6
1955/1956	125	32	27	33	20
1957/1958	145	17	28	51	− 1
1959/1960	131	9	23	57	− 16
1963/1964	110	14	20	71	2
Troughs of Agricultural Cycles					
1952/1953	69	30	21	66	24
1954/1955	89	29	24	51	20
1956/1957	83	23	24	59	16
1958/1959	89	19	22	47	9
1960/1961	90	14	23	80	− 1
1965/1966	91	15	17	. .	8

*The first year in each pair refers to the index of agricultural
production, and the second to all other data.
  Sources: SZS, Jugoslavija 1945-1946, pp. 86, 97.
  SZS, Statistički Godišnjak Jugoslavija, 1967, pp. 131, 208.

in good years results in net surpluses. Since the balance of payments deficit increased still further along with the expansions in
1961 and 1964, the reasons for it must be sought in the cycles and
structure of industrial production. It is necessary to examine this
indication in more detail later.

Notes

1) SZS, <u>Medjusobni odnosi privrednih delatnosti Jugoslavije u 1962. godini</u> (Belgrade, 1966).

2) The eternal balance of trade, with a usual lag of one year, reflects the situation on the internal market. "Until 1957," states V. Stipetić, "consumption of food products increased more rapidly than agricultural production. That was especially the case with nourishment in the village after the abolition of compulsory deliveries" (<u>Jugoslovensko tržište poljobprivrednih proizvoda</u>, Zadr. Knj. Belgrade, 64, p. 78).

Chapter 7

REGIONAL CYCLES

Because of very uneven development in the territory of Yugoslavia — per capita social product is five times less in Kosmet
than in Slovenia — and very uneven distribution of productive power, it will be useful to briefly examine regional differences in economic fluctuations. First we shall consider the summary picture
of regional differences given in Table 7.1.

Seven Yugoslav regions are classified in three groups: underdeveloped regions, developed regions, and Serbia proper,* whose
per capita production corresponds to the Yugoslav average. The
developed regions have 40% of the population, and they produce
53% of total production. Given the proclaimed goal of economic
policy to reduce the differences in degree of development, one
would have to expect that the rate of growth would increase with
the degree of underdevelopment. The table shows that this goal
was achieved only in the developed group for the economy as a
whole, as well as for industry and agriculture. There were no
such regular movements in the underdeveloped regions. Moreover, in the course of the 13 years under consideration, the productive position of the entire underdeveloped area worsened. That
occurred because of the relatively slow development of Kosmet
and Bosnia-Herzegovina. In Kosmet, development was very slow
at the beginning of the period and accelerated later. In Bosnia-
Herzegovina the movements were the reverse: the rate of growth
constantly fell from a relatively high value at the beginning of the
period. In both cases the average development was slow. The

---

*Serbia proper is the Republic of Serbia excluding the autono-
mous provinces of Kosovo-Metohija (Kosmet) and Vojvodina.

73

	Per Capita Social Product in 1,000 Old Dinars	Economy		
		Rate of Growth %	Percent Share in	
			1952	1965
Kosovo-Metohija	81	8.2		
Macedonia	136	9.6		
Bosnia-Herzegovina	154	8.2		
Montenegro	164	11.2		
Underdeveloped regions	139	8.8	22.8	22.4
Serbia proper	208	9.2	23.8	24.8
Vojvodina	222	9.8		
Croatia	256	8.7		
Slovenia	410	8.5		
Developed regions	280	8.8	53.4	52.8
Yugoslavia	213	8.9	100.0	100.0

Source: Statistički Godišnjak-Jugoslavia (1967), pp. 326, 355.

relative position of the underdeveloped regions worsens more perceptibly when population indices are considered, for the growth of population in that area is twice as fast as in the developed regions.

It is of interest to observe that, contrary to expectations, the shares of agriculture in the social product are not much different in the underdeveloped and developed regions (28.5% and 25.7% in 1952, 17.1% and 16.8% in 1965). Accordingly, the eventual greater instability of production cannot be attributed to a greater share of agriculture.

Since quarterly data exist only for industrial production, we shall carry out a comparative analysis of cyclical movements only for industrial production. And there too, because of lack of data, we shall have to omit Kosmet from the group of underdeveloped regions and Vojvodina from the developed group. The underdeveloped regions

Table 7.1

Growth of Social Product by Regions, 1952-1965
1960 prices)

Industry			Agriculture		
Rate of Growth %	Percent Share in		Rate of Growth %	Percent Share in	
	1952	1965		1952	1965
10.1			5.2		
14.2			5.7		
12.9			4.0		
20.8			3.5		
13.3	19.9	23.2	4.6	23.7	22.1
13.7	19.3	23.3	5.3	26.7	27.3
13.8			6.8		
10.9			5.0		
9.9			3.5		
10.9	60.8	53.5	5.3	49.6	50.6
12.0	100.0	100.0	5.1	100.0	100.0

thus determined (Macedonia, Bosnia-Herzegovina and Montenegro) accounted for 21% of the total industrial output of the country in 1965, while the developed regions (Croatia and Slovenia) accounted for 45%. The movements are shown on Graph 7.1, and the basic measured characteristics are given in Table 7.2. Aggregation from the original data is carried out so that unweighted arithmetic averages of chain indices are used.

It can be seen from the table that the amplitudes of industrial fluctuations in the underdeveloped regions are significantly greater than in the developed ones, and the graph shows that the path of the chain indices has a much more irregular shape for underdeveloped regions. It follows from both facts that the instability of industrial production is significantly greater in the underdeveloped regions than in the developed regions. The oscillations are also

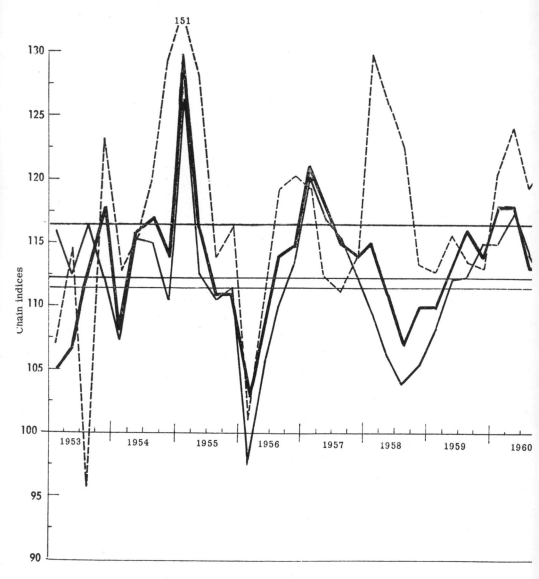

Graph 7.1   Regional

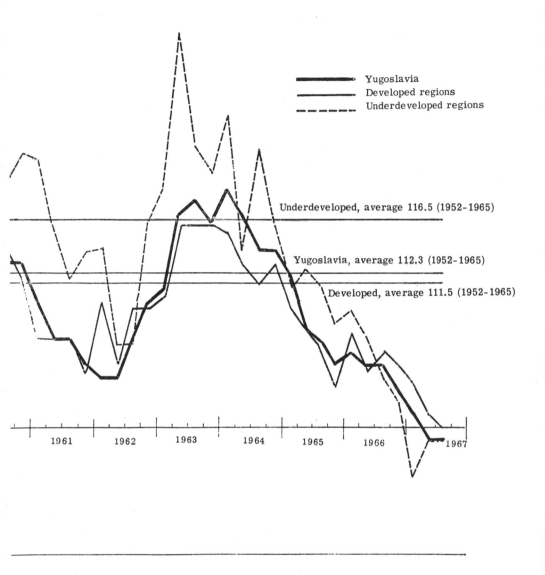

Underdeveloped, average 116.5 (1952-1965)

Yugoslavia, average 112.3 (1952-1965)

Developed, average 111.5 (1952-1965)

Yugoslavia
Developed regions
Underdeveloped regions

1961   1962   1963   1964   1965   1966   1967

Industrial Cycles

Measured Characteristics of Industrial Cycles

	Turning Points			Indices
	Yugoslavia	Developed Regions	Underdeveloped Regions	Yugoslavia
Peak	I/1955	I/1955	I/1955	130
Trough	I/1956	I/1956	I/1956	103
Peak	I/1957	I/1957	I/1958	121
Trough	III/1958	III/1958	I/1959	107
Peak	II/1960	II/1960	II/1960	118
Trough	I/1962	IV/1961	II/1962	104
Peak	I/1964	I/1964	I/1964	119
Trough	III/1967*	III/1967*	I/1967*	99*

*Forecast of turning point.

greater in agricultural production, for which there exist only annual data. (1) Thus, the entire economy of the underdeveloped regions is more unstable than the economy of the developed regions and demands special attention on the part of agencies concerned with economic policy.

The increase of general industrial instability from 1960 on that was observed earlier can now be explained by the increase of instability in underdeveloped regions (in the developed regions the amplitudes of fluctuations decrease up to the last peak as can be seen in Table 7.2). That holds especially for the period beginning with the implementation of the last reforms. In the entire earlier period the path of the index of growth of the underdeveloped regions lies above the path of the developed regions (see Graph 7.1). However, in the middle of 1966 the rate of industrial expansion of the underdeveloped regions fell below the rate of the developed regions, and in 1967 there was even an absolute decline in industrial production.

Except in the second cycle, the turning points of the developed and underdeveloped regions coincide with the turning points of industrial production as a whole. Accordingly, the industrial cycles are synchronized in all regions of Yugoslavia. The exceptional occurrence in the second of the mentioned cycles, i.e., in 1958, was

Table 7.2

of Developed and Underdeveloped Regions

at Turning Points		Amplitudes		
Developed Regions	Underdeveloped Regions	Yugoslavia	Developed Regions	Underdeveloped Regions
128	151	—	—	—
98	102	27	30	49
121	130	18	23	28
104	113	14	17	17
118	124	11	14	11
105	107	14	13	17
116	125	15	11	18
100*	96*	20*	16*	29*

that a sharp acceleration of production took place in the underdeveloped regions just at the time when the retardation of production
in the developed regions deepened. And that is precisely the reason for the exceptionally mild recession in 1958.

Note

1) See the monograph by M. Bazler, Klasifikacija jugoslavenskih
područja po stepenu privredne razvijenosti, Yugoslav Institute of
Economic Studies, Belgrade (1968). That monograph deals with
regional cycles in much greater detail.

Chapter 8

REGULARITIES IN THE TREND OF LABOR PRODUCTIVITY

Economic stability depends upon stability of prices, among other things. But price stability is to a significant degree conditioned by the increase in efficiency of economic activity. Thus we arrive at the problem of productivity of labor and the efficiency of capital. In addition, the cyclical movements of the economy make possible empirical verification of a widely circulated hypothesis related to labor productivity.

"With a given volume of employment, the growth of labor productivity results in an increase of production. In addition, the growth of productivity of labor always represents a positive phenomenon. Now, when the volume of employment changes, statistical data do not always show unambiguously whether the causal connection is that production grows because of increased labor productivity or, conversely, productivity of labor — which represents the ratio of production to employment — grows because production can increase faster than employment. Establishing an approach to the causative conditions in this case is of great importance for the formulation of economic policy. Insofar as the process begins with an increase in the productivity of labor, then it is a matter first of all of utilizing the internal reserves of economic organizations. Insofar as the predominant influence is fulfillment of the possibilities of increasing production, then the Archimedean lever must be sought in the organization of the economy as a whole and, in general, in the institutional framework of production." Five years have elapsed since this was written in the "Yellow Book" (Žuta Knjiga) (1), and this permits the positions brought out there to be more strongly substantiated empirically.

In the meantime, the daily press and official materials appear to have made the following three positions one of the maxims of economic policy:

1) rapid growth of labor productivity is the precondition for inclusion in the international market, i.e., for increased exports;

2) rapid growth of labor productivity — i.e., a greater contribution to production from increased productivity than from increased employment — is the precondition for greater expansion of production;

3) in order to attain goals (1) and (2) it is necessary to reduce the present rate of employment growth.

The question arises as to whether that three-point maxim is correct.

As far as point (1) is concerned, Ricardo has already shown that it is mistaken. Inclusion in the international market does not depend upon absolute productivity — on that score the underdeveloped countries would have no chance whatever — but on relative productivity which, in the theory of international trade, is known as "comparative advantage." In addition to comparative advantage, the exportability of products, which again depends upon the structure and expansion of world demand for imports, plays a key role.

It is also a mistake to believe that an increase of the share of labor productivity growth in the increase of production in relation to the share of increased employment is, in itself, positive. In slowly growing economies, such as the British, the share of productivity of labor is greater than in Yugoslavia, but the rate of economic growth is several times lower. Also, in developed countries that have exhausted their reservoirs of labor from agriculture, the contribution of productivity is greater. In fact it is only for such economies that there is validity to the conclusion that there is an identity between rapid increases in labor productivity in nonagricultural sectors and the general rate of economic growth. In underdeveloped economies with large reserves of labor, the contribution to production of new employment will be greater. There is not only nothing bad in that, but on the contrary it represents the rational way to maximize the increase of social production. The expansion of production will in fact be maximal only if the growth of labor productivity is also sufficiently high. What the relative contributions of productivity and employment will be is entirely irrelevant: they are not determinants of growth; they are determined by growth. The faster the rate of economic development, the faster the reserves of labor will be exhausted and the faster the proportions will change in favor of productivity of labor.

Points (2) and (3), moreover, represent empirical propositions.

Insofar as they are correct, then a rapid growth of labor productivity will be accompanied by relatively little employment growth, and vice versa. What do statistical data show concerning that?

Table 8.1 aggregates years in which the growth of labor productivity was above the average (Group I) and those in which it was below the average (Group II), considered in relation to what happened to employment. The result obtained is that in years of high gains in production, industry employed 10% more workers than in years of low gains. The tendencies are similar in the economy as a whole (measured by the social product, agriculture excluded), but they are not as pronounced. Accordingly, empirical verification turned out negative, and our maxim must be turned about so that it reads: the faster the growth of production, the faster will be the growth of labor productivity, even if a great many new workers are employed.

The accuracy of this conclusion can be seen clearly especially if we group the data according to maximum and minimum growth of production, i.e., according to the peaks and troughs of our graphs. In addition, the conclusion is accurate not only for labor productivity, but holds also for efficiency of use of capital. We will measure that efficiency by the marginal production coefficient, i.e., the ratio of the increase of the social product to the increase of fixed capital ($\Delta P / \Delta K$).

Table 8.1

Growth of Productivity of Labor and Employment in
Years with Above-Average (I) and Below-Average (II)
Increase in Labor Productivity

		Average Annual Index of Labor Productivity	Average Annual Employment (in thousands)
Industry*	I[a]	107	66
	II[b]	103	60
Economy, excluding agriculture**	I[c]	107	129
	II[d]	101	122

*Period 1952-1965 a 1953, 1957, 1959, 1960, 1963, 1964.
                     b 1954, 1955, 1956, 1958, 1961, 1962, 1965.
**Period 1952-1964 c 1956, 1957, 1959, 1960, 1963, 1964.
                     d 1953, 1954, 1955, 1958, 1961, 1962.

Table 8.2

Growth of Productivity of Labor and Efficiency of
Capital in Years of Maximum and Minimum Growth
of Production

		Average Annual Index of Growth of Productivity	Average Annual Increase in Employment	Average Annual $\dfrac{\Delta P}{\Delta K}$	Average Annual Index of Growth of Fixed Capital
Industry:	peaks a	106	81	0.75	108
	troughs b	103	50	0.47	108
Economy, excluding agriculture:	peaks a	106	167	0.71	106
	troughs b	103	88	0.35	106

a) 1955, 1957, 1960, 1964; for fixed capital, excluding 1964 for
lack of data.
b) 1956, 1958, 1962.

At the peaks of the cycles the economy employed almost twice
as many new workers as at the troughs and, at the same time, attained twice as high a growth rate of labor productivity. Since
fixed capital is not as mobile as the labor force — investment activity must be completed once it has begun — it expanded at equal
rates at the peaks and troughs. Consequently, the efficiency of its
utilization depends first of all on the variation of the social product. It can be seen that the marginal production coefficients are
twice as high at the peaks than at the troughs. In both cases the
differences are extreme: a high rate of growth means high productivity and efficiency as well, while a low rate of growth reduces both.

Since there are quarterly data for employment, it is possible
for us to consider cycles of employment and labor productivity in
more detail. Graph 8.1 presents the necessary data. One can see,
first of all, that there is a close connection in industry between
movements of employment and movements of production: when
production grows, employment also grows. The maximum value

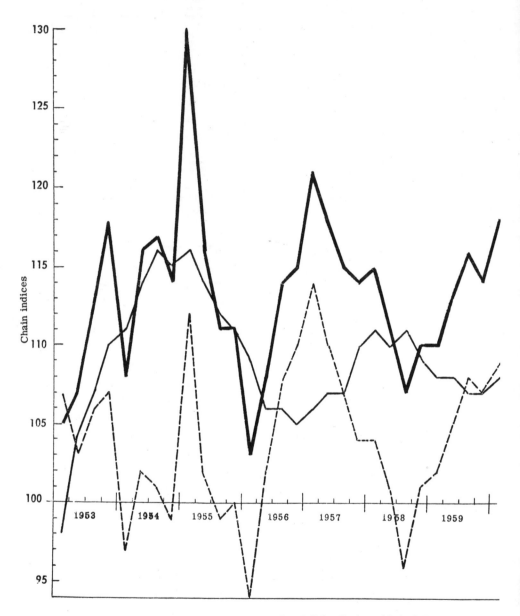

Graph 8.1   Cycles of Industrial Production,

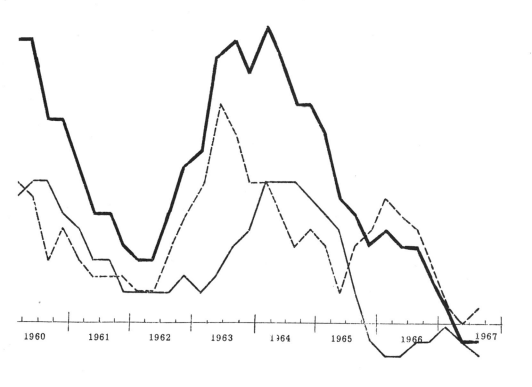

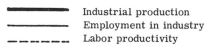 Industrial production
Employment in industry
Labor productivity

Employment, and Labor Productivity

of the coefficient of correlation $r = 0.54$ is obtained when a lag of one quarter is assumed. This means that the cycle of employment lags behind the cycle of production by about one quarter, which is also evident on the graph. The lag of employment behind production at the peaks of the cycles can be explained by the optimism of enterprises that the upswing will continue, while at the troughs it is caused by depressive pessimism and accumulated excess labor force, which must be utilized first by an increase of production.

Since the index of labor productivity is obtained as the coefficient of the index of production and the index of employment, the growth of labor productivity is narrowly correlated with the growth of production ($r = 0.66$, period I/1953-II/1955). In this case there is no lag, but all the peaks except one and all the troughs correspond. At the peaks the productivity of labor grows 9-14%, and at the troughs it falls by 0-6%. The variations are, naturally, significantly greater than with annual data, and they persuasively demonstrate the thesis that an expansion of production not only increases employment but accelerates the growth of productivity of labor as well. If we possessed quarterly data for fixed capital, we would undoubtedly obtain the same picture of the movement of efficiency of investment in relation to the utilization of fixed capital. We shall see later that acceleration of production also reduces the volume of inventories in the production unit. Thus, acceleration of production enhances the general efficiency of economic activity, and retardation reduces it.

However, the problem is more complicated than the analysis up to now has indicated, and therefore to avoid misunderstanding it may be necessary to point out still other aspects. Industrialization means, among other things, the transfer of labor force from the village to the city. Historically there have been two types of such transfer. Capitalist transfer — with the pushing of the peasants off the land by force or by economic differentiation — created slums and an army of unemployed whose pressure kept wages low, and industrialization was carried out from the increased profits. In our century that process of agrarian differentiation and depopulation in the developed countries is mitigated and slowed by state subsidization of small farms. The second type of transfer was carried out in the Soviet Union, where collectivization was completed by administrative measures and where the flow of labor to the city was checked by administrative

measures. In this connection it is of interest to cite a study by
Rudolf Bićanić, in which he takes as the end of a characteristic
phase of development a year in which the active agricultural population fell absolutely. The Soviet Union reached that turnabout in
1956, with 41% of the active population in agriculture. In Yugoslavia the turnabout already occurred in 1948, when two-thirds of
the active population was still employed in agriculture. (2) In fact
the Yugoslav turnabout took place with the highest percent of agricultural population of all countries considered, and therefore at
one of the lowest levels of economic development.

It is rather obvious that neither of the two mentioned types of
transfer has any relevance in Yugoslavia. That does not mean, of
course, that the present rate of employment of the labor force from
the village — which, as we have seen, is one of the highest, and
perhaps even the highest in the world — is necessarily optimal.
Unqualified workers come from the village; they do not have industrial habits, disturb labor discipline, and do not show interest
in workers' self-management, especially to the extent that they
also keep their property; insofar as the peasant is completely pro-
letarianized and cast into the city, then an apartment must be built
for him, and that burdens and otherwise strains investment balances; massive employment growth reduces the potential growth
of real personal incomes; to the extent that labor productivity depends on the size of personal income, then low income reduces
not only productivity of labor but also total potential production.
This customary argument is accompanied by the assertion that
low productivity prevents integration into the international division
of labor. Since adequate economic measurements are not carried
out, it is difficult to say what the quantitative significance is of the
effects described in this argument. Therefore, all that can be done
in this situation is to present other argumentation, and then experience and intuition are left to determine the relative weight of each
argument.

It is undoubtedly true that an inadequately nourished worker
without adequate housing and with poor education achieves less
working effectiveness than a worker whose conditions of life are
better. But it does not follow necessarily that greater personal income also means greater productivity. Adequate education, rational housing construction, and workers' nourishment can be efficiently organized even with lower personal income. The conclusion concerning income and productivity would follow only if

haphazard development were assumed and it were expected that every individual would resolve the above problems himself. In a planned economy there is no need for such an assumption. Furthermore, it is taken as obvious that a high standard in and of itself means an incentive for increasing the productivity of labor. In fact that is not only not obvious, but can be entirely erroneous, for it confuses static and dynamic phenomena. Income levelling at a high level which does not increase probably represents the extreme disincentive situation for an increase in labor productivity. This implies therefore that stimulation depends on the following two elements: income distribution according to work performed, and anticipation of rapid and continual increases in the standard of living. The first implies a certain spread in income distribution, and the second stands in contrast to the present situation, which in no way can be essentially changed.

Increases in the standards of industrial workers depend, naturally, not only on their labor productivity, but on the productivity of labor in the entire economy. And there again agriculture is excluded. The growth of agricultural production depends on the development of socialized farms, but these cannot develop on tiny peasant property. Accordingly, the social transformation of agriculture will progress at the rate by which labor is transferred from the village to the city. In addition, because of the big difference between the marginal productivity of labor in the city and the village, even the low productivity of the newly-hired in the city will still be significantly greater than the opportunity cost that arises from their departure from the village, which means that general Yugoslav productivity is increased. However, employment has both a sociopolitical and a productive aspect. We cannot separate the city from the village. If incomes in the city grow faster than those in the village — and they cannot grow fast in the village if the collective production structure does not change rapidly — then inflationary pressures will constantly come from the village along with the growth of unemployment of those whom the urban standard has drawn from the village. Let us add that the retardation of production during 1965 resulted in registered unemployment of about 300,000 at the beginning of 1966, which represents 8.8% of the number employed. In all, during 1965, 54,000 people were hired. At that rate of hiring, six years would be necessary to absorb those who are today registered for employment. However, each year it is also necessary to employ the 110,000 new

88

entrants to the labor force. But in the following year, 1966, not only was there not new hiring, but the number employed even fell by 84,000. In 1967 the number employed fell still further.

Doubtless it is correct that the flow from the village dilutes the working class in some manner. And probably it is also correct that the migration to the city, especially to the factory, represents the best possible school for building socialism. It is a question, naturally, of scale. Comparing the rate of economic growth of Yugoslavia and of other countries, it appears that this scale has not been surpassed. Industrial productivity of labor grows faster in Yugoslavia than in, for example, France and many other countries; the general national productivity is increasing faster in Yugoslavia than in the majority of countries in the world. Furthermore, it is true that the large flow of labor force creates very serious problems in housing and urbanization. But it is also true that the village youth have the same right to a high living standard as manual workers and white-collar employees. Community construction for their housing has its costs, but at the same time the general living standard of the country is raised, which is the purpose of overall economic growth.

Without detailed research and quantification of the effects, it is impossible to define the optimal economic policy in the area that we have just outlined. But some conclusions are fairly clear. An increase — not of labor productivity and of the efficiency of capital utilization — but of the rate of the increase is desirable, necessary, and probably possible. In that respect there are still large unutilized reserves in economic organizations. However, from the point of view of economic policy the main reserves lie in the increase of production, or more precisely, in the increase in the rate of economic expansion. And in that respect the individual enterprise is not able to accomplish much. The enterprise can plan the dynamics of inventories by the most modern statistical technique, but what good will that do if at any moment the delivery of materials can be interrupted, if somewhere in the production chain someone has not succeeded in bringing about an essential import. The experts of an enterprise can faultlessly program an optimal plan of production and then, for example, there is a reduction of the supply of electrical energy or the transportation channels are blocked somewhere. The workers' council can very conscientiously work out a long-range investment and business policy, and then prices, interest rates, taxes and other instruments are changed administratively, so that what appeared very profitable becomes unprofitable, and vice versa. The work collective* can, like a good householder, set aside substantial funds in the investment account from the personal incomes account, and then the state blocks those funds and coercively converts them into long-term deposits. And when this is how things are, the enterprises are not interested in modern statistical methods, or in a thoroughly prepared investment program, or in a solid long-run business policy, but they respond to bureaucratic demands to the same degree. The political bodies are obviously responsible for the creation of conditions for more efficient business activity, and thus for an increase in the rate of production. To that theme we will have to return.

Notes

1) Uzroci i karakteristike, op. cit., p. 10.
2) R. Bićanić, "Zaokreti u ekonomskom razvoju i agrarna politika," Ekonomski pregled, 1965, No. 11-12, pp. 739-740.

---

*A work collective consists of all the people who earn their living in a particular enterprise, from the director to the cleaning women — Translator.

Chapter 9

INVENTORY CYCLES

Since the flows of production and consumption cannot be absolutely synchronized, the differences that appear are absorbed by
inventory changes. However, that does not mean that inventories
only passively absorb shocks that come from imbalances of supply and demand. There is also a reflexive link by which changes
in inventories influence changes in the production program. In that
respect various economies react very differently, and even in diametrically opposite ways. Thus, a response by the economic system that involves the formation of inventories can be either a stabilizing or a destabilizing reaction.

9.1 Some Characteristics of Inventory Formation in the Yugoslav Economy

First of all, it is important to observe that in Yugoslavia a huge
amount of capital is continually tied up in inventories. About one-
half of the entire economy's social product is continuously in inventories. (1) Furthermore, in the last fifteen years total inventories have constantly grown faster than the social product, so
that the proportion of inventories to social product has increased
from one-third at the beginning of the 1950s to almost one-half in
the mid-1960s. In that period about two-thirds of the social product of industry and almost 100% of the social product of collectiv-
ized agriculture and trade lay in inventories. (2) The proportion
of inventories increased in all economic sectors except in communications and construction where, because of the nature of the
production process, inventories do not play a significant role.
  The second statement is related to the recorded fact that inven-

tories are significantly greater in the Yugoslav economy than in many other countries. This indicates definite inefficiency in economic activity. Since comparable data on inventories in various countries are very scarce, it is difficult to set forth any reasoned hypothesis on the determinants of the size of inventories in national economies that would enable us to judge the Yugoslav situation. It appears that the size of inventories depends upon the following circumstances.

1) Underdeveloped countries have larger inventories than the developed ones. That is partly true because of a greater share of agriculture in the production of those countries, and agriculture has larger inventories than other productive sectors. But it appears that this holds for each productive sector separately. Thus Madžar shows that the coefficient of inventory turnover in India is 50% lower than in Yugoslavia. The same holds also for individual phases of development of one and the same country. Thus in the USA the proportion of inventories to industrial production fell 25% from 1920-1929 to 1947-1954 (3) (industrial inventories amounted to 49% before the war, and in 1960 to 39% of the social product of industry, excluding indirect business taxes). (4) By way of explanation, one can say that less developed economies are more primitively organized, channels of supply do not function reliably, and the enterprise must insure itself by maintaining large inventories. (5)

2) Centrally planned economies have larger inventories than market economies. According to the data of the American economist Campbell, Soviet industrial inventories are twice as large as the American. According to the data of the Soviet economist Bunich, the difference is less but still significant. Bunich's data for Czechoslovakia and East Germany show the same picture. Madžar's estimate indicates that Yugoslav inventories are somewhat smaller than those of centrally planned economies, but significantly larger than in market economies. Because the data are not precise, it can probably be assumed that the Yugoslav economy, according to its performance, belongs in the centrally planned group. The explanation as to why centrally planned economies require larger inventories is fairly obvious. In those economies the enterprises have an interest in completing the production plan, but are not stimulated to deliver goods then and there, just when they are needed. Since all details in practical situations cannot be foreseen far in advance by a plan, nor can the

latter react flexibly to unforeseen changes in the situation, that necessarily results in significant separation of the structure, and even the volume, of supply and demand; so the enterprise must protect itself by maintaining large inventories. The enterprise also accumulates inventories because they cost less due to a low or nonexistent rate of interest.

3) It appears justified to assume that accelerated growth, which multiplies bottlenecks, requires larger inventories than slow growth. Madžar presents a table for twelve countries at the head of which, in terms of accumulation of inventories, are the world's two best performers in rate of growth, Yugoslavia and Japan, and at the bottom — a slowly-growing economy, Belgium (in the period 1955-1964, these three economies absorbed 65%, 65% and 10% of the social product by accumulation of inventories). However, the remaining countries in the table do not provide strong support for our hypothesis. Thus, slowly-growing Great Britain accumulated twice as much inventory as fast-growing Italy. It follows that at least within a certain interval, the effect of the growth rate can be significantly modified by other factors.

4) In addition, an unstable economy will require larger average inventories than a stable economy. Later, in the chapter "International Comparisons," the coefficients of instability are calculated for individual countries. If those coefficients are compared with Madžar's data on the accumulation of inventories for three countries which appear in both tables — Japan, France, and Italy — it can be seen that the order of inventory accumulation is the same as the order of instability. However, it is also necessary to have in mind that economic instability is closely correlated with the rate of growth.

5) Finally, the size of inventories also depends on the specific reaction of individual national economies to disturbances that produce fluctuations.

Hypothesis (5) leads us to the third key contention. At least some capitalist countries, of which the USA is the most well-known and investigated case, accumulate inventories in the upswing phases and reduce inventories in the downswing phases. In fact, the four-year American cycles begin by reduction of inventories, which releases the recession mechanism and results in cumulative contraction of demand. Therefore, fluctuations of inventories represent a factor of instability in the American economy, and the four-year cycles have been called inventory cycles. The Yugoslav

Table 9.1

Inventory Formation in the Yugoslav Economy,
1952-1964
(in 1962 prices)

	Increase of the Social Product (billion din.)	Inventory Investment (billion din.)	Share of Inventory Investment in Growth of the Social Product %	Growth Rate of the Social Product %
Fat Years				
1953	291	22	7.6	17.8
1955	280	63	22.5	14.1
1957	495	129	26.1	22.7
1959	454	145	36.3	16.4
1963	459	179	39.0	12.2
1964	546	237	43.4	12.9
Total	2525	775	30.7	—
Lean Years				
1954	71	36	50.7	3.7
1956	-82	230	—	-3.6
1958	84	232	276.2	3.1
1960	205	223	108.8	6.4
1961	192	180	93.8	5.6
1962	156	259	166.0	4.3
Total	626	1160	185.3	—

economy reacts in an entirely opposite way. In the upswing phases inventory accumulation slows down, and even results in an <u>absolute reduction</u> of inventories (for example, in industry in 1953, in the fourth quarters of 1959 and 1963, and in the first quarter of 1964). In the downswing phase the cycle of inventory accumulation accelerates. Accordingly, in recessions and depressions inventories function as one of the economic stabilizers of the Yugoslav economy.

In connection with what has just been said, some data that I have taken from Madžar are very illustrative. The twelve years of the period 1952-1964 can be divided into two equal groups: "fat" years with growth rates of the social product of about 12% annually, and "lean" years with growth rates below 6-1/2%. Inventory formation is carried out very differently in "fat" and "lean" years, as can be seen in Table 9.1.

Until 1960 every odd year was productive, and every even year was unproductive. Since at that time agriculture contributed a significant part of total production, those were predetermined "fat" and "lean" years for the economy as a whole. After 1960 the behavior of agriculture and its influence on the rest of the economy changed significantly, but the pattern of inventory formation still remained the same: contrary to the Bible, in "lean" years inventories accumulated and in "fat" years they were depleted. In the entire period considered, recession years accumulated half again as much inventories as expansive years. In years of economic upswing somewhat less than one-third of the annual growth of the social product entered into inventories. However, in lean years investment and inventories absorbed not only the entire annual increase of production, but also a good part of the current production beyond that.

It is obvious that the years when the warehouses were empty and the market was chronically unsupplied in quantity are now far behind us. From that point of view we may be satisfied. However, comparative analysis shows that inventories in Yugoslavia are significantly larger than in other countries and, what is more serious, that they constantly increase in relative terms. That process was intensified in the period 1965-1967 (at this moment there are no comparable data for expressing that statement precisely). Our current economy is significantly more developed than the economy of 1952. Industrial production has increased five times. Administrative central planning has been replaced to a large extent by the market mechanism. Therefore, in accordance with hypotheses (1) and (2), derived from comparative analysis, and with the improvement of market supply, inventories ought to decrease relatively. That actually occurs in phases of cyclical upswings. But in the retardation phases which follow and which become longer and deeper, the positive effects are annulled and the process of accumulating inventories continues. Naturally, if one must still choose between production for inventories and stopping production, then the spontaneous choice of the Yugoslav economy was economically rational. For stopping production and reducing inventories — i.e., the American reaction — would lead to cumulative contraction of demand and thus to an absolute reduction of production — i.e., to American effects. The mechanism of inventory formation thereby saves the unstable Yugoslav economy from cyclical catastrophes. It is also understandable why relative reductions of inventories do not occur, which we would otherwise have had to expect. And it also becomes clear that it is necessary to formulate economic policy that will solve the problem. It would be a mistake to drive out inventories from enterprises by means of credit restriction. Such forced imitation of American behavior would lead to American effects. What we must work out is the levelling of cycles, eliminating or at least mitigating instability, and the economy will then spontaneously channel inventories in the right direction.

9.2 Cycles of Components of Industrial Inventories

Industrial inventories include about 60% of nonagricultural inventories, so that a study of the movements of those inventories is sufficiently representative of the behavior of inventories as a whole. Inventories have three components, which behave very differently. There are inventories of raw materials and semi-finished products (intermediate goods), of unfinished production, and of final products. The structure of total and industrial inventories at the beginning and end of the period under consideration was as follows:

Table 9.2

Structure of Inventories

	Intermediate Goods	Unfinished Production	Final Products
Total Inventories			
1952-1954	46	14	40
1962-1964	39	17	44
Industrial Inventories			
1952-1954	59	21	20
1962-1964	49	23	28
Industrial Inventories in the USA*			
1919-1938	40	20	40
1952-1953	38	29	33

*Source: Stanback, Postwar Cycles in Manufacturers' Inventories, p. 25.

It can be seen that because of the reduction of the share of intermediate goods inventories, there was growth in inventories of unfinished production and especially of final products. On the other hand, Madžar shows that the coefficients of turnover of inventories of intermediate goods remained approximately unchanged in the period considered, while the coefficients of turnover of the other two components of inventories were reduced. It follows that inventories of intermediate goods move in step with production. Since according to general belief the supply of raw materials and semi-finished products is today significantly better than at the beginning of the period, in this area there has been an advance in the economy's business activity in the sense of hypotheses (1) and (2) of the preceding section. The contrary conclusion may be drawn for the movement of inventories of final goods. The inadequately organized and unstable market results in their relative increase. This conclusion appears to contradict the American data, which show an even greater share of final products. However, in making a definitive judgment it is necessary to keep in view the following two facts: (1) in the USA the share of final products falls, while in Yugoslavia it rises; (2) the import element of production is several times lower in the USA than in Yugoslavia. And importation of materials requires longer terms of delivery, and hence also larger inventories. With significantly larger imports, American inventories of intermediate goods would be larger, and that would automatically reduce the share of final products. Thus, it can probably be said that the increase of the share of final products was in part necessary because of the filling up of inventories, and in part it was the result of increased economic instability.

The relative increase in inventories of unfinished production represents a regular phenomenon, and we can expect the same trend in the future as well. It is a matter, namely, of a regular change in the structure of industrial production in the direction of a greater proportion of durable consumer and producers goods.

Table 9.3 shows that the durable goods industries (the metals complex and the lumber industry) increased their share of total industrial inventories in twelve years from 42% to 51%. And it is precisely those industries, because of the nature of the technological process, that have a significant share of unfinished production, while in addition that share increased. Thus, the growth of the average share of unfinished production from 21% to 23% is explained.

We may now state the following three hypotheses: (1) since

Table 9.3

Structure of Industrial Inventories
(in current prices)

	Interme-diate Goods	Unfinished Produc-tion	Final Products	Total	Share
Inventories, durable goods industries					
1952-1953	61.7	23.9	14.4	100	41.9
1964-1965	54.7	27.5	17.8	100	51.4
Inventories, other industries					
1952-1953	51.6	19.0	29.4	100	58.1
1964-1965	49.0	18.0	33.0	100	48.6
Industry, total					
1952-1953	55.8	21.1	23.1	100	100.0
1964-1965	51.9	22.9	25.2	100	100.0

inventories of raw materials and semi-finished products materially precondition production, there will exist a tendency for inventories to follow trends of production and to behave like production; (2) since unfinished production is technologically conditioned and, moreover, precedes finished production, this component of inventories will also move like production with a short lead; (3) since inventories of final products serve to absorb disturbances in demand, fluctuations of those inventories and of production will be phasally shifted so that the troughs of production correspond to the peaks of inventories, and vice versa; i.e., the behavior of inventories must be just the reverse of the behavior of production in every phase of the cycle. There are no data on movements of unfinished production, but research carried out in the USA completely supports hypothesis (2). Graph 9.1 presents the data for verifying the other two hypotheses. Those data are then summarized in Table 9.4.

Let us begin with inventories of intermediate goods. As we expected, the cycles of these inventories correspond on the whole to

Table 9.4

Cycles of Industrial Production and Inventories

	Turning Points (quarter/year)			Indices at Turning Points			Amplitudes of Cycles		
	Industrial Production	Inventories of Intermediate Goods	Inventories of Final Products	Industrial Production	Inventories of Intermediate Goods	Inventories of Final Products	Industrial Production	Inventories of Intermediate Goods	Inventories of Final Products
Peak	I/1955	I/1955	IV/1954	130	122	79	–	–	–
Trough	I/1956	I/1956	II/1956	103	111	168	27	11	89
Peak	I/1957	III/1956	III/1957	121	135	102	18	24	66
Trough	III/1958	II/1958	IV/1958	107	102	131	14	38	29
(Peak)		IV/1958			116			14	
(Trough)		IV/1959			98			18	
Peak	II/1960	IV/1960	I/1960	118	109	100	11	11	31
Trough	I/1962	II/1961	II/1962	104	101	127	14	8	27
(Peak)		IV/1961			111			10	
(Trough)		I/1963			100			11	
Peak	I/1964	I/1964	I/1964	119	127	88	15	27	39

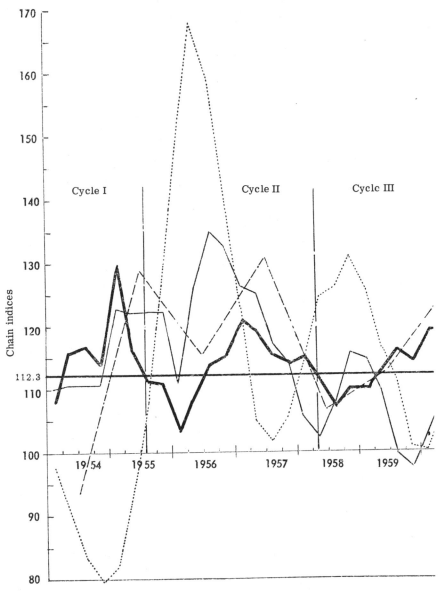

Graph 9.1 Cycles of Industrial

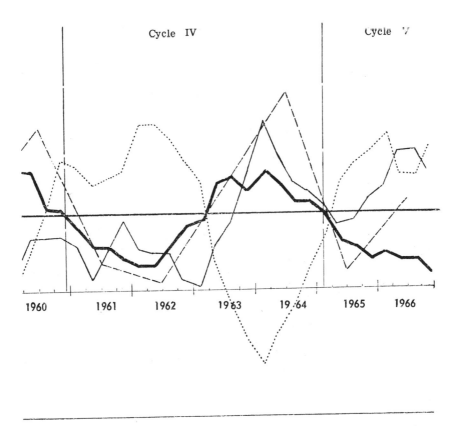

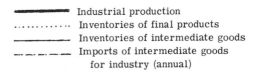

Industrial production
.... Inventories of final products
_____ Inventories of intermediate goods
_ .. _ .. _ .. _ Imports of intermediate goods
for industry (annual)

Cycle IV

Cycle V

1960   1961   1962   1963   1964   1965   1966

Production and Inventories

the industrial cycles. The amplitudes are also equal. An interesting tendency of decreasing expansions and amplitudes of intermediate goods inventories can also be seen from the graph before
1960-1962, and of increasing expansions and amplitudes after
those years. The changes in amplitudes can be explained by the
reduction of general economic instability before 1960 and by increased instability after that year. And the changes in the expansion of inventories can, it appears, be explained by the reduction
of imports of intermediate goods for industry before 1962, as is
seen from the movements of annual chain indices of intermediate
goods imports drawn on the graph. The reduction of imports of
intermediate goods is an indication of the substitution of domestic
production for imported materials, which together with better organization of supply, reduced the terms of delivery and thus the
size of the required inventories. The opposite is true with the increase of imports and disorganization of the market. It is worth
noting that the amplitudes of the annual indices of imports of intermediate goods are greater than the amplitudes of the quarterly indices of inventories and production. This is explained by the fact
that the elasticity of imports of intermediate goods is greater than
one at a high rate of growth of industry and less than one in recession periods.

The correspondence of the cycles of intermediate goods inventories and production is interrupted in the third production cycle.
In 1958-1959 an intracycle of inventories whose meaning is not
entirely clear is interpolated. Perhaps the rapid growth of inventories in the second half of 1958 can be explained by the relatively
large credits for working capital immediately prior to that, along
with the simultaneous growth of imports of intermediate goods,
and the fall in 1959 by the contraction of credit expansion which
lasted until the beginning of 1960 and may have stopped the expansion of intermediate goods in a situation of relatively good supply.
Similarly, in the fourth production cycle another cycle of inventories of intermediate goods is interpolated. That mildly expressed
cycle, with a tendency to fall, can probably be explained by the
slowing of expansion of imports of intermediate goods for industry in 1961 and 1962. (6)

Four cycles are insufficient for drawing more certain conclusions about the eventual time shift of the turning points of cycles
of inventories and production. However, they give some indications
and it is necessary to note them. Thus, the peak of intermediate

goods inventories corresponds twice to the peak of production, precedes once and follows once, and it is therefore probable that in the general case the peaks of both cycles correspond. The troughs of the cycles correspond once, and the troughs of inventories precede twice, which makes probable a lead in the general case. Insofar as these observations are correct, it can be said that cycles of materials inventories and production are, on the whole, synchronized with an eventual short lead of the inventory troughs. The latter may mean that the equipping of industry with intermediate goods, stimulated by the previous growth of credit, gives an impulse to the upward turning of the production cycle.

The movement of inventories of final products presents, natually, an entirely different picture. The amplitudes of fluctuations are several times greater, especially at the beginning of the period, when inventories were relatively small. The correspondence of the inventory and production cycles is almost perfect with the expected phasal shift of 180°. The trough of the inventory cycle corresponds once, precedes twice, and lags twice with respect to the corresponding peak of production. In three cases the peak of the inventory cycle lags behind the corresponding turning points of the production cycles. The lagging of the peaks of inventories of final products, as well as the leading of troughs of intermediate goods inventories, indicates that the departure from depression is achieved at first by production for inventories.

The place on the graph where the line of inventories of final products cuts the abscissa or closely approaches it indicates situations in which inventories remain unchanged or even fall absolutely. It can be seen that this happens when the expansion of industrial production exceeds a rate of about 14%. We will see later that at this rate the tempo of industrial exports and imports is equalized with the tempo of industrial production. The graph also shows the rates of industrial expansion at which there results a relative reduction of final products inventories (i.e., inventories increase more slowly than production). That happens when the line of inventories moves below the line of production, i.e., at a rate of industrial expansion of about 13%. One is strongly tempted to conclude that at a rate of 13-14%, long-run industrial expansion could be stabilized so that cycles are smoothed, inventories increase moderately, and the export-import gap remains closed.

It is interesting that this is also the rate that is obtained as the arithmetic mean of average attained expansion of the social product

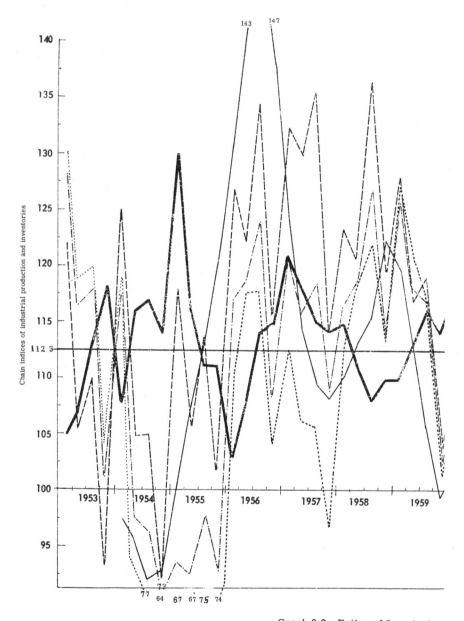

Graph 9.2   Ratios of Inventories

104

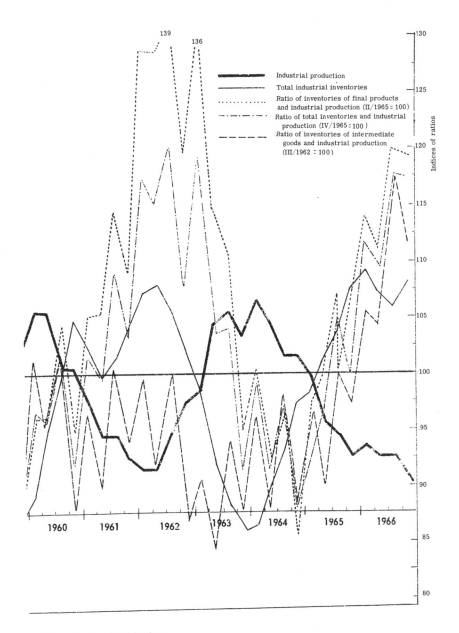

139
136

Industrial production
Total industrial inventories
Ratio of inventories of final products
  and industrial production (II/1965 = 100)
Ratio of total inventories and industrial
  production (IV/1965 = 100)
Ratio of inventories of intermediate
  goods and industrial production
  (III/1962 = 100)

Indices of ratios

130

125

120

115

110

105

100

.95

90

85

80

1960   1961   1962   1963   1964   1965   1966

and Production in Industry

(excluding agriculture) in the course of the last full cycle and of expansion during the upswing, which was used as one of the elements in calculating the losses of production in Section 1.1. Thus the realism of that calculation obtains still another substantiation, and the economic analyst and planner are given yet another indication of the structural constants of the Yugoslav economy.

The coefficients of turning points in relation to their reciprocal values, the proportions of inventories and production, provide useful information on inventory movements. Those proportions are shown in Graph 9.2. The proportions are shown as indices in relation to base values, which are again selected as average values for the whole period, and the scale of proportions of inventories and production is shifted so that the index 100 corresponds to the average index of growth of industrial production of 112.3. In that way the base indices of proportions (in relation to the average proportions) are centered on the average value of industrial expansion (for the period 1952-1964).

The usual assumption is that producers attempt to maintain inventories in some fixed proportion with respect to production. We saw earlier why this tendency is condemned to failure when it is a matter of inventories of final products. Because of that the huge fluctuations of proportions of final goods inventories are not surprising. However, now it can be seen that the proportion of intermediate goods is also very unstable. The large growth in the proportion of inventories of intermediate goods to production in 1956 is the result of large imports of intermediate goods in that year. In the succeeding years, imports of intermediate goods slow down, and the proportion of inventories of intermediate goods also decreases, with large fluctuations. The proportion attains its minimum in the first half of 1963 and then again grows by leaps. The large fluctuations in the proportion of intermediate goods inventories from quarter to quarter show how irregularly Yugoslav industry is supplied with materials. And the shifts between acceleration and deceleration of imports in somewhat longer periods, along with a similar increasing and decreasing of the proportions of intermediate goods inventories to production, show that not only is the market extremely disorganized, but also that there is not any kind of developmental program for Yugoslav industry. The reduction of the quarterly changes of proportions of intermediate goods inventory after 1960 shows that the supplying of intermediate goods had become more regular. The rapid increase of the proportion after 1964, along with the corresponding movements of intermediate goods imports, indicates the presence of an effective program to produce goods that would replace imports. And the very noticeable tendency from 1957 on for the proportions of intermediate goods to fall in prosperous years and to increase in depression years (which can be seen on the graph, as the lines of intermediate goods inventories are below the line of production in prosperous years but above the line of production in depression years) points to the possibility that depletion of intermediate goods inventories results in a break at the peak of the cycle, and the renewed normalization of intermediate goods supply prepares the way for a new upswing.

9.3 Cycles of Total Industrial Inventories

Unfortunately, since in Yugoslavia we do not have statistics of the quarterly movement of the social product and of total inventories, we cannot analyze cycles of total inventories. We will therefore have to limit ourselves to the examination of cycles of industrial inventories. Table 9.5 gives an idea of the significance of industrial inventories.

Table 9.5

Nonagricultural Inventories by Economic Sectors
(structure on the basis of current prices)

	USA*	Yugoslavia	
	1928-1939	1952-1953	1964-1965
Industry and mining	53.5	63.9	56.8
Trade	38.9	25.5	28.2
Other sectors	7.6	10.6	15.0

*Source: M. Abramovitz, Inventories and Business Cycles, p. 36.

It can be seen that 90% of nonagricultural inventories are found in industry and trade. Inventories of agricultural producers represented 12.3% of total inventories in the USA in the period cited, while comparable data are lacking for Yugoslavia. Because of a certain uneconomic management of trade, inventories in that sector are less than what economic processes demand, and that well-known assertion is illustrated here by the American data. Relatively larger inventories in trade probably would enable inventories

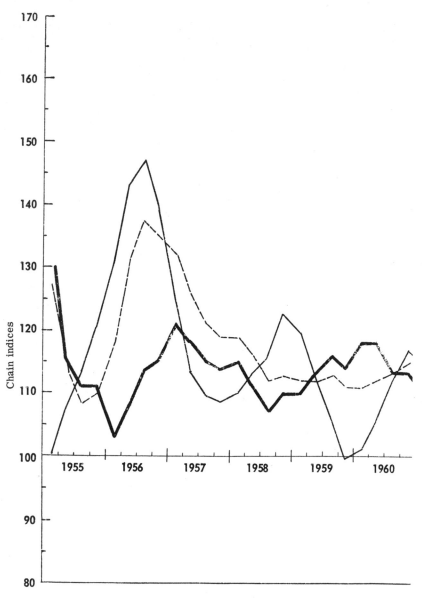

Graph 9.3   Production, Inventories, Credits for

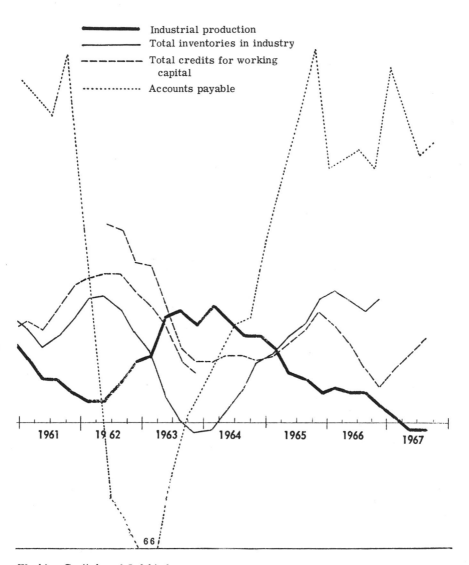

Industrial production
Total inventories in industry
Total credits for working
capital
Accounts payable

1961   1962   1963   1964   1965   1966   1967

66

Working Capital, and Indebtedness

in industry, as well as total inventories, to fall <u>absolutely</u>. Since
we do not know of a single empirical study of cycles of trade inventories, and there are no domestic data, we will have to be satisfied with the assumption that inventories in trade move approximately like inventories of intermediate goods in industry, since
sales determine supply in both cases. In that way we can immediately approach an examination of movements of total industrial
inventories (Graph 9.3).

Table 9.6

Turning Points of Industrial Production and Inventories

	Industrial Production	Total Industrial Inventories	Lead (−) or Lag (+) in Quarters
Peak	I/1955	Trough III/1954	−2
Trough	I/1956	Peak III/1956	+2
Peak	I/1957	Trough IV/1957	+3
Trough	III/1958	Peak IV/1958	+1
Peak	II/1960	Trough IV/1959	−2
Trough	I/1962	Peak III/1962	+2
Peak	II/1964	Trough IV/1963	−2

Considering the divergent movements of individual components
of inventories, total industrial inventories behave with surprising
regularity. Additional cycles of intermediate goods are on the
whole eliminated, and the large amplitudes of final products inventories make total industrial inventories move inversely to production in spite of the lesser weight of final products. All the
peaks of inventories lag one to two quarters behind the troughs of
production, which supports the earlier thesis that the departure
from recession is paid for by accelerated accumulation of inventories in the first few months. The inventory troughs, except in
1957, precede the peaks of industrial cycles by two quarters respectively, which at first leads to the conclusion that renewed accumulation of inventories is the signal for producers that the market is oversaturated and that it is necessary to reduce the expansion of production. We will see later in fact the explanation is
otherwise. Explosions of the foreign trade deficit at peaks of the
production cycles check the further acceleration of production —

and, with it, also demand — while enterprises which do not depend
upon imports or which in the preceding period were well supplied
with imports continue to expand production; that output, for lack
of buyers with means of payment, begins to overflow into inventories.

Table 9.7

Time Lags of Industrial Inventories at the
Turning Points of Industrial Production
(based on constant prices)

Industrial Cycle	Lead (−) or Lag (+) in Months							
	Intermediate Goods		Unfinished Production		Final Products		Total Inventories	
	USA*	Yugo-slavia	USA*	Yugo-slavia	USA*	Yugo-slavia	USA*	Yugo-slavia
Peaks	+2.8	0	−4.0	...	+8.8	0	+2.7	−2.2
Troughs	+5.8	−4	+3.3	...	+6.0	+1	+5.0	+5.0
Average	+4.5	−2	−0.3	...	+7.4	+0.5	+3.8	+3.6

*Source: Stanback, op. cit., p. 101.

Note: The American data relate to the period 1948-1958, and the
Yugoslav to 1955-1964. They are not entirely comparable, for
Stanback measures deviations in relation to the so-called reference cycle and I measure in relation to the production cycle. In
addition, Stanback works with series of absolute values and I use
rates of growth. For Yugoslav data on final products and total inventories, the lag (lead) is measured from peak of production to
the trough of inventories and from the trough of production to the
peak of inventories, while in the American series the lags (leads)
are measured from the same turning points.

It will be useful now to summarize our observations concerning
the comparison of movements of inventories and production and
to compare them with a similar approach in a foreign study, i.e.,
with Stanback's data for the USA. This material is presented in
Table 9.7. It can be seen that the cycles of inventories and of
production are better synchronized in Yugoslavia than in the USA.
And differences appear in the direction of time displacements
that must be examined.

Let us begin with final products, which comprise the most complicated category of inventories. Stanback (op. cit., p. 63) distin-

guishes the following components of final products inventories:

	USA	
	1939	1947
Goods made to order	15-25	15-25
Goods made for stock	75-85	75-85
Goods whose production cycles are governed by demand		
Perishables	*	*
Nonperishable staples	50-60	41-51
Goods whose production cycles are governed by supply		
Perishables	*	*
Nonperishable staples	16	23
Total industrial inventories	100	100

*Total perishable goods account for 9%. Their structure is un-known.

Inventories of goods made to order (machines, transportation equipment, etc.) fluctuate along with production. The same is true of demand-governed perishable goods. Supply-governed inventories (agricultural raw materials and the products derived from them) are not sensitive to the business cycle. Inventories of nonperishable goods governed by demand, which constitute the largest single component of final goods, move inversely in relation to the production cycle; therefore total inventories of final goods move in the same way as in Yugoslavia. The inversion is complete to the extent that cycles are short, but it turns into a lag when they are longer, which is the normal case in the USA. This observation indicates the possibility that in Yugoslavia an interruption of the inversion of inventory movements will also result to the extent that the cycle is prolonged. In other words, insofar as the present depression is prolonged, it may be that the expansion of inventories will weaken before the lower turning point of production. Reduction of the share of nonperishable demand-governed staples resulted, in the USA, in reduction of the lag of total industrial inventories from 8.6 months before the war to 3.8 months after the war.

Inventories of intermediate goods largely move together with production; they lag behind production in the USA, but they lead in Yugoslavia. This has, as we shall see, significant consequences for the explanation of the cyclical mechanism. It follows from the above considerations that inventories of intermediate goods, unfinished production, final products made to order, and final perishable goods governed by demand — in all, 75% of industrial inventories in the USA — move in conformity with the production cycle, inventories of nonperishable staples governed by demand (16% of total inventories) move inversely, and the rest move randomly. As a result, total industrial inventories change in conformity with the cycle of industrial production in the USA, while they move inversely in Yugoslavia, for those components of inventories which move directly with the cycle are relatively small, and the reactions of economic decision-making units are different.

Stanback and Abramovitz explain the functioning of the cyclical mechanism as follows. (7) At the beginning of the upswing, sales increase and orders similarly grow rapidly. Enterprises place orders (a) to cover the requirements of increased sales, (b) to increase disposable inventories, and (c) to obtain a place in time on the waiting lists of suppliers, who prolong their delivery schedules with the growth of demand. At the beginning of the decline in production, sales fall, enterprises reduce orders to adjust inventories to the lower volume of business activity, and the increase in available goods shortens the delivery schedules, by which the desired ratio of unfilled orders to inventories is reduced. The cycle is determined by such behavior. At the beginning of the upswing it appears to result in a relative, and even an absolute, reduction of inventories (troughs of inventories lag: see Table 9.7), and producers increase orders. After some time inventories begin to increase and grow faster than production, for producers try to restore the normal relation between inventories and sales. At some point in the course of the upswing a situation emerges in which producers consider that they are sufficiently insured with respect to inventories and orders, and they begin to reduce new orders. The inventory accumulation also slows down, and the reduction of demand results in a downward turning of the cycle. After the turning point inventories still increase for some 2-3 months (see Table 9.7), for producers are in the course of fulfilling unfinished orders for intermediate goods and because producers of final nonperishable staples made for stock cannot reduce production quickly because of the great costs involved in such rapid adaptation. But inventories also begin to fall after 2-3 quarters, and the rapid decumulation of total inventories deepens the depression. Later, inventory decumulation begins to slow down and that — i.e., the trough in negative changes in inventories — gives the impulse for the upward turning of the cycle. The fact that in all three postwar cycles the peaks of inventory investment preceded the peaks of the business cycle — as was also true in two or three troughs — indicates that in the American economy inventories initiate the upswing from recession and then check that upswing at a certain point.

It would doubtless be useful to consider in like manner the functioning of the cyclical mechanism in a centrally planned economy. In this respect the sole work published so far is the short paper of Goldmann and Flek on waves in the movement of the growth rate and inventory cycles in Czechoslovakia. (8)

Analyzing the period 1950-1966, the authors establish that in the years when the social product grew only a little, inventory decumulation resulted by which consumption greater than production was covered, and that the reverse was true in years of great growth of the social product. In other words, high growth rates generate inventory accumulation, and low rates — decumulation; in "fat" years inventories accumulate, while in "lean" ones they are depleted, just exactly as in the Bible. Such reactions of producers are similar to those of the American producers. Some difficulty in interpreting Goldmann's results is introduced by the statistical data, which include in inventories uncompleted investments in fixed capital and which allocate to the social product new capacity put into operation in the course of the year without regard to when they are completed investments. Goldmann and Flek see "socialist speculation" as the prime mover in Czechoslovak inventory cycles. That is, in the accelerative phases of the production cycle, difficulties in supplying intermediate goods increase and each enterprise attempts to protect itself with larger inventories. The result, of course, is that the scarcity increases still more. When, finally, import possibilities are also exhausted, the turning of the cycle downward results. Now the enterprises complete and throw into production objects that were started in earlier years. Thus capacity is increased, which, along with slowed expansion of demand and reduction of the foreign trade deficit, improves conditions of supply; enterprises reduce their inventories, which still further stabilizes the situation; and at a certain moment acceleration of growth begins again. These cycles last six to eight years.

Thus Abramovitz, Stanback, Goldmann and Flek explain inventory cycles by the same "speculative" behavior of producers conditioned by the gap between demand and supply. But the causes of that gap are diametrically opposed in the two economies. The Czechoslovak economy, like every centrally planned economy, is oriented toward production. Because it comes up against capacity barriers — i.e., because of the deficiency of supply in relation to existing demand — a recession results. The American economy, like every market economy, is consumption oriented. Therefore insufficient demand will stipulate the end of the upswing. The same argument holds for the emergence from depression: increased supply in the centrally planned economy and increased demand in the market economy spur on the new upswing.

Since in both economies the inventories change in conformity with the production cycle, but in such a way that inventory changes absorb a smaller percentage of the growth of production in the accelerative phase and a relatively greater part of the fall in production in the retardation phase, consumption is more stable, fluctuating less than production. It is precisely in this respect that the behavior of the Yugoslav economy is different. In the Yugoslav economy inventories move inversely to the production cycle, resulting in reduction of fluctuations of production at the expense of increased fluctuations of consumption. And thus we have established in fact a third, hitherto unknown, type of mechanism of inventory fluctuations. As the result of the inverse movement of inventories and production, in the accelerative phases of the cycles the investment in total industrial inventories absorbs about 25% of the growth of production, and in the retardation phases it absorbs the entire increase in industrial production. (9) The latter means that in the retardation phase of the Yugoslav industrial cycle, production growth is possible only if it is production exclusively for inventories. And insofar as it may be attempted, for example by credit restriction, to prevent the formation of a certain volume of inventories, an absolute reduction of production will result. Evidence of the correctness of this last hypothesis is provided by economic policy in 1967.

Now we are finally able to consider in detail the mechanism of inventory fluctuations in Yugoslavia. The necessary information is given in Graph 9.3. Slowing down of production corresponds to acceleration of accumulation of total inventories and to the reverse in phases of accelerated production. Total credits for working capital on the whole follow inventories (the coefficient of correlation $r = 0.75$ for the period 1955-1965) but have somewhat smaller amplitudes. The curve of chain indices of credits has a discontinuity in the second quarter of 1962, since a year earlier — in May 1961 — significant institutional changes occurred: initial funds of working capital transferred to enterprises that had earlier been in the form of a debt were now paid in part from blocked amortization funds and in part were turned into credits from the general investment fund. In order to obtain an approximate idea of the actual movement of available sources of working capital in the disrupted year of 1962, we extended the curve several quarters on the basis of the construction of comparable movements of chain indices. The credit curve shows an interesting feature. In the entire thirteen-year period considered, it was only in the second half of 1955 and in the last three quarters of 1966 that credit expansion slowed down below 10% annually. And in both those cases it resulted in stagnation of industrial production. With the exception of the beginning and end of the period considered (1954-1958 and 1966) — which were both abnormal, although for different reasons — credit policy was to a certain degree anticyclical in relation to industry. Following inventories, which move inversely to production, in depressed periods credit expanded more rapidly than production; in periods of high growth rates the credit expansion was slower. However, even when it was objectively anticyclical, it was delayed; it is obvious that economic movements were not anticipated and that, especially in retardations, credit therapy was undertaken under the pressure of self-protective reactions of economic organizations.

Direct credits of producers, i.e., accounts payable, represent the third component of our cyclical mechanism. The data, taken from periodic reports of the Social Accounting Service, extend back only to 1960. In years of prosperity accounts are settled promptly and indebtedness to suppliers is reduced relatively. When retardation of production begins, it results in a sharp increase in accounts payable. Since it is a question of an expedient in necessity, and since accounts payable, especially earlier, were significantly less than bank credits in absolute terms, they fluctuate several times more intensively. The deep trough at the end of 1962 is the consequence of an action to settle mutual outstanding debts by a multilateral clearing operation with significant credit support, which was extended in the first half of that year.

116

If we now consider the interplay of all the above-mentioned factors, we may be able to describe the industrial cycles in the last thirteen years in the following way. In the course of 1955 there was a retardation of production, which evoked inventory accumulation supported by significant credit expansion. As we saw in Graph 9.1, there accumulated not only inventories of final products but, to a large extent, also inventories of intermediate goods. In that way industry, well supplied and relatively liquid, entered the mildest of all cycles in 1957-1959. The upswing in 1959 resulted in an absolute reduction of inventories and relatively stable credit expansion that was relatively close to the critical rate of 10%. The first half of 1960 saw the beginning of a retardation of production, an abrupt growth of inventories, mild credit expansion, and a sharp slowing down of debt payments to suppliers. The unprepared and inconsistent radical institutional changes in 1961 deepened the recession, producing a piling up of inventories, and despite relatively large credits the economy became illiquid. After the illiquidity was resolved in 1962 by special measures, there was a new upswing of production and a fall of inventories. The retardation in 1964 renewed the already familiar sequence of events. Inventories increased abruptly and, since credits did not follow that increase, indebtedness grew by leaps and bounds. In 1965 credits began to follow inventories, the expansion of indebtedness slowed somewhat, the line of inventories turned downward, industrial production attained some sort of plateau and, to all appearances, a turning upward of the cycle would ensue. However, just at that time, contrary to all principles of anticyclical policy, the National Bank began a sharp restriction of credit that lasted a year, reduced the rate of growth to production below zero, and brought the economy to the same condition of illiquidity as in 1962.

How, accordingly, does the typical Yugoslav industrial cycle develop? The results of investigations up to now present us with this picture. In the upswing, inventories relatively — and at the peaks even absolutely — decline, credit expands by some well-balanced rate of about 10%, liquidity of industry increases, and it pays its debts. When, for various reasons, a downward turning of the cycle occurs, practically at the same time inventories begin to pile up, liquidity is reduced, and the economy becomes indebted very quickly. After production reaches the lower turning point, inventory accumulation accelerates still another one or two quarters, accompanied by expansion of credit and reduction of illiquidity, which means that revival begins with production for inventories, which must be financed by additional money supply.

This picture of the functioning of the cyclical mechanism is still incomplete. There remain, especially, the unexplained upper and lower turning points. It is not clear what happens with prices, nor what the role of international trade is. Investigation of these problems is the task of the following chapters.

Notes

1) All data in this chapter that are related to inventories are taken from the doctoral dissertation of Ljubomir Madžar, Mesto zaliha u procesu društvene reprodukcije.

2) In relation to sales, inventories comprise 16% in trade, 20% for the economy as a whole, and 20% in industry.

3) T. M. Stanback, Postwar Cycles in Manufacturers' Inventories (New York: NBER, 1959), p. 15.

4) M. Abramovitz, Inventories and Business Cycles (New York: NBER, 1959), p. 109; Stanback, op. cit., p. 132; UN Statistical Yearbook, 1966, p. 569.

5) W. Stolper remarks: "Textile factories that in England would keep two days' supply of spare parts on hand must in Nigeria keep enough to last nine months. Similar figures apply to tobacco factories and steel mills. It takes that long to order and get the parts from overseas" (Planning Without Facts [Cambridge, Mass.: Harvard University Press, 1966], p. 111).

6) Op. cit., pp. 123-127, 270.

7) J. Goldmann and J. Flek, "Vlnovitý pohyb v tempu růstu a cyklus v dynamice zásob," Plánované hospodárstvi, 1967, No. 9, pp. 1-16.

8) In the USA these percentages for the prewar and postwar period amount on the average to 9% in the expansion and 44% in the contraction (Stanback, op. cit., p. 13).

9) For a more extended explanation and corresponding analysis, see my book Ekonomska nauka i narodna privreda, Part II (Naprijed, 1968).

Chapter 10

MONETARY-CREDIT FACTORS AND PRICES

10.1 <u>Fluctuations in the Aggregate Values of</u>
<u>Industry and the Economy as a Whole</u>

Essentially all the movements which we will analyze in this chapter are shown in the next three graphs. Let us begin with a description of industrial movements, by which we extend the analysis in the preceding chapter (Graph 10.1).

The data on sales have been taken from the statistical bulletins of the National Bank and the Social Accounting Service. Those nominal sales are then deflated by an index of producers' prices for industrial products in order to obtain chain indices of the physical volume of paid-in-full shipments. On the basis of our earlier analysis of inventory fluctuations, we may expect that sales fluctuations will be significantly greater than fluctuations of industrial production. That expectation receives full confirmation in Graph 10.1. The segments for 1962 and 1965-1966 on the graph, where the sales line resembles the line of a seismograph, are striking. And indeed it is a matter of two economic shocks, the reforms of 1961 and 1965.

Sales of the economy as a whole (Graph 10.2) behave similarly to industrial sales and have the same two earthquake-like periods, but the amplitudes of fluctuation are significantly greater. In this case the general index of retail prices was utilized as a deflator; this is not the most adequate deflator, but it is the best available. Since there are no quarterly indices of movements of the total social production, it would be interesting to examine the extent to which sales can act as a proxy for those indices, with respect to the degree to which the indices of sales and of the physical volume

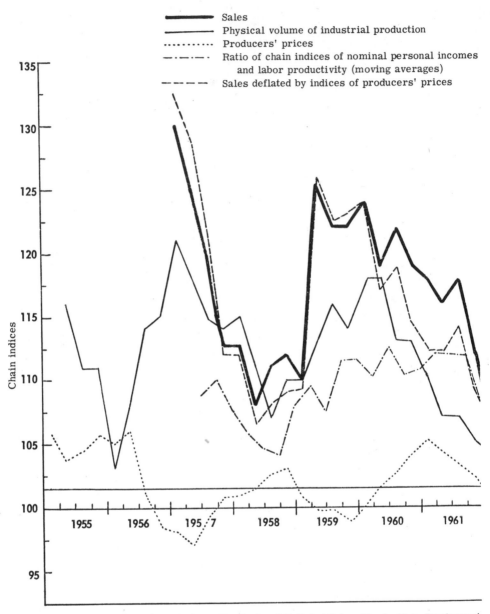

Graph 10.1 Industry: Nominal and Deflated Sales, Production, Producers'

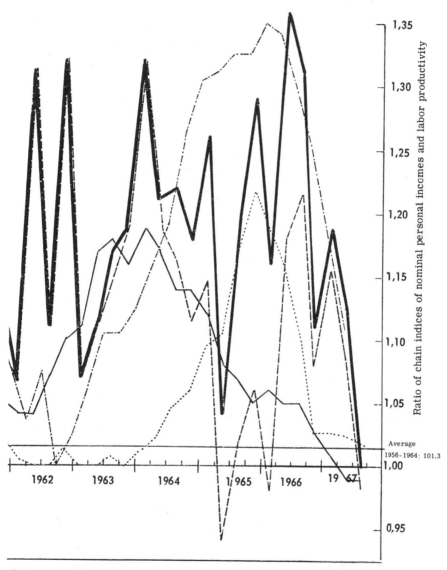

Average
1956-1964: 101.3

Prices, and Relations of Nominal Personal Incomes and Labor Productivity

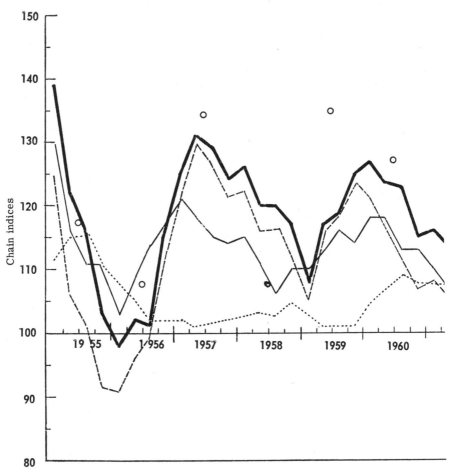

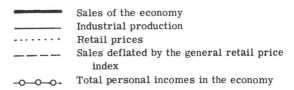

Graph 10.2 Nominal and Deflated Sales of the Economy, Retail Prices,

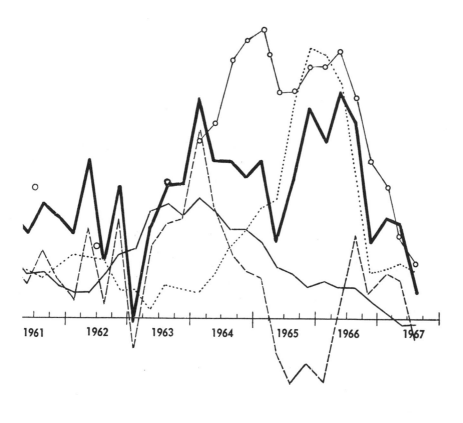

Total Personal Incomes of the Economy, and Industrial Production

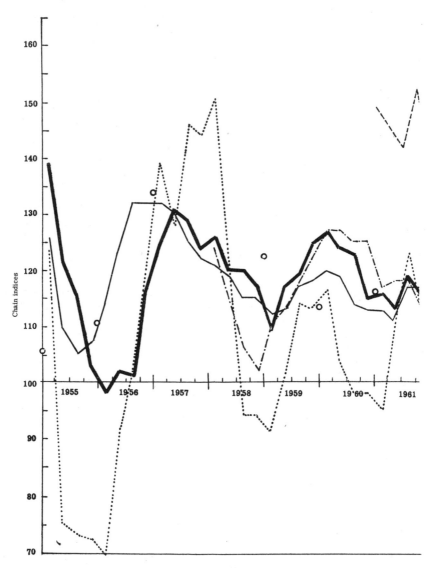

Graph 10.3   Sales, Credits, Inventories, Demand Deposits,

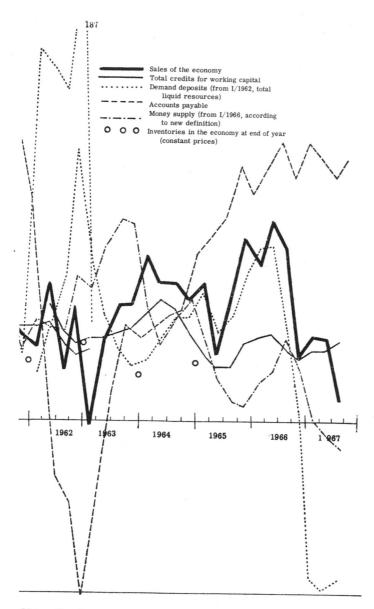

187

Sales of the economy
Total credits for working capital
Demand deposits (from I/1962, total
   liquid resources)
Accounts payable
Money supply (from I/1966, according
   to new definition)
Inventories in the economy at end of year
   (constant prices)

1962   1963   1964   1965   1966   1967

Money Supply, and Accounts Payable

of production agree. The correlation between deflated industrial sales and the physical volume of industrial production is r = 0.52 for the entire period and r = 0.72 for the same period without the two reforms; and between deflated sales for the economy and the physical volume of industrial production — r = 0.63 and r = 0.66 respectively. Regression equations show that the indices of sales and of physical volume move approximately at the same rate, and that their level is corrected by a positive or negative value of the constant term. (1) The regression coefficients are highly significant even at the level of 1%.

Table 10.1

Chain Indices of the Social Product
(in 1960 prices)

	Economy (excluding agriculture)	Industry	Other Sectors (excluding agriculture)	Difference 2-3
	1	2	3	4
1953	107.4	109.5	105.3	4.2
1954	112.4	114.4	110.5	3.9
1955	110.2	114.1	106.3	7.8
1956	103.5	109.7	96.7	13.0
1957	115.2	117.3	112.5	4.8
1958	109.7	111.8	106.9	4.9
1959	111.2	111.6	110.6	1.0
1960	113.7	113.6	113.9	−0.3
1961	108.7	107.0	109.6	−2.6
1962	105.4	107.3	102.8	4.5
1963	113.7	115.6	111.0	4.6
1964	114.4	116.0	112.0	4.0
1965	106.1	108.4	102.9	5.5

Source: SZS, Statistički godišnjaci.

Analysis of annual data gives additional information (Table 10.1). It can be seen that the economy, excluding agriculture, and industry move at about the same rate, which is not surprising when one bears in mind that industry contributes a significant part of total production excluding agriculture — 36% at the beginning of the period considered and almost 50% at the end (in constant 1960 prices).

The data in column 4 show that the physical volume of industrial production grows faster than the production of other sectors. In that respect the table shows a tendency for the differences to decline up to 1961, when they even become negative, and to increase after that year. What is particularly interesting is that at high rates of growth the differences decline, while in depressed years they are significantly greater than the average. An important conclusion follows: fluctuations of economic activity of other sectors are greater than fluctuations of industry; accordingly, other sectors are a more unstable element of the Yugoslav economy than industry is.

The same conclusion can also be drawn from the data in Table 10.2 on turning points and amplitudes of fluctuations. The amplitudes of deflated sales are greater for the economy than for industry, and in both cases they are greater than for industrial production. Furthermore, it is very significant that the amplitudes systematically increase from cycle to cycle for all three aggregates; this means that from 1957 to the present the instability of the Yugoslav economy has systematically increased. In that respect the phenomenon of the constant lowering of the cyclical troughs is especially dangerous. In the last cycle all the troughs fell below 100, which means that there was an absolute reduction of both production and sales, the first since the time of the Cominform blockade.

Our knowledge about monetary-credit phenomena, which we acquired by the analysis of fluctuations of industrial inventories, will now be supplemented by analysis of certain aggregate values for the entire economy. It can be seen from Graph 10.3 that total credits for working capital follow total inventories at the outset, and from 1957 they follow total sales in the economy (the coefficient of correlation is 0.62 for the period 1957 to the second quarter of 1965). However, as credits are not well synchronized with the requirements of sales, the economy is aided by mutual indebtedness and variations in liquidity. Both variations are extreme. Liquidity of the economy is shown on the graph by chain indices of funds in demand deposits (žiro računi) up to 1963, and by indices of total liquid resources (demand deposits, depreciation funds, funds for common consumption, and other money deposits) from 1962 on. This statistical discontinuity is necessary in order to neutralize institutional changes as much as possible. That is, depreciation funds and other liquid resources had been strictly assigned and often blocked; changes in the financial system after 1961

Table 10.2

Turning Points and Amplitudes of Physical Volume of Production and Deflated Sales

| | Industry Production | Industry Sales | Sales of Economy | Lag (+), Lead (−) in Relation to Industrial Production In Quarters | | Indices at Turning Points | | | Amplitudes | | |
				Sales of Industry	Sales of Economy	Industry Production	Industry Sales	Sales of Economy	Industry Production	Industry Sales	Sales of Economy
Peak	I/1957	I/1957*	II/1957	0	+1	121	133*	130	—	—	—
Trough	III/1958	II/1958	I/1959	−1	+2	107	107	105	14	26	25
Peak	II/1960	II/1959	IV/1959	−4	−2	118	125	124	11	18	19
Trough	I/1962	I/1962	I/1963	0	+4	104	107	95	14	18	29
Peak	I/1964	I/1964	I/1964	0	0	119	130	130	15	23	35
Trough	III/1967*	II/1965	I/1966	−9	−5	99*	94	90	20	36	40

*Estimate and forecast respectively.

(when business funds of economic organizations were created) gradually abolished restrictions, and other funds approached the liquidity of demand deposits.

At high rates of credit expansion, liquidity increases still faster, at low rates — even slower. When credit expansion exceeds the rate of 20% annually, liquid funds grow faster than credit; when credit expansion falls below 15%, liquidity not only deteriorates relatively, but even the absolute amount of liquid resources falls. Naturally, the reverse is true of movements of indebtedness of the economy, which are shown on the graph by chain indices of accounts payable that are based on the periodic calculations of the Social Accounting Service. Since credits move with sales, along with extreme oscillations (in opposite directions) of liquidity and indebtedness, it is completely clear that anticyclical credit policies had not been devised for the Yugoslav economy as a whole. What is more, as we shall see a little later, credit policy resulted in increased instability. Only in emerging from depressions, particularly in 1962, did credit policy play a positive role.

It is interesting that the money supply is much more weakly correlated with economic movements than credits for working capital (the coefficient of correlation with total sales is $r = 0.21$). The cause of that is probably at least partially the earlier inadequately precise definition of money supply, which includes in money those funds which do not serve for payment.

Although all three recessions shown on Graph 10.3 occurred basically in the same way, the recessions that began in the first half of 1960 and 1964 deserve special attention because of their severity. In both cases the expansion of sales and credit slowed down and the liquidity of the economy fell sharply, while the indebtedness of the economy increased enormously. When in the first of these recessions the illiquidity of the economy became more than critical, remedial action was taken in the first quarter of 1962 — debts were mutually cleared, and relatively large (in relation to the volume of production) credits and other financial measures during 1962 liquidated indebtedness and increased liquidity, so that in the second half of that year an economic upswing began anew. The recession of 1964 is different from the preceding one, inasmuch as large administrative increases in prices were introduced in 1965; the price increase raised nominal sales and, along with the support of somewhat accelerated credit expansion, increased nominal liquidity. However, since the expansion of liquid resources only follows the expansion of nominal sales, liquidity per unit of monetary transactions did not increase. In 1966 there was a slowing down of credit expansion, and then an absolute reduction of money available for economic transactions. As a result, the growth of nominal sales slowed down sharply, the physical volume of sales — which in the second half of 1965 and the first half of 1966 fell absolutely, and then recovered somewhat — again showed a tendency to fall absolutely, and the liquidity of the economy fell far below the lowest point of 1961. From the middle of 1965 the indebtedness of the economy increased by a rate of 45-50% annually and in 1967 reached the level of indebtedness of 1961 with respect to the volume of transactions.

There can be observed, it appears, yet another interesting difference between the last two recessions. In the recession of 1960 the expansion of indebtedness and liquidity of resources moved in reverse directions; in the recession that started in 1964, they moved in the same direction from the middle of 1965 to the middle of 1966. The latter phenomenon can be explained by the fact that in the middle of the recession, in mid-1965, reforms were adopted which: (a) cancelled various taxes, thereby increasing the liquidity of the economy as a whole; (b) drastically changed prices and the structure of demand, and thus produced unexpected and unearned profits for some enterprises and undeserved losses for other enterprises; and (c) treated low-profit and unprofitable enterprises less generously than hitherto. Consequently, some enterprises accumulated liquid resources normally while others had to incur debt in order to continue production. Since the economy is an interdependent system, every stronger disturbance in one segment of that system will lead to a stoppage in the functioning of the whole system. In a system of intersectoral links, low-profit enterprises are — directly or indirectly — customers of high-profit enterprises. To the extent that the first group abruptly stops or reduces production, that will also have to be done by the latter group. For that reason the high-profit enterprises will use their own and borrowed funds to grant credit to their weaker partners, at least so long as the process of readaptation of the economy to the initial disturbance is uncompleted. Since, as our graphs show, the initial disturbance was violent, the normal unfolding of the process of readaptation ordinarily would require a longer period of time, at least several years, along with a systematic campaign to strengthen and replace weak links in the economic chains. However, weak enterprises were left more or less to themselves, emissions of money and credit were slowed instead of accelerated, and thus after only one year the weak pulled themselves and the strong into the abyss of nonliquidity. In 1967 the economy again found itself in the situation of 1961.

10.2 The Volume of Transactions, Money and Indebtedness

Although we established in the preceding section that quarterly movements of the money supply (according to the appropriate definition) are not closely correlated with quarterly movements of the economy, it can be assumed that the correspondence is significantly better in longer time periods. Therefore it would be useful to attempt to supplement the conclusions from the preceding section with a summary analysis of the supply and demand for money. We will carry this out for the period from 1958 on, when the Yugoslav economy had already assumed the characteristics of a market economy. We can begin this task conveniently by a comparative analysis of some economic movements in the eleven most expansive market economies in the world over the last twelve years. Those economies that grow by rates of 5% or more annually have been selected as expansive. The data were taken from statistical publications of the International Monetary Fund, whose definition of money supply approximates the Yugoslav definition.

Table 10.3 permits the statement of an entire series of hypotheses concerning monetary and real movements. First of all, the unweighted averages show that accelerated growth is accompanied by an increase in prices, and to some extent, the elasticity of the supply of money. In all the countries, the elasticities of the money supply in relation to the physical volume of production are significantly greater than one; however, in relation to the money value of final production they sometimes fall below one, and on the average are not significantly greater than one. This means that the velocity of turnover of money in relation to the money value of transactions was constant for the period considered. In all the countries, prices on the internal market — represented by the costs of living — increased relatively fast. In all there were two quite significant exceptions — Portugal in the first group and West Germany in the second. Both countries also have below-average elasticities of money supply. The example of West Germany, because of its high rate of economic development, is particularly instructive. The

Table 10.3

Rate of Growth of the Social Product, Money Supply and
Cost of Living in Twelve Expanding Economies in the
Period 1953-1965

	Social Product		Supply of Money	Cost of Living	Coefficients of Elasticity	
	In Constant prices	In Current prices			3:1	3:2
	1	2	3	4	5	6
I Medium Expansive Economies						
Netherlands	5.0	9.1	6.3	3.3	1.26	0.69
Italy	5.0	9.0	11.6	3.3	2.32	1.29
France	5.0	9.7	11.8	3.9	2.36	1.22
Portugal	5.1	6.7	7.4	1.8	1.45	1.10
Austria	5.5	9.2	8.4	2.8	1.53	0.91
II Highly Expansive Economies						
Greece	6.0	10.9	16.2	3.4	2.70	1.49
West Germany	6.0	9.8	9.9	2.1	1.57	1.01
Spain	6.4[a]	9.1[b]	13.5[b]	6.9[b]	2.11	1.48
Mexico	6.6	12.7	11.6	5.0	1.76	0.91
Japan	9.3	13.2	15.0	3.6	1.62	1.14
Israel	10.5	18.7	16.7[c]	6.1	1.59	0.89
Average, Group I	5.1	8.7	9.1	3.0	1.78	1.04
Average, Group II	7.5	12.4	13.8	4.5	1.89	1.15
Yugoslavia, 1958-1964	9.5	20.6	24.9	8.8	2.62	1.21
Yugoslavia, 1958-1967	7.4	23.5	17.8	12.2	2.40	0.76

a) 1956-1964, b) 1955-1964, c) 1954-1964

Sources: a) For foreign countries and Yugoslavia during 1958-1964,
data are taken from International Monetary Fund, International Financial Statistics, Supplement to 1966/
1967 Issues; and UN Statistical Yearbook, 1966.

Table 10.3 (continued)

b) For Yugoslavia, according to columns of the table:
(1) SZS, Statistički godišnjak, 1958-1965, estimate of
SZPP for 1966 and my estimate for 1967 (–1%). (2)
SZS, Statistički godišnjak, 1958-1966, my estimate
for 1967 on the basis of the estimate of the dynamics
of total values of production (+6.3%). (3) As under (a)
for 1958-1965, SDK, Statistički bilten 11/1967 for
1965-1967. (4) Indeks, 12/1967.

ordering of internal finances, along with a significantly slower
movement of prices in relation to all her main partners, made it
possible for Germany to have a revaluation of the mark and great
export expansion. The case of Japan is similar. Its economy is
certainly less stable than the German, but attains a rate of growth
half again higher and, in terms of price movements and coefficients of money supply, is below the average of her group.

Two countries at the extremes of the table, the Netherlands and
Israel, are striking because of their unusual behavior — prices
rising significantly above the average, but the supply of money expanding significantly below the average. Accordingly, these countries fundamentally contradict that quantitative theory of money
according to which prices are lower the less money there is in
relation to the volume of transactions. The explanation is probably similar to the one for the same phenomenon in Yugoslavia.
Both countries are small and very open — the Netherlands exports
half of its production — and the rate of price inflation is a basic
peril to their economic growth. Having exhausted other methods
of controlling prices, they resorted to restricting the supply of
money.

Yugoslavia, with a rate of growth of 8.5% in the 1958-1964 period, enters at the very peak of group II. Emissions of money were
above the average for the group, especially in relation to the physical volume of production. However, those emissions were still
lower than, for example, in Greece, and the second coefficient of
elasticity (in relation to the nominal social product) was less than
in a number of countries, while at the same time prices increased
faster not only than the average but also in relation to any other
country in the table. In connection with this statement it is necessary to have in mind that, because of institutional changes, the

same stock of money was able to clear a greater volume of economic transactions in 1964 than six years earlier. But there remains a very strong indication that the price increases had an autonomous cause, that monetary-credit policy cannot be blamed in that respect, and that the supply of money was, on the whole, the same as in other countries.

The above-mentioned indication is further strengthened when the period considered is extended to cover three more years of the last reform. Monetary emissions slowed down drastically, so that for the three years the average second coefficient of elasticity fell to the Netherlands-Israel level. At the same time, administrative increases of prices significantly raised the average price increases for the entire period. A drastic monetary shock had to be drastically reflected in the liquidity of the economy, concerning which we present data on financial flows of the National Bank (Table 10.4).

As regards the changes in the composition of money during the period considered, judgments cannot be made concerning the changes in the turnover of money in the possession of economic organizations, except that the obvious sharp increase of liquidity in 1962 was the result of measures to deal with the illiquidity of the economy, and the drastic reduction of liquidity after 1965, when the money supply fell not only relatively but absolutely, was the result of a policy of monetary restriction. Direct credits to buyers, by which the availability of money as a means of payment is corrected, naturally move cyclically. In the expansive years (1959, 1963, 1964) accounts receivable were lower (10.5-11.4% of the value of production); in recession years (1961, 1965-1967) they increased (11.8-15.9%). In that respect the situation in 1967 was the same as in 1961. In 1962, as a result of measures to improve the financial condition of the economy, accounts receivable fell by 330 billion old dinars, or 21%.

Short-term bank credits, as can be seen in column 9 of Table 10.4, move in the same way as the business cycle, thereby deepening the latter. In 1967 bank credits reached by far their lowest value for the entire period. The extent to which credit restriction was severe is seen from the data that accounts payable surpassed indebtedness to banks; the economy substituted its credit for that of the banks.

Total means of payment (money and accounts receivable) and total credits (i.e., bank and direct) represent fairly steady proportions of the value of production: first they move in the interval

134

Table 10.4

Value of Production, Supply and Demand for Money,
1958-1967 (million new dinars)

	Means of Payment	Credits Short-run			Relationships According to Value of Production (%)					
Value of Production^a	Money^b	Accounts Receivable	Credits of Banks	Accounts Payable	Means of Payment			Credits		
					2:1	3:1	Total	4:1	5:1	Total
1	2	3	4	5	6	7	8	9	10	11
1958	60,810	3,174	7,085	9,481	5,657	5.2	11.6	16.8	15.6	9.3	24.9
1959	71,030	3,190	8,094	11,822	7,158	4.5	11.4	15.9	16.6	10.1	26.7
1960	85,983	3,859	11,277	13,413	8,961	4.5	13.1	17.6	15.6	10.4	26.0
1961	99,882	4,827	15,823	14,924	12,873	4.8	15.8	20.6	14.9	12.9	27.8
1962	107,547	6,398	12,522	16,856	9,965	5.9	11.6	17.5	15.7	9.3	25.0
1963	131,197	7,305	14,925	19,904	11,732	5.6	11.4	17.0	15.2	8.9	24.1
1964	167,185	8,546	17,605	21,514	14,706	5.1	10.6	15.7	12.9	8.8	21.7
1965	212,744	10,419	25,185	24,194	20,159	4.9	11.8	16.7	11.4	9.5	20.9
1966	263,322	9,776	34,309	26,742	28,592	3.7	13.0	16.7	10.2	10.9	21.1
1967	279,900	7,455	42,700	29,200	34,400	2.7	15.3	18.0	10.4	12.3	22.7

Notes

a) Sales of goods and services of economic organizations, plus inventory investment and changes in accounts receivable.

b) Cash, demand deposits [žiro i tekući računi], and funds in financial transactions of economic organizations.

Source: For 1958-1966, Godišnji izveštaj Narodne Banke Jugoslavije (1966); for 1967, my estimate.

between 15.6 and 20.7%, and later in the interval between 21.4 and 27.9%, with a tendency to fall. However, the movements within the intervals are not random but systematic, and such that the velocity of turnover falls in retardation phases of the cycle and increases in accelerative phases. At the trough of a depression, a total volume of money of 21%, or total credits of 28%, of the value of production will not be sufficient; in periods of economic upswings, even means of payment of 16% and credits of 22% can be entirely satisfactory. However, the total volume of money and credit required depends also on their composition. Money turns over faster than accounts receivable, and similarly, it would appear, bank credits turn over faster than accounts payable. And that is one more indication, among the others observed earlier, of the exceptional importance of correct doses of money and credit in maintaining the normal rhythm of economic transactions.

10.3 Price Movements

Variations in the volume of money are immediately linked in popular and expert opinion with the movement of prices. Our analysis has given some indications that this conception, at least as far as the Yugoslav economy is concerned, is mistaken and that price movements have a specific and autonomous cause. Discovery of the cause which satisfactorily explains current, quarterly price movements in the Yugoslav economy would be of great importance in establishing stabilization policy on a scientific basis. And, indeed, the research that follows is dedicated to resolving that problem, insofar as it falls within the framework of this study.

Table 10.5 gives us, first of all, a general conception of price movements in Yugoslavia. The implicit deflators of the social product and the direct price indices show that the dynamics of industrial prices are significantly more stable than the dynamics of prices either in agriculture or in other sectors. This means that industry succeeded in absorbing the even greater variations and price increases of other sectors and, until 1964, kept its own prices quite stable. There is little doubt that industry achieved this as a result, first of all, of the rapid growth of labor productivity and the efficiency of investment; that is, in turn, the result of rapid expansion of production, as was established in the chapter on the productivity of labor.

Comparison of the implicit deflators and the direct indices shows

Table 10.5

Implicit Deflators of Components of the Social Product and Some Price Indices, 1953-1967

| | Chain Indices of (Implicit) Deflators of the Social Product | | | | Chain Indices | | |
| | | | | | Producers' Prices | | Retail Prices |
	Economy	Agriculture	Industry	Other Sectors	Agriculture b)	Industry a)	General Index a)
1953	101.4	97.6	98.4	113.8	109	98	100
1954	110.4	114.7	101.6	114.5	111	98	94
1955	104.8	110.8	106.8	97.0	114	105	110
1956	107.8	124.2	95.2	110.6	104	101	105
1957	100.7	99.3	96.0	108.1	110	99	101
1958	96.9	96.8	98.7	94.7	88	101	102
1959	105.3	97.7	106.4	112.7	104	100	101
1960	111.0	115.8	106.4	113.2	109	102	107
1961	110.4	121.6	104.9	110.0	113	104	108
1962	107.5	116.7	101.1	109.7	118	100	107
1963	108.2	113.2	103.8	111.3	110	101	104
1964	118.2	123.6	115.0	120.1	124	105	109
1965	126.0	146.0	113.9	131.5	143	115b)	129b)
1966	..	..	..	..	118	111b)	123b)
1967	..	..	..	..	97*	102b)**	107b)***
Average							
1953-1964	106.9	111.0	102.9	109.6	110.2	101.	104.0

*January-September **January-October ***January-November
Sources: a) SZS, Statistički godišnjaci. b) Indeks.

the existence of the same tendencies and order of magnitude of variations, but otherwise the agreement is by no means ideal. The differences can be the result of more fundamental differences in the indices (for the indices measure different phenomena), but they can also stem from methodological and other errors. Since I am not familiar with the research in this field, it is impossible to make a judgment at this point. It is necessary to warn, however, that the statistical methodology has a peculiarity that can have significant effects: producers' prices include the turnover tax which, until the last reforms, was paid mainly by producers. Thus, since the turnover tax changes from time to time, and changes independently of the producers, these in fact are not producers' prices, i.e., producers do not determine them.

Our table shows at the bottom that, after the proportioning of prices on a higher level in 1965, the chain indices of prices in 1967 almost returned to the average of the period 1952-1964, and agricultural prices were even below that average. We shall elaborate on the analysis of movements of producers' prices in agriculture and industry, industrial retail prices, and the general index of retail prices. In that connection, in interpreting the graphs it is necessary to keep constantly in mind that the lines of chain indices do not represent quarterly indices of the changes of prices in successive quarters but (in order to eliminate seasonal influences) the index of the same quarters of successive years, as has been generally done in our graphs.

Let us begin with agricultural prices, which are easier to analyze. The economy came out of the administrative period with large disparities between industrial and agricultural prices, to the detriment of the latter. Development of market relationships demanded the elimination of those disparities, so that in the period under consideration there was a constant and rapid increase of agricultural prices. For the period 1952-1964, that increase amounted on the average to almost 10% annually. Since food absorbs about half of family budgetary resources, the increase of agricultural prices produced a significant increase in the cost of living which, through pressure to raise personal incomes, evoked strong inflationary tendencies.

Where annual changes are concerned, it can be expected that a good harvest causes a fall in prices (in our case, a fall in the rate of increase of prices) in the third and fourth quarters of the same year and in the first two quarters of the next year. Graph 10.4

138

supports that expectation. As good and bad harvests appeared in alternate years, the troughs and peaks of the price curve, with a small phasal shift, coincided with the troughs and peaks of the curve for agricultural production. That correspondence stopped after 1959, for after that year the two-year cycle of good harvests was interrupted. But the general regularity of the reverse movement of rates of increase of production and prices remained, with a certain lag. One cannot discern any sort of connection between annual changes of industrial and agricultural prices. However, from time to time there occurred a coincidence of inflationary periods, as in 1954-1955, 1960-1961, and 1964-1966, and then a strong inflationary wave ensued throughout the country (see Table 10.5).

What strikes one first about industrial prices is something that we have already emphasized — their very small increase, an over-all average of about 1% annually in the period 1952-1964. There are not many countries in the world with such mild movements of industrial prices. That result is even more significant because, in the same period, there was strong inflationary pressure from agricultural prices, as well as the pressure of frequent economic reorganizations. By rapid increases in labor productivity, as well as efficiency in the use of capital, industry succeeded in absorbing those pressures. But in 1954-1955 industrial prices began to follow agricultural prices. When that tendency attained its culmination in 1955, the Federal Price Bureau was founded and permission had to be obtained to raise prices. Those measures, accompanied by the establishment of some maximum price ceilings and aided by corresponding credit policy, stabilized industrial prices in the following eight years. Reduced fluctuations express certain market laws. High industrial production lowers industrial prices and low production raises them (or the chain index of prices). That is a very important statement. It follows that in Yugoslav conditions industrial expansion does not lead (within certain sufficiently large limits) to inflation but to better satisfaction of chronically unsaturated consumer demand. And the reverse also holds: in depressed periods there will be strong inflationary pressure because there is a tendency in those periods to carry out administrative increases in prices (1962, 1964 and 1965), as well as because of a (for now) still unidentified cause. These are not necessarily normal characteristics of the market, but they are the reflection of a certain institutional system. (2) The effects are stronger when the

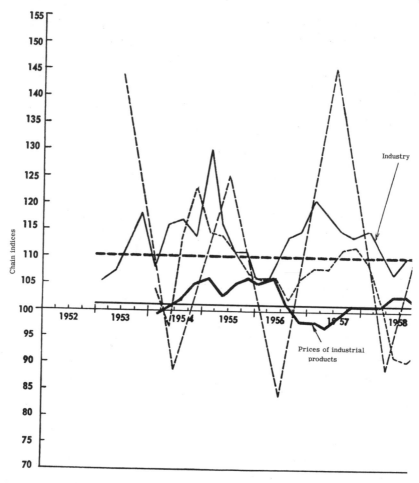

Graph 10.4   Indices of

peaks and troughs of industrial and agricultural production correspond.

The picture described changed abruptly at the end of the period,
when there was an explosion of prices, agricultural as well as industrial. That explosion was probably in part prepared by the excessively rigid price policy in the preceding eight stable years.
Some prices remained fixed too long and the profitability of production fell, while real personal incomes began to lag. In a number of industries price stability was attained by subsidization, either direct or indirect (through reduction of tax obligations). Elec-

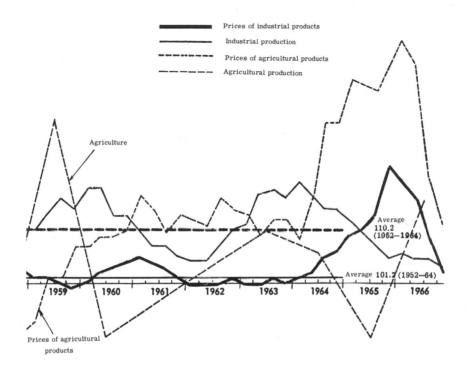

Agriculture

Average
110.2
(1952—1964)

Average 101.2 (1952—64)

1959   1960   1961   1962   1963   1964   1965   1966

Prices of agricultural
products

Producers' Prices

tric power production, coal, iron and steel, railroads and other industries operated with subsidies, on the borderline of profitability or even with a loss. Instead of developing market relations, the more convenient but dangerous path was taken of expanding every year the sphere of administrative price control. (3) And thus disparities accumulated underneath the apparently smooth level. In 1961 industrial enterprises presented the Federal Price Bureau with demands for increasing the prices of 12,800 industrial products; in 1964 the number of demands exceeded 69,000. (4) As a result, when ways of equalizing conditions of economic activity and

of relieving the federal budget of various subsidies were emphasized, it was possible to achieve a harmonization of prices only at
a significantly higher level. Then there is the question of drastic
administrative intervention, and whether it was necessary to wait
eight years, or did there exist some more efficient solution? Administrative harmonization can eliminate only the most gross disparities and, in addition, it simultaneously creates new ones.
Freezing of prices, which is the natural consequence of administrative intervention, and which lasts for months, intensifies disparities and also creates new ones, for in a dynamic economy the
relative relationships of costs of production constantly change.
Therefore, in the succeeding period we can expect further disturbance in the market. In fact, already in 1966 the Federal Price
Bureau received the same number of demands for price increases
as it did in 1964.

Viewed from a longer perspective, however, the following conclusion appears to be indisputable. Since in a turbulent twelve-
year period, in which agricultural prices increased 10% annually,
success was achieved in maintaining the stability of industrial
prices, that stability can be preserved by an adequate price policy
in the future to an even greater degree. That is so because the
main disparities between agricultural and industrial prices have
declined, and the significance of agricultural production in the social product is decreasing. The adequacy of that policy depends
on the factor which directs changes in industrial prices, and we
shall now undertake to identify that factor.

The recessions of 1961 and 1965-1967 showed that, along with
all the monetary restriction and piling up of inventories, prices
continued to increase, and even more than before. That paradox
remained unexplained. It was believed — and experts hold the same
opinion even today — that it is a matter of the deformation of an
insufficiently market-oriented economy, a deformation that the National Bank has been attempting already for two years to correct
by the artificial "limbs" of rigid monetary-credit restriction. It
would seem more logical to me, however, to assume that the differences in the reactions of the Yugoslav economy in comparison
to classical capitalist market economies do not result from the
former's deformations, but from differences in the institutional
system. Let us consider for a moment what happens in the course
of a cycle.

With the slowing down of the expansion of production, capacities are insufficiently utilized, fixed costs (depreciation, overhead) per unit of output rise, and variable costs also rise, for the collectives — quite normally and quite properly — avoid dismissing their fellow workers. Furthermore, in a rapidly growing economy average personal incomes increase rapidly, and they continue to rise with a certain inertia even when the recession has already begun. Employment growth also continues after the beginning of the recession, for producers do not react immediately at the turning point of the cycle and, so it appears, it is a social-psychological characteristic of the decision-makers to make short-run forecasts by extrapolating tendencies of the recent past. As a result of the phenomena we have described, nominal personal incomes rise faster than the productivity of labor and, under the pressure of increased unit costs, prices also rise. Since, fortunately, bankruptcy and massive dismissals of workers do not enter into consideration, the economy rapidly becomes illiquid; then, when the unavoidable credit injections set it back on its feet, a new economic expansion begins in which all the cited reasons operate in the reverse direction, the pressure of costs slackens and prices stabilize or even fall.

We must now submit this theory to an empirical test. Price movements are drawn on Graphs 10.1 and 10.2, which we analyzed earlier. The correlation between deflated total sales and the general retail price index is strong and negative. It follows that retail prices are in some way related to the physical volume of sales, but the relationship is such that prices rise when sales slow down and they fall (or rise more slowly) when sales accelerate.

Graph 10.2 also presents data on increases in total personal incomes in the economy. Unfortunately, we have at our disposal only annual data until 1964. But even that data is sufficient to observe that with the exception of 1958, when the points for personal incomes were below the line for sales (and when, therefore, all price indices were exceptionally low, as can be seen from Table 10.5), personal incomes constantly rose faster than sales, and accordingly also rose faster than production. There is therefore little doubt that the Yugoslav economy is so constructed that there are huge pressures to increase personal incomes. But the case of 1958 shows that those pressures can be held in check even in a recession year.

Since we have more data for industry, the line for the ratios between nominal personal incomes and productivity of labor is drawn on Graph 10.1. Those ratios show the extent to which personal incomes per employed person increase faster than the achieved increase in labor productivity in particular years. In order to eliminate random deviations, four-quarterly moving averages of the original ratios are drawn. Since those ratios are continually greater than one, this means that incomes constantly rise faster than production, thus confirming the statement made for the economy as a whole. The sole exception is 1962, when the ratio fell to one and — despite the depression, large credits, and great liquidity — industrial prices stabilized (see Table 10.5).

The above analysis and careful study of Graph 10.1 show that there must be a quite strong connection between producers' prices and the ratios of income excess — the shortened expression we use for the ratios of chain indices of nominal personal incomes to productivity of labor. The connection is such that high indices of producers' prices correspond to high ratios, and vice versa. Regression and correlation computations entirely support this hypothesis:

$$x_1 = 49.7 + 47.3 \; x_2, \quad r = 0.84 \atop (4,9) \tag{10.1 a}$$

$$x_1 = 81.8 + 17.8 \; x_2, \quad r = 0.57 \atop (4,8) \tag{10.1 b}$$

Variable X_1 represents the producers' price index for industrial products; X_2, the average ratio of income excess shifted in time by half a quarter ahead of the price index. Equation (a) refers to the whole period for which there are data, i.e., for 1957-1967; equation (b) excludes the last reform, i.e., the period from January 1965 on. The standard errors are given in parentheses, as is customary. The regression coefficients are highly significant, even at the 1% level. Interpretation of the results is very simple. Let us take case (a): when the ratio of income excess is exactly equal to one ($X_2 = 1$), the index of producers' prices equals 97; accordingly, it is possible for incomes to rise faster than production and for prices nevertheless not to increase. The limit of income excess over productivity beyond which prices will increase is 6.5%; below that limit prices will fall. Finally, every increase of the ratio by 0.1, i.e., an acceleration of the increase of incomes in relation to production by 10%, increases prices by 5%, or approximately half of the percent of income excess. These effects hold for some average rates of growth and are modified to the extent that rates deviate from the average.

144

The results just obtained, as well as the earlier fundamental consideration, show the possibility of further improvement in explanations of variations in producers' prices. Namely, the pressure on prices does not depend only on how much the increase of average money incomes exceeds the increase of productivity, but also on the phase of the cycle in which that happens. The same ratio of income excess will exert more pressure on costs when productive capacities are underemployed than when they are fully utilized. In order to take this influence into account, we will construe variable X_2 as the difference between the index of growth and the index of income excess; therefore X_2 equals the index of the physical volume of industrial production minus the ratio of income excess times 100. And this hypothesis is confirmed, for the correlations improve further.

$$x_1 = 102.3 - 0.425 \; x_2, \quad r = 0.89 \qquad\qquad (10.2 \text{ a})$$
$$(0.036)$$

$$x_1 = 101.9 - 0.239 \; x_2 \quad r = 0.72 \qquad\qquad (10.2 \text{ b})$$
$$(0.043)$$

The interpretation of equation (a) is now this: if the difference between the index of growth and the index of income excess in-creases by one, $X_2 = 1$, the price will fall by 0.4; that difference must amount to at least 5.4 for producers' prices not to change. This means, then, that in periods of prosperity the ratio of income excess can be fairly high (e.g., 1.10 if the rate of growth is 15.5%) — in those periods the productivity of labor and average incomes both rise so fast that the pressure of income excess is not great — and that prices nevertheless do not increase; and conversely, in depression even a small increase of the ratio, e.g., a ratio of 1.01 with a rate of growth of 5%, will lead to price increases. To the extent that average incomes surpass productivity (and total incomes — production) by the same rate at which production increases, there is no difference between them and therefore $X_2 = 0$, and the increase of prices is determined by the constant term. Since the constant term corresponds approximately to the average rise in producers' prices for industrial products, the equation can be interpreted (heuristically) as representing some average trend of prices (the constant term) about which prices oscillate downward or upward depending upon whether the index of production or the index of income excess is greater ($X_2 \lessgtr 0$).

Comparing equations (a) and (b) in both pairs of equations shows that inclusion of the reforms in the period considered raised the correlation and regression coefficients. That may mean two things: (1) either there were changes in the reactions of economic decision-makers, so that the factor of income excess has an even greater quantitative effect on prices and explains them to a greater extent; or (2) the index of producers' prices in the last nine quarters which correspond to the reform (when the turnover tax was removed from production) is a better expression of true producers' prices. A combination of both factors, by which the effects are strengthened, is naturally also possible. It will not be possible to answer this question until more time has elapsed or we obtain reconstructed series of the index of pure producers' prices from the Federal Statistics Bureau.

The coefficient of correlation $r = 0.89$ between the index of producers' prices and the complex variable X_2 means that by use of the difference between the index of growth and the index of income excess we have succeeded in explaining about 80% of current variations in producers' prices. That undoubtedly establishes the dominant factor in the formation of producers' prices. The earlier mysteries as to how prices rise when money is in short supply and inventories are increasing are now easily explained. However, it would be useful if we could explain some of the remaining 20% of price variations.

It is natural to assume that credit emissions influence prices, and therefore that price variations can be explained at least partially by variations in credit. It is also obvious that credit must be placed in relation to something that it serves. We ascertained earlier that, in industry, credit follows inventories. Accordingly, our second independent variable, X_3, may represent the ratio of chain indices of total credit for working capital and of the physical volume of industrial inventories. It seems plausible to assume — in fact it is a very widespread assertion upon which all justification of restrictive credit policy is founded — that prices will rise with values of that ratio above one, and that prices will fall when credit expands more slowly than inventories. However, this assumption not only cannot be verified, but in the conditions of the Yugoslav economy it is shown to be mistaken. Inserting X_3 in equation (a) shows that the corresponding regression coefficient is insignificant even at the 10% level. Inserting X_3 in equation (b) yields a regression coefficient that is significant at the 5% level, but is negative, which is contrary to the assumption. The latter result means in effect that <u>faster</u> expansion of credit in relation to inventories results in a <u>fall</u> in prices. This paradox is easily solved when we recall that credit stimulates production, expansion of production reduces costs, and lower unit costs exert less pressure on prices.

As we have already emphasized, there are no quarterly data for the economy as a whole, as there are for industry, and therefore it is not possible to draw such strong conclusions. It is necessary, nevertheless, to try to determine what can be done with the existing data. We will therefore attempt to explain the movements of industrial retail prices and the general retail price index.

$$x_1 = 42.1 + 56.4 \ x_2, \quad r = 0.77 \qquad (10.3)$$
$$(13.0)$$

$$x_1 = 103.4 - 0.574 \ x_2, \quad r = 0.88 \qquad (10.4)$$
$$(0.085)$$

In both equations the variable X_1 represents the retail price index for industrial products. X_2 in equation (10.3) signifies the ratio of the chain index of total personal incomes in the economy (excluding the private sector) to the index of the total social product (excluding the social product of agriculture), and therefore it refers to the already familiar ratio of income excess. X_2 in equation (10.4) is constituted in the same way as in equation (10.2), i.e., it represents the difference between the index of growth of the social product (excluding agriculture) and the index of income excess as defined in (10.3). All data are annual and relate to the period 1952-1967. From the definition of the variables used it can be seen that they are by no means theoretically ideal. However, the results are surprisingly satisfactory. Now the correlation is high and increases in moving from the simple to the complex variable X_2. Accordingly, the interpretation and conclusions drawn from the analysis of equations (10.1) and (10.2) hold.

$$x_1 = 36.27 + 64.16 \ x_2, \quad r = 0.90 \qquad (10.5)$$
$$(6.70)$$

$$x_1 = 107.73 - 0.436 \ x_2, \quad r = 0.90 \qquad (10.6)$$
$$(0.046)$$

The general retail price index is explained by equations (10.5) and (10.6), where it is the dependent variable. X_2 in (10.5) is defined as the ratio of chain indices of personal incomes to deflated total sales. X_2 in (10.6) signifies the difference between the index of growth of deflated total sales and the index of income excess as defined in (10.5). The data are annual for the period 1955-1963, and quarterly for 1964-1967. Given the apparently chaotic movement of sales and the crudity of the deflator adopted, the correlation coefficients obtained are all the more surprising. The difference between the use of the simple and complex variable X_2 is now combed out. The strength of the correlation may possibly be explained by the fact that quarterly data are used for the period from 1964 on, and therefore that period receives four times greater weight in relation to the preceding period, for which we have only annual data. And precisely for the period 1964-1967, as we saw earlier, there are strong indications that a firmer link emerged between relative movements of personal incomes and price variations.

It is useful, next, to verify the hypothesis about credit. Therefore variable X_3, which in one variant represents the ratio of chain indices of credit for working capital to chain indices of the social product in constant prices (excluding agriculture), is also inserted in equation (10.4). The meaning of the first variant is the assumption that credits cover inventories, and of the second that they are proportional to the physical volume of sales, and that deviation from these norms affects prices. In equation (10.6) the ratio of credit to deflated sales is inserted as X_3. In all three cases the regression coefficients with the credit variable are insignificant even at a level of 10%.

Thus it is fairly certain that credit movements do not explain price variations. Are there other, additional factors that explain that remaining 20% of variation of producers' and retail prices? At this moment the answer to that question is not known. However, it is entirely possible that, with corrected indices of producers' prices, the ratio of income excess explains more than 80% of the variation, of which we mentioned one indication before. In that case it may be that there are no additional systematic individual factors. (5) But only further research can bring greater certainty to this question.

One of the very popular candidates for explaining variations in prices is investment. It is said that a high level of investment inflates demand and the latter, when it exceeds supply, results in price increases. The lack of satisfactory quarterly series for investment prevents us from directly examining this hypothesis. In addition, here an entire economic model, whose construction lies

148

outside the framework of this study, would be necessary for an adequate analysis. However, something can still be said as of this moment. The entire social demand in a period consists of intermediate goods, personal and public consumption, exports, and investment. Juxtaposed to that demand are the flows of production and import capabilities. To the extent that the two spheres are not equal, there will be disturbances that will be reflected in prices. However, the component of demand which contributed to that situation is not known in advance. Accordingly, the frequently drawn conclusion that the existence of an overall surplus of demand indicates that there has been excessive investment represents an economic non sequitur. What is more, it can happen that the two spheres are the same in volume but diverge significantly in structure — for example, in 1966-1967, when investment was sharply reduced — and result in large disturbances, scarcity of one commodity, and unsalable stocks of another. Investment can therefore function as a disturbance factor on the market only if it further increases even when producers of investment goods are already fully utilizing their capacity while import possibilities are exhausted. I do not know of any serious study in this area, and the existing empirical analyses give no indication whatever that, in relation to available capacities and the possibilities for imports, the surplus of investment demand is greater than the surplus of demand for intermediate goods or consumer goods.

We can now proceed one step further. Since investment is synchronized with business cycles, i.e., expands in upswings and falls in the downturns of the cycles, while prices fall in upswings and increase in downswings, it is hardly probable that expansion of investment results in a rise in prices as a whole (although, let us say, producers of some construction materials can temporarily exploit the boom by inflating their prices, etc.). But viewed in the longer run, investment naturally reduces prices because it accelerates production and raises labor productivity.

Finally, it is necessary to note that this examination of the mechanism of fluctuations of producers' prices and retail prices represents only the beginning of a study of the inflationary mechanisms in the Yugoslav economy. Our task was limited by the framework of this study. Improvement of data and the construction of new time series will make possible increased accuracy in the explanation of price formation. Construction of economic models will make it possible to discover new relationships. Experimen-

tation with averaging and lags will improve regression relationships. And in the meantime economic policy can rely dependably
upon the following conclusion: if average personal incomes do not
increase faster than the productivity of labor, other things being
equal, prices in the Yugoslav economy will be perfectly stable.
Monetary-credit policy has no direct connection whatever with the
realization of that task. Efficient control of overall movements of
personal incomes can most probably be attained by fiscal measures.
And the task of monetary-credit policy must be limited exclusively
to providing the economy with money when and where the rational
allocation of resources demands it.

Notes

1) Industry:
   a) $X_1 = 23.9 + 0.820 X_2$, X_1 = the index of deflated sales of
         (0.211)   industry

   b) $X_1 = 13.7 + 0.910 X_2$, X_2 = the index of the physical vol-
         (0.159)   ume of industrial production

   Economy:
   a) $X_1 = 0.510 + 0.982 X_2$, , X_1 = the index of deflated sales of
         (0.193)   the economy

   b) $X_1 = -1.34 + 1.008 X_2$, X_2 = the index of the physical vol-
         (0.184)   ume of industrial production

In equations (b) the periods of both reforms are omitted, which reduces the standard errors of the regression coefficients and increases the correlations.

2) In fact, just the reverse effects have been considered up to
now as normal reactions of the market: growth of production leading to inflation, and retardation of production conditioning deflation.

3) In 1958, prices were controlled in 10 industries out of a total
of 20; in 1962 — in all industries except shipbuilding. In 1962, in
16 industries 60-100% of the value of production was included in
price control (K. Džeba and M. Beslać, Privredna reforma, Zagreb,
Stvarnost, 1965, p. 71). In 1964 about 60% of industrial products
were under control; in the first quarter of 1965 industrial and other
prices were frozen, and up to the end of 1965 less than 50% of
prices were liberalized, so that the situation in that respect was

not essentially better than in 1964.

4) I. Karli, Kritički prikaz režima cijena prije i poslije reforme (Zagreb: Institute of Economics, 1967), p. 27.

5) In investigations such as ours it is always useful to test the influence of an eventual time trend. That testing showed that in all the equations, with the single exception of equation (10.2 a), the co-efficient of the time variable is insignificant even at a level of 10%. In the exception mentioned it remains insignificant at 1% (increasing the previous coefficient of correlation by 0.90). Thus we can conclude that there is no time trend in the explanation.

CHAPTER 11

CYCLES OF EXPORTS AND IMPORTS AND THE INFLUENCE OF INTERNATIONAL TRADE

11.1 Introductory Theoretical Considerations

It can be assumed that in an economy which has a relatively large and chronic balance of payments deficit and which works without the necessary foreign exchange reserves, fluctuations in exports and imports will significantly affect economic fluctuations. Let us begin our analysis with one of the standard considerations in the theory of international trade.

The basic economic balance that equalizes sources and the use of resources can be represented by this equation:

$$\begin{array}{ccc}
\text{Sources} & = & \text{Use} \\
C + G + S + M & = & C + G + I + X
\end{array}$$

$$(11.1)$$

where C represents that part of personal income which is spent on consumer goods, G is governmental expenditures on noninvestment goods, S is saving (1) (accumulation), I represents investment, and M and X are imports and exports. Since $C + G$ are the same on the left and right sides, equation (11.1) reduces to

$$S + M = I + X \qquad (11.2)$$

and net saving = net exports:

$$S - I = X - M \qquad (11.3)$$

Let us assume for a moment that investment is determined by a plan — as, in fact, it is, even though these plans are usually not carried out — and that the saving function of national income is, for the sake of simplicity, a linear function. Let us then assume that exports are fixed, for they are determined exogenously by the possibilities of sale on the international market (which is only partially correct), and that imports are a linear function of production. Let us draw such a graph.

The most frequent situation in the Yugoslav economy is represented by the thick line on Graph 11.1. In that situation production amounts to Y_1, and is achieved with a balance of payments deficit that is financed by negative internal accumulation. We can define economic equilibrium as the absence of a balance of payments deficit: $X - M = 0$. Under the assumption that we <u>do not change anything in foreign markets</u>, equilibrium will be restored at $\overline{Y}_2$, where either internal accumulation will be increased at the expense of personal and governmental consumption or investment will fall. Since the new production is less than the preceding amount $\overline{Y}_2 < Y_1$, such an economic policy, whether in its first or second variant, is not desirable. We see further that equilibrium can be attained also at production $\overline{Y}_3$, which is greater than both preceding levels: $\overline{Y}_3 > Y_1 > \overline{Y}_2$. We can attain that desirable result by an economic policy that <u>changes the conditions of foreign trade</u>, whether by an increase of exports with a given level of imports, or a reduction

Graph 11.1 ESTABLISHING ECONOMIC EQUILIBRIUM

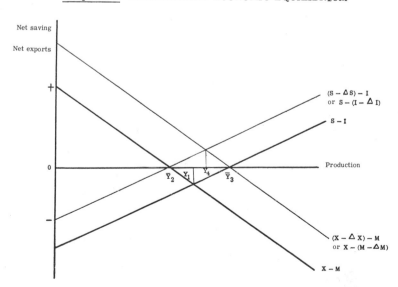

of imports with a given level of exports, or a combination of both. Such an economic policy is realized, first of all, by an adequate change in the productive structure of the economy: reinforcement of those sectors of the economy in which the country has comparative advantages, as well as those which produce import substitutes. It is important to observe an asymmetry in the two groups of economic policies cited: the latter requires significantly more time than the former because it is necessary to change the structure of production, and not only to correct the volume of consumption by financial instruments. It is not surprising, therefore, that policy-making bodies, especially in unplanned economies, take the path of least effort and orient themselves toward the first group, which results in contraction of production. In connection with our graph we must still call attention to level of production Y_4 which, along with the application of both groups of economic policies, results in a balance of payments surplus, but with a lower level of production than is objectively possible.

Having made these preliminary remarks, we can proceed to an empirical analysis of the effects of imports and exports on industrial cycles. Since we considered imports and exports of agricultural products earlier, we will now analyze foreign trade in industrial products. This separation of agricultural products is justified because the agricultural deficit was financed to a large extent by noncommercial means. We take into account imports of all industrial products, and not only those that are used in industry. This involves the exclusion of some agricultural raw materials, such as leather, wool and cotton, which we will correct somewhat later. But investment and consumption goods are included, which is important for observation of the total effect of industrial variations; the total effect consists of the primary effects of changing production on the expenditure of intermediate goods and of the secondary effect on income from which investment and consumption are financed.

First we must solve yet another statistical problem. Along with the index of imports and exports, it is necessary to construct an instrument that will measure the aggregate effect of exports and imports. That can be achieved by correlating either the absolute quantities of exports and imports or their rates of growth. Since with sufficient time the economy can adapt to various sizes of the foreign trade deficit, the relationship of the absolute quantities would be a biased measure of the effects of foreign trade on short-run economic movements. Consequently it would be necessary to use the indices of change of those relationships. But then it is simpler to work directly with the relationships of the index of growth of imports and exports. Accordingly, our indicator, which we will call the index of divergence in the growth rates of imports and exports of industrial products, will appear thus:

$$\frac{\text{chain index of imports}}{\text{chain index of exports}} \times 100.$$

An increase in the index, i.e., a widening of the divergence, means that imports have accelerated — and not simply increased absolutely — in relation to exports; similarly, a reduction of the index, a narrowing of the divergence, shows a retardation of imports in relation to exports. The reason why we place imports in the numerator and exports in the denominator will be clear from the analysis of Graphs 11.2 and 11.3. Since the random fluctuations of imports and exports are not the same, it is necessary to achieve comparability by use of moving averages. The industrial indices are given, as earlier, on the basis of 4-quarter moving averages.

11.2 Basic Empirical Findings

On the basis of the above considerations, Table 11.1 and Graphs 11.2 and 11.3, which tell an unexpected tale about the functioning of the Yugoslav economy, are worked out. To the extent that I am able to read from the graphs, that tale has ten parts.

1. The index of divergence represents a concentrated expression of international trade. For the sake of comparability, the scale of the index of divergence is shifted so that the average index of divergence — which amounts to 99 for the period considered — corresponds to the average index of annual growth of industrial production — which amounts to 112.3 for the period under consideration. It is noticeable that exports and imports fluctuate significantly more than industrial production, and that the amplitudes of the index of divergence are even somewhat greater. Industrial imports and exports fluctuate significantly more than total exports and imports. From these observations it follows that:

a) international trade is an additional factor of economic instability (2);

b) imports and exports do not change in a parallel direction; there is a tendency for fluctuations of imports and exports to

155

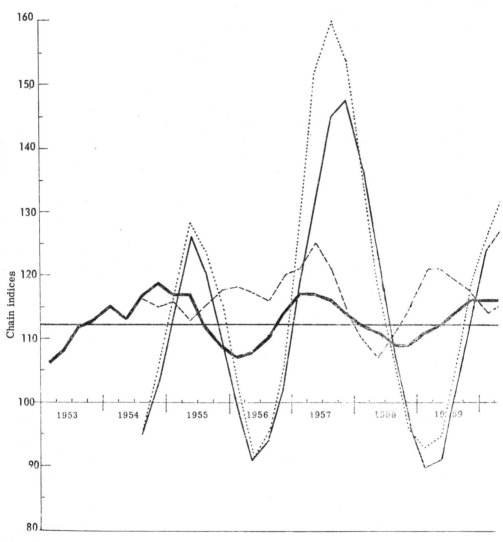

Graph 11.2 Cycles of International

(Chain Indices on the

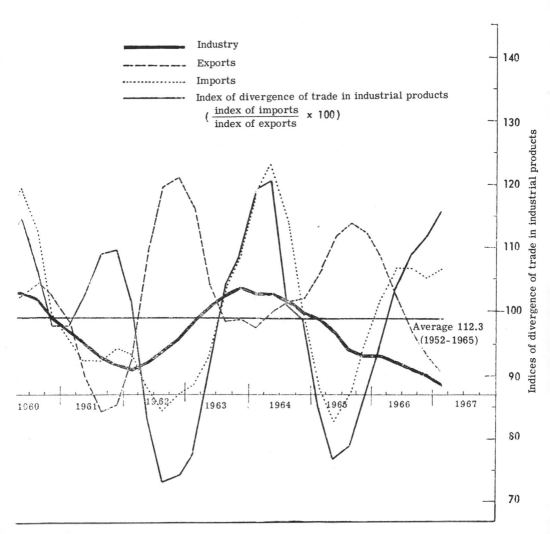

Legend:
- **———** Industry
- **– – – –** Exports
- **············** Imports
- **————·—** Index of divergence of trade in industrial products

$$(\frac{\text{index of imports}}{\text{index of exports}} \times 100)$$

Indices of divergence of trade in industrial products

Average 112.3
(1952-1965)

Trade in Industrial Products

Basis of Moving Averages)

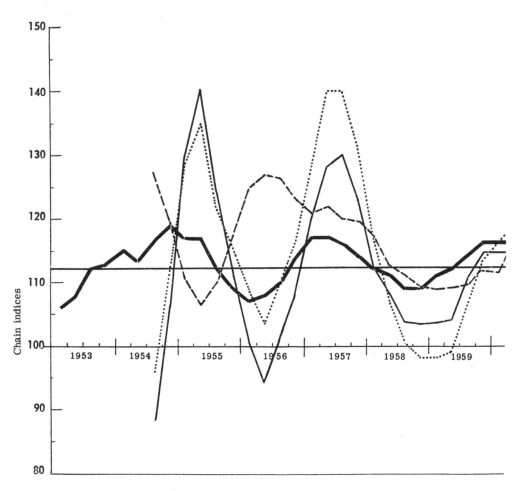

Graph 11.3   Cycles of Total Exports

(Chain Indices on the

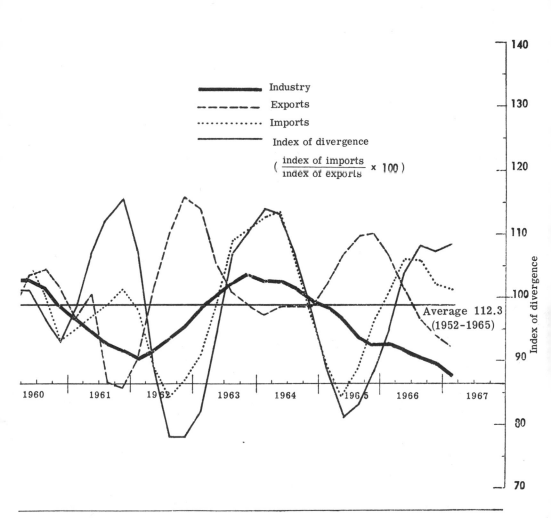

Industry
Exports
Imports
Index of divergence

$$\left(\frac{\text{index of imports}}{\text{index of exports}} \times 100 \right)$$

Average 112.3
(1952-1965)

Index of divergence

and Imports of Goods

Basis of Moving Averages)

occur in different directions;

c) since exports fluctuate significantly less than imports, and fluctuations of industrial imports are especially large (four times larger than production), the cause of refractions in economic movements must be sought especially in imports.

2. There is exceptional correspondence between industrial cycles and the index of divergence: accelerative and retardation phases conform with a certain lag. The peaks of the index of divergence lag behind the peaks of industrial cycles by 1-3 quarters. It follows that acceleration of industrial production leads to a relative increase in the trade deficit. Pressure on foreign exchange reserves increases, foreign exchange is all the more rigidly allocated, and it is increasingly difficult to obtain the necessary imports on time. This strain at a certain moment brings on the turning point of the cycle. As a result of the pressure of earlier orders, imports still increase for some time at the expense of the balance of payments deficit, but it is already late and, besides, the payments deficit becomes insupportable. The solution is found in reducing the tempo of importation, which further reduces the rate of growth of industrial production. We obtain the cycle.

The troughs of the index of divergence lag behind the troughs of industrial production by 1-2 quarters. These troughs correspond to the troughs of the import cycles. That fact indicates that imports probably do not contribute fundamentally to the turning upward of the cycle. Besides, it can be assumed that imports are at least partially a technological function of production. The position of exports is otherwise.

4. To the extent that exports are determined by the possibilities of sale on the international market, they will reflect fluctuations of that market. Since until recently the Yugoslav market was separated from the world market to a considerable degree, external and internal economic fluctuations would have to be distinguished. We see, however, that export cycles show definite regular behavior in relation to industrial cycles. Accordingly, they are at least partially internally conditioned. Furthermore, when production capacity is uniformly utilized, and investment is carried out in cycles, the investment potential would be increased in cycles with a shift equal to the gestation period. Graphs 5.4 and 5.5 show that the investment and industrial cycles correspond very well. Now, it is known that the average gestation period of investment in Yugoslav industry is shorter than $3\frac{3}{4}$ years — as long as the duration

of the production cycle. It is also known that industrial capacities are utilized very unevenly. Consequently, investment cycles do not condition export cycles.

The next assumption is related to aggregate demand. To the extent that the rate of growth of industrial production increases, the expansion of internal production also increases and — through incomes — investment and consumption demand increase. Insofar as exports represent residual quantities — which until now has often been the case in the Yugoslav economy — then expansion of internal demand means a reduction of export potential. The graphs show that this assumption is justified. For similar reasons imports move in the opposite direction. Therefore the peaks (troughs) of import cycles often approach or correspond to the troughs (peaks) of export cycles.

5. In accordance with the just-mentioned assumption, it is to be noted that the peaks of the export cycles precede the peaks of the industrial cycles. Accordingly, reduction of the tempo of exporting strengthens the negative effects of the increased tempo of importing and the combined effect leads to a turning of the cycle downward. One can see, however, that the troughs of exports also precede the troughs of industrial production. It can therefore be concluded that expansion of exports represents one of the factors which transform the retardation phase of the industrial cycle into the accelerative phase. Both effects point to the exceptional importance of exports for the stability and expansion of the Yugoslav economy.

6. The graphs show that until 1961 there was a tendency for exports to grow at a declining rate, and that from 1961 until 1966 the expansion of exports again accelerated. In the period 1953-1961 the rate of growth of the value of industrial exports was cut in half: from about 20% at the beginning of the period to about 10% at the end. For the whole period 1952-1965 the rate of growth, according to current foreign trade prices, amounted to about 15%. The acceleration of export expansion in the last cycle was obviously the consequence of economic policy which, from the end of 1960 on, was oriented toward pressing ahead with the inclusion of Yugoslavia in the world economy. The analysis thus far unambiguously confirms the correctness of that orientation. But from 1959 the rate of industrial imports also increased (1952-1965, 10.5%; 1959-1965, 11.9%) because of inadequate changes in the productive structure (the lagging of industries that produce import substitutes),

Table 11.1

Turning Points and Amplitudes of Cycles of Industrial Production, Exports and Imports, and Index of Divergence (4-quarter moving averages)

	Industrial Production	Exports		Imports		Index of Divergence	
		Industrial	Total Turning	Industrial Points	Total	Industrial	Total
Peak	IV/1954	—	—	II/1955	II/1955	II/1955	II/1955
Trough	I/1956	—	II/1955	II/1956	II/1956	II/1956	II/1956
Peak	I/1957	II/1957	II/1956	III/1957	II/1957	IV/1957	III/1957
Trough	III/1958	II/1958	I/1959	I/1959	IV/1958	I/1959	IV/1958
Peak	I/1960	II/1959	III/1960	II/1960	II/1960	II/1960	IV/1961
						(IV/61)	(II/60)
Trough	I/1962	III/1961	IV/1961	III/1962	III/1962	III/1962	IV/1962
Peak	IV/1963	IV/1962	IV/1962	II/1964	II/1964	II/1964	I/1964
(Trough)	—	I/1964	I/1964	II/1965	II/1965	II/1965	II/1965
(Peak)	—	III/1965	IV/1965	II/1966*	II/1966*	?	?
Trough	III/1967*	?	?	?	?	?	?
Lag (+) or Lead (−) in quarters in relation to industrial production:							
Peak	—	−2.0	−1.7	+1.8	+1.5	+2.0	+3.0
Trough	—	−1.5	−2.0	+1.7	+1.3	+1.7	+1.7

Amplitudes (Differences Between Indices at Turning Points)

Peak	—	—	—	—	—	—	—
Trough	12	—	—	37	31	36	45
Peak	10	—	20	68	36	57	35
Trough	8	18	18	67	42	58	27
Peak	7	14	9	40	21	38	27
Trough	12	24	19	36	21	42	38
Peak	13	38	30	40	29	48	36
(Trough)	—	24	18	41	29	44	33
(Peak)	—	16	12	24	22	?	?
Trough	18	?	?	?	?	?	?
Average	11	22	18	44	29	46	34

*Forecast

Source: Indeks, 1952-1967.

so that the index of divergence in the two subperiods was not essentially changed. One must also add that in the second subperiod there was a reduction in the rate of growth of agricultural production, which meant that the expansion of industrial exports — together with the expansion of invisible exports — was neutralized by the expansion of industrial imports and the lagging of agricultural exports. Therefore, despite all the beginnings in that direction in the period 1961-1966, it was not possible to achieve a freer internal market, liberalization of foreign trade and currency regulations, and stabilization of the economy on the level of a high rate of growth. And the most recent economic measures unfortunately fall in the first group, which yields quick results but leads to a reduction of production.

7. It is of interest to call attention to an anomaly in the movement of industrial imports and, especially, of industrial exports during 1961. After the acceleration of exports at the beginning of 1959 abruptly ceased, a drop occurred that continued in the following year. In the middle of 1960 export acceleration began again, but was no more able to stop the economic retardation which began at approximately the same time. An insufficiently prepared reform of foreign trade and exchange regulations was carried out at the beginning of 1961. The reform conditioned a sharp retardation of exports and some acceleration of imports. Because of that the trade deficit, financed by loans obtained to implement the foreign exchange reforms, increased — which is shown on the graph by a temporary upswing of the index of divergence. The fall of the divergence index continued until 1962. That lag of one year resulted in a widening of the trough of the cycle for one year. Total exports and imports also had very similar movements, and for the same reasons. The reform of 1965 had somewhat different effects. By then the economy was already to a much greater degree a market economy, and devaluation immediately led to an acceleration of exports and a deceleration of imports. However, the effects of devaluation were soon exhausted, and the insufficiently thought-out liberalization opened the door to uncontrolled imports, so that the divergence between exports and imports quickly began to widen.

8. For the reasons cited, the reform of 1965 is interpolated by an additional cycle of exports and imports. It is characteristic, however, that the export expansion and import contraction in 1965 did not succeed in stopping the retardation of general economic movements. It is obvious, therefore, that although foreign trade

164

expansion aids the recovery from depression, it is not sufficient by itself to reverse economic movements.

9. Agricultural imports and exports are included in total imports and exports. Earlier, aid was included in agricultural imports, a practice by which economic relationships are distorted. Agricultural exports depend substantially upon weather conditions. Since to a great extent agricultural trade involves food, which has priority in consumption, total trade will be more stable than industrial, as is shown especially by import amplitudes in Table 11.1. However, the more sensitive industrial trade will more precisely reflect economic interdependence. But it is interesting that the lags and leads in total and in industrial trade are approximately equal. That probably occurs because industrial trade accounts for a very high percentage of total trade (75% of exports and 86% of imports in 1959-1960).

10. It remains for us to look at still another phenomenon that appears to be regular. With the exception of the second peak for industry and the first for the economy as a whole, the peaks of the divergence index move in the region of 114-121 for industry and 114-117 for the economy. The troughs of the divergence index move in the region of 78-73 and 90-78 respectively. This hypothesis may therefore be stated: in a situation in which import expansion exceeds export growth, the former growing at a rate of 14-21% and the latter at 14-17%, there emerges an unrestrainable retardation of development; after the revival has begun, export expansion can exceed import growth by a maximum of 28-37% (1/0.78, 1/0.73) compared with 11-28% (1/0.90, 1/0.78). But since import expansion lags behind production by 4-5 months, a still significantly smaller widening of the divergence in exports and imports than that cited will condition refractions of economic movements and turn the cycle downward. The graphs show that this happens when the divergence widens to 106-111. Accordingly, when in the course of the boom the increase of imports exceeds the increase of exports by about 6%, it is necessary to sound the alarm and to take energetic measures to prevent further widening of the divergence in trade. Insofar as this is not done, the economy will quickly enter into a cumulative retardation of growth.

11.3 Intermediate Goods Imports and Other Questions

After having examined, along with industrial exports, the behavior of total imports of industrial products, it would be useful to study imports of raw materials and other intermediate goods for industry. We can assume that this importation is to a large degree technologically determined, and that it will therefore be closely correlated with industrial production. In this analysis we will use the work of S. Stamenković and D. Pirec. (3)

The authors calculate their regressions on the basis of semi-annual data for the values of imports and exports and of the physical volume of production of industrial goods for the period 1957-1964. As a function of imports they use a cubic parabola, as a function of exports — a quadratic parabola; in both cases the independent variable is industrial production, and the variables are expressed in annual rates of growth. The coefficient of determination for imports is 0.8, and for exports — 0.5. That difference in correlation must be expected because exports are much less technologically determined than imports.

Research shows that with a slow expansion of industry, imports of intermediate goods increase more slowly than production, and the difference widens up to an industrial rate of growth of about 9.8% and then narrows; with a rate of growth of industrial production of 13.5%, imports of intermediate goods rise at the same rate, but if the expansion of industry accelerates still further, the rate of increase of imports exceeds the rate of growth of production even faster. As regards exports, the differences between exports and productive power decrease after a rate of industrial growth of 11.2%, and beyond a 13.7% growth of industry the expansion of exports of industrial products begins to slow down (the maximum is 14.8%). Since exports rise slower but imports increase faster, at a certain rate the result is a maximum difference between these rates of growth. That happens when industry grows at a rate of 10.5%, which determines a 12.7% increase in exports and a 5% increase in imports; this represents the most favorable possibility for the foreign trade balance of industry. When the rate of growth of industry increases to 13.7%, the rates of increase of exports and imports equalize.

From the above data the authors draw the conclusion that the optimal rate of growth of industrial production is somewhere around 10.5%. (4) That conclusion is mistaken. What appears as optimum is the result of a particular economic structure and the rate of its adjustment. Given more adequate changes in the production structure, the "optimal" rate of growth may be raised significantly; given poor economic policy, it may also be lowered significantly. Indeed, if in order to achieve short-term effects, industrial expansion were reduced by financial measures to 10.5%, and nothing were done to change the production structure, the economy would adjust to the new rate and the "optimal" rate would be perceptibly lowered. Instead of the optimal solution we would have a retardation of economic growth.

But a second conclusion which corresponds to the facts is possible. If the rates of export and import expansion equalize when industry grows at a rate of 13.7%, industry cannot grow by a higher rate than that in the longer run. Indeed, in the longer run we can expect a lower rate. And in fact in the 1957-1964 period, industry expanded at a rate of 12.1%, and in the 1952-1964 period — at a rate of 12.4%. It is evident that these are not the highest possible rates of industrial growth since Japan and Bulgaria achieved rates of 14.1% and 13.7% in the 1952-1963 period. (5)

There remains, finally, still another question that must be considered. Reduction of the excessive expansion of imports at high rates of growth depends upon the possibility of developing import-substitute industries. In that regard the potentialities of the Yugoslav economy have obviously not been utilized; agriculture, the iron and steel industry, and the entire sector of intermediate goods lag behind the needs and possibilities for development. With respect to exports, however, it is not only a matter of pressing export-oriented industries; there is also the question of the possibilities for sales on the world market. Since the Yugoslav economy expands significantly faster than the world average, that must also hold for Yugoslav trade. In the decade 1955-1964, world exports increased at a rate of 6.5% annually. In that decade the physical volume of total Yugoslav exports grew at a rate of 13.5% (12.5% in the period 1951-1964) (6), or twice as fast as the world average. This means that it is necessary to conduct a very aggressive export policy, for it is not only a question of penetrating new markets, but of wresting markets from exporters who were there earlier. To what degree is that possible in the longer run? That is obviously a practical rather than a theoretical question, and the answer must be sought in the results achieved by other countries. In the same period Japan achieved an annual average rate of growth of exports of

14.8% (7), and the rates for West Germany and Italy in the decade 1950-1960 were 14.8% and 12.1%. (8) Since these cases involve a significantly greater volume of exports than in the case of Yugoslavia, it is obvious that such rates of export expansion can also be attained by Yugoslavia. And since the highest rates of export expansion are achieved by the countries with the highest rates of economic growth, we have additional support for our earlier conclusion that exports are a precondition of growth.

However, exports cannot be achieved irrespective of price. If, for example, we stroll through Rome and compare the prices of consumer goods with the prices in Belgrade, we notice that they are, with some exceptions (e.g., automobiles), equal. However, the exchange rate of the dinar is twice as unfavorable as that of the lira. The impression of the tourist is confirmed by systematic research carried out in the Yugoslav Institute of Economic Studies. (9) In 1962 the internal purchasing power of the French franc was, overall, 14% greater than that of the new dinar and the exchange parity was 52% more favorable, while today it is 150% more favorable. Part of the difference is explained by the regular deviations of exchange parity from the parity of purchasing power in less developed countries in comparison with the more developed countries. But there is still a large part of the difference that must be explained by other factors, such as: (a) the exporting of products in which the country does not have comparative advantages; (b) substandard quality; (c) poor organization of foreign trade (10); (d) the costs of capturing and wresting away the market. It would be important for correct economic policy to examine and quantify the comparative effects of all these factors. To the extent that the differences cited are not economically justified, Yugoslavia is giving the substance of its production to its trading partners without payment.

Notes

1) The term "saving" seems to me scientifically more accurate than "accumulation," for it is a question of ex ante analysis. Accumulation is an ex post phenomenon. Ex post saving and accumulation are identical.

2) A. Maddison comes to the same conclusion in his analysis of postwar fluctuations in 14 West European and North American countries: "The coincidence of the timing of fluctuations in trade in re-

lation to movements of production clearly indicates that those fluctuations in trade and production are closely connected in almost all the periods and countries" ("Growth and Fluctuation in the World Economy, 1870-1960," Banca Nazionale del Lavoro Quarterly Review, June 1962, pp. 32-33).

3) S. Stamenković and D. Pircc, "Analiza medjuzavisnosti nekih agregatnih veličina u jugoslavenskoj privredi," Ekonomist, 1965, No. 3, pp. 429-439.

4) Ibid., pp. 438-439.

5) Z. Popov, "Zemlje s najbržim privrednim razvojem," Ekonomska analiza, 1967, No. 1-2, pp. 112-122.

6) SGS 1965 and 1962, pp. 231 and 185.

7) See A. Maddison, "Japanese Economic Performance," Banca Nazionale del Lavoro Quarterly Review, December 1965, p. 36.

8) A. Maddison, "Growth and Fluctuation in the World Economy," op. cit., p. 18.

9) S. Stajić, Kupovni paritet dinara, work in progress.

10) K. Džeba and M. Beslać state: "... in England our bacon is sold 10-15% cheaper than Danish bacon because of poorer quality, while in Vienna and Munich our fruit is 10-20% cheaper than Italian fruit — also because of poorer quality and bad packing. In international markets many of our machines and other industrial goods also obtain prices that are lower by 10-20% in comparison to those of other producers because of construction, quality, and their being out of date" (Privredna reforma, [Zagreb: Stvarnost, 1965], p. 24).

Chapter 12

ADMINISTRATIVE CYCLES AND THE INFLUENCE OF ADMINISTRATIVE INTERVENTIONS

12.1 Cycles of Legal Regulation

The meaning of decentralization in the economy lies in extension of the autonomy of direct producers. The actual degree of autonomy and, accordingly, the real success of decentralization depend on the degree to which administrative interventions are absent. There are probably various ways of measuring the extent of administrative interventions. One of the simplest and most obvious follows from the assumption that the scope of administrative interference in the economy is reflected in the size of the Official Gazette. (1) We will use that measure in further analysis. Let us begin with the assumption that the Federal Official Gazette sets in motion — and at the same time indicates — waves of administrative regulation in general.

However, measurement of the organizational state of the Yugoslav economy is not simply a matter of academic interest. It is clear that frequent reorganizations and waves of new regulations (not infrequently, regulations that are retroactive and mutually incompatible) must have a negative effect on the efficiency of business activity. Often unforeseeable changes in the parameters of business activity introduce unrest and uncertainty into the economy, and forecasts and long-run calculations become impossible; economic organizations are oriented toward the extraction of privileges from economic policy bodies instead of serious programming, toward consciously irrational expenditures instead of an economically substantiated investment program, toward speculation with loopholes in the regulations instead of the organization

of production. Moreover, every wave of new regulations demands
a period of adaptation during which the efficiency of business activity falls — instead of growing; and, because of the inherent instability of the economy, such adaptations can cause cumulative
retardation of growth. Our task is to examine the correctness of
such an assumption and to quantify the effects.

Let us first consider the lawmaking activity of the Federal Parliament and Federal Executive Council.

In the fourteen years covered, every three days brought a regulation issued at the level of the Administration or Parliament. In
addition, the Federal economic secretariats and banks produced
rules, orders, instructions, decisions, and solutions (245 in 1965).
When we take into account the regulations of the republics and lo-
calities, and subtract holidays and vacations from the annual time
available, it follows that every working day brought some administrative surprises. However, this does not exhaust all the possibilities for administrative pressure. State bodies (2), the National
Bank, and the Social Accountancy Service also have their internal
regulations; they also change and, by the nature of things, even
faster and more often than legislative acts. Economic organizations and their leading cadres bear a huge burden, and therefore
it would not be surprising to us if this led to refractions. Let us
verify this.

Table 12.1

Legal Regulations Governing Relations in the Economy
(1952-1965)

	Federal Parliament			Federal Executive Council			
	Laws	De-cisions	Total	Decrees	De-cisions	Total	Grand Total
1952	11	2	13	29	9	38	51
1953	2	2	4	39	27	66	70
1954	12	8	20	36	79	115	135
1955	4	5	9	36	72	108	117
1956	8	9	17	32	115	147	164
1957	7	10	17	35	87	122	139
1958	5	12	17	33	79	112	129
1959	21	24	45	28	62	90	135
1960	11	12	23	18	36	54	77

Table 12.1 (continued)

| | Federal Parliament | | | Federal Executive Council | | | |
	Laws	De-cisions	Total	Decrees	De-cisions	Total	Grand Total
1961	34	29	63	23	83	106	169
1962	34	18	52	26	86	112	164
1963	30	16	46	12	58	70	116
1964	33	25	58	15	66	81	139
1965	102	20	122	11	60	71	193
Average	23	13	36	27	66	93	129

Source: Službeni List SFRJ (Chronological Register)

We will compare the number of regulations in the years that had peaks and troughs of business cycles. Since all regulations need not equally represent administrative encumbrances, we will cite, alongside the total, the number of acts of Parliament and only the decrees of the Federal Executive Council:

| In Years of Peaks | | | In Years of Troughs | | |
| Number of Regulations | | | Number of Regulations | | |
Year	Total	Excluding Administra-tive Deci-sions of F.E.C.	Year	Total	Excluding Administra-tive Deci-sions of F.E.C.
1955	117	45	1956	164	49
1957	139	52	1958	129	50
1960	77	41	1962	164	78
1964	139	73	1965	193	133

The regularity is rather pronounced: except in 1958, which is also the mildest retardation of all cycles, the troughs of the cycles are accompanied by a significantly larger number of regulations than the peaks. That regularity is even more clear in Graph 12.1, which shows the quarterly movement of legal regulations in relation to the quarterly movement of the annual rate of growth of industrial production. Seasonal fluctuations in lawmaking activity are eliminated by moving averages. It can be seen that the cycles of the economy and of lawmaking activity are differentiated from each other in phase, so that "bad" years in Parliament correspond to good years in the economy, and vice versa.

Table 12.1 reflects an important tendency in Yugoslav political life: the shifting of economic regulatory activity from the Administration to Parliament. At the beginning of the period considered, Parliament accounted for 26% of the total number of regulations, and at the end, for 63%. Such a development is undoubtedly positive, since it eliminates arbitrariness and introduces the public to economic regulatory activity. In addition, one would expect that under public pressure Parliamentary acts will be more thoroughly prepared, that they will therefore be more permanent, and hence that they will bring greater stability in the functioning of the economy. However, that assumption has not proven true up to now. It was precisely in the latter years of the period, when there was special insistence on the elimination of administrative interference in the economy, that the number of regulations reached a record level and the rate of growth of production fell to one of the lowest levels. Simultaneous changes in normative regulative activity and in economic movements point to another possibility: instead of increased expertness and preparation, there was a greater lag in undertaking adequate measures, because of which the rate of growth was reduced and the duration of the cycle was prolonged. Some indications of the accuracy of this observation are cited in the following section, but at this moment I do not see analytic possibilities of proving it.

Comparison of Table 12.1 and Graph 12.1 shows that the number of regulations rose until the end of 1956. That can be explained by the emergence from the administrative period, when internal regulations of economic organizations replaced public ones and when the regulative function of Parliament began to develop. In the period 1946-1951, Parliament brought forth an annual average of 7 regulations (as compared with 36 in the next 14 years) and the Federal Executive Council issued 52 (compared to 93 later). The number of regulations fell from the beginning of 1957 to the end of 1960. That can be considered the stabilization phase of the new economic system. There is reason to repeat that it was, at the same time, the period of Yugoslavia's fastest economic growth. But the number of regulations began to increase again in 1961, which probably indicates that the state apparatus and economic policy bodies fell behind in the mastering of techniques for regulating the ever more complex mechanism of the Yugoslav economy.

Graph 12.1   LEGAL REGULATIONS

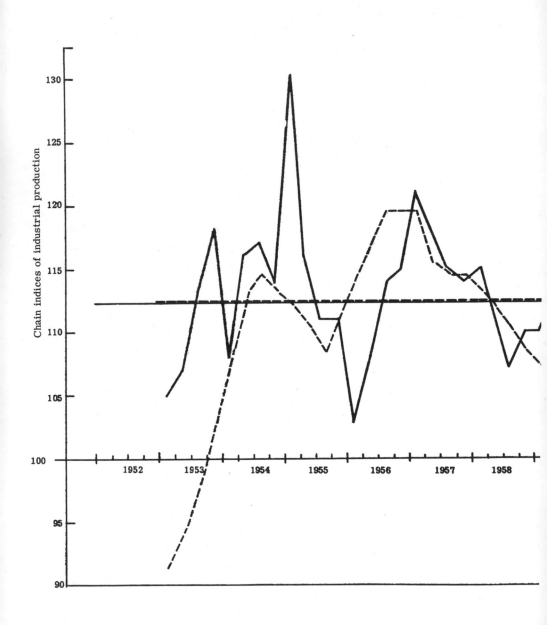

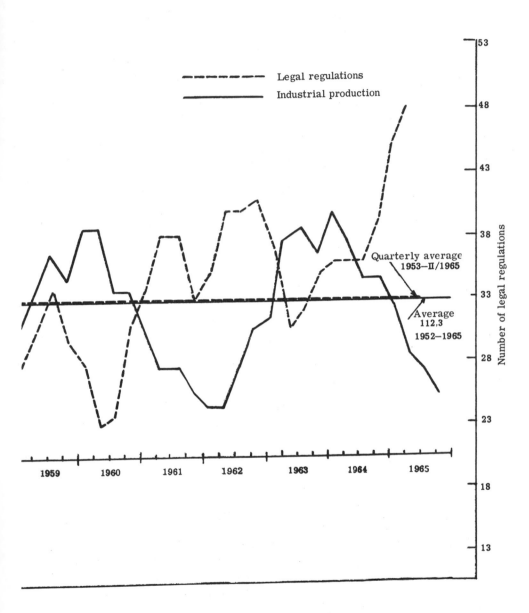

It is of interest to observe that a "long" cycle in legal regulations (upswing to 1956; decline, 1956-1960; upswing after 1960)
corresponds to the long cycles, noted earlier, in the Yugoslav
economy with a certain phasal shift. Agricultural production accelerated in the period 1956-1960, and after that it slowed down;
the expansion of industrial exports decreased in the period 1956-
1961, and then accelerated; the rate of economic growth attained
its maximum in 1956-1960 and the five-year plan was declared
completed in four years, and after that the economy slowed down
along with the postponement of the new five-year plan. On the basis of these statements it would not be necessary to conclude that
it is desirable to return to the economic system of 1956-1960; and
indeed that would be senseless, for today's economy is no less
different from that of 1956-1960 than the latter was different from
the economy before 1956. What is more, it is necessary to seek
the causes of today's difficulties in part in the successes of 1956-
1960: there has been a failure to make changes in the productive
structure in a sufficiently intensive way, and on time; there has
been a failure to prepare thoroughly and on time a program of institutional changes, the need for which could be foreseen with the
further development of a market economy.

In addition to the simple comparisons that we have made so far,
we can express the close connection between administrative interventions and economic fluctuations somewhat more formally. We
will begin with the hypothesis that low rates of growth correspond
to a large number of legal regulations and vice versa, and that
therefore there is a significant negative correlation.

Since every legal regulation does not have the same effect on
the economy — and every discrimination or weighting would be
arbitrary, and we will therefore not carry them out — it can be
expected that the number of regulations will explain a lesser part
of economic fluctuations than would correspond to the real effect
of administrative interventions. Furthermore, since until some-
time in 1958, when there was a definite settlement of the distribution of incomes of economic organizations, the economy was always to a large extent administratively regulated by direct interventions which bypassed Parliament, we can expect that the connection between legal regulations and the rate of growth will not
be particularly strong. We can also expect that the connection
from quarter to quarter will become all the stronger, until some
maximum at which it will temporarily stabilize. All these assump-

tions are shown to be justified.

| Period | Coefficient of Correlation Between the Rate of Growth and Number of Regulations | |
	Industry	Production
I/1953-II/1965	−0.01	—
I/1954-II/1965	−0.18	−0.20
I/1955-II/1965	−0.21	−0.23
I/1956-II/1965	−0.22	−0.28
I/1957-II/1965	−0.26	−0.28
I/1958-II/1965	−0.37	−0.42
I/1959-II/1965	−0.44	−0.47
II/1959-II/1965	−0.47	−0.50
III/1959-II/1965	−0.47	−0.49
IV/1959-II/1965	−0.47	−0.49

The series are correlated until the second quarter of 1965, for which the last data are available for moving averages of legal regulations. For both industry and production the coefficients of correlation attain the maximum in the second quarter of.1959. In that quarter both coefficients of correlation are significant at the 2% level. Accordingly, by the usual statistical criteria it can be said that there is a significant connection between the number of legal regulations and the rate of growth.

Correlation, naturally, does not reveal causation. Therefore we still do not know whether an increase of regulations reduces the rate of growth or, conversely, if a retardation has occurred, it is cured by the normative acts of Parliament or the Federal Executive Council. The latter is most often the explanation of the Yugoslav press and economic policy bodies. There are certain statistical indications for the accuracy of the first explanation — larger correlation coefficients when the series of legal regulations (without removal of seasonal effects) precedes the series of growth rates — but that is entirely inadequate. The dilemma can be resolved only by detailed analysis of economic policy in the last fifteen years. Let us see, therefore, when the most significant changes in the Yugoslav economic system occurred, and what those changes were.

12.2 Institutional Content of Business Cycles

1. The new economic system (1). In 1950 a law was passed concerning workers' councils. This law inaugurated the relinquishment of administrative planning and began the building of a new, specifically Yugoslav economic system. The far-reaching reorganizations caused a retardation of growth, and the economic blockade transformed that retardation even into an absolute reduction of production. After nearly two years of preparation, the new system began to function in 1952. The general and main directorates were abolished and, in addition to self-management, the enterprises also received a certain amount of operational independence. Administrative planning was replaced by planning of global proportions. Distribution of income between the community and the enterprises was resolved on the basis of a single and, therefore, rather primitive instrument: the rates of accumulation and funds.* But those rates — which were abolished after two years — along with some operational independence, played an almost revolutionary role in increasing the efficiency of business activity. Almost overnight the chronic shortage of labor was transformed into surpluses, labor productivity began to increase, and the efficiency of utilization of fixed capital began to grow. A sharp and unrestrainable economic upswing began.

It is necessary to add one more remark. In the chapter on industrial cycles we mentioned that before the end of the prolonged first cycle there was a smaller cycle, which started at the beginning of 1954 and lasted some seven quarters. Now we may add that at the beginning of that year there was a change in the system of business activity which, at the time, was called the "new economic system." "Rates of accumulation and funds" were superceded as an instrument for the distribution of income of enterprises by calculation of the basis of "accounting wages and profit." Government financing that did not include an interest charge for new enterprises was abolished. Investment funds for communities were established. Sales of fixed capital were permitted, with the sole obligation that

---

*Translator's note: these rates were centrally determined and varied according to industry and, ultimately, according to individual enterprises; they were used to determine the enterprise's tax base and had the effect of giving the enterprise an incentive to economize on the use of labor.

enterprises maintain the value of fixed capital. A rate of interest on fixed capital was introduced. But all those changes meant the direct freeing of the hitherto shackled potentials of the economy, so that they only slightly retarded growth and therefore a full cycle did not develop.

2. Transition to the second five-year plan. At the end of 1955, in M. Popović's report to the Federal Chamber of Nationalities, he asserted: "One period of our economic development is completed.... In a certain sense the year 1956 is a transitional year in our economic policy. During the coming years we must make all the preparations for a more successful economic development in the future.... Therefore, the basic task which runs through our economic policy in 1956 is stabilization of the market." (3) In the course of 1956 there were strong inflationary movements, in fact so strong that they were not repeated until 1965 (see Graph 10.4). The inflation reached its culmination two quarters after the peak of the divergence index of industrial production and three quarters after the toppling down of the industrial rate of growth. The economy began to feel the consequences of the disproportions of prior development — the neglect of investment in agriculture and transportation, as well as the lag in production of consumer goods and of noneconomic activities. The rapid development in the preceding period led to expansion of demand which, however, did not encounter a corresponding structure of supply. After it was no longer possible to correct disproportions by imports, there was a retardation of growth and inflation. The reaction was price control, credit restrictions, compulsory reserves, blocked funds, and reduction of investment. Investment not only slowed down, but in 1955 it constantly fell absolutely and reached its lowest level in the middle of 1956. (4) The reduction in industrial investment was especially sharp: in 1955 it amounted to 77% of the volume of investment in 1953. Thus, at the beginning of 1955, when the economy had already entered a retardation phase, economic policy strengthened that downward movement still more. Prices stabilized, and an attempt was made to revive the economy by credit expansion. (5) Investment in fixed capital grew rapidly. The structure of investment was significantly changed by the new five-year plan: noneconomic investment grew at the expense of economic; investment in transportation and agriculture, at the expense of industrial; investment in consumer goods industries, at the expense of basic industries. (6) While the first five-year plan was oriented

toward basic industries, the second was oriented toward processing industries. That orientation was shown to be fundamentally
correct, for it led to exceptionally rapid growth. But inadequately
controlled, it went to the other extreme, so that the second five-
year plan was completed with new disproportions and, naturally,
with the occurrence of a new cycle. But in the meantime there
was a smaller cyclical disturbance.

3. The new system of distribution of total income of economic
organizations. In the course of 1957 there was a record increase
in industrial imports (see Graph 11.2) and, because of the bad harvest the preceding year, a large increase in agricultural imports.
Since exports lagged, the index of divergence of industrial trade
attained a maximum (see Graph 11.2). The balance of payments
and trade deficits were the maximum for the entire period until
1960. (7) That determined the turning of the cycle and the retardation in 1957. In the midst of the downward phase, at the beginning of 1958, a new system of distribution of the total income of
economic organizations was introduced. After the use of rates of
accumulation and funds, which were abolished at the end of 1953,
and some experimentation with various instruments of income
distribution in the following years, in 1958 the basic system that
is still in effect today was instituted. (8) The essential characteristic of the new system is that the enterprise acquired the right
of independent distribution of net income, which it autonomously
divides into personal incomes and enterprise funds. Adaptation to
the new conditions required some time and probably also contributed to the deepening of the cyclical fall. But since prices of industrial and agricultural products increased relatively little, investment expansion continued, credit policy was conducted well,
and the new law did not bring after it the usual wave of other regulations and changes (see Table 12.1), the retardation phase was
checked relatively quickly and was the mildest of all the cyclical
drops.

4. The new economic system (2). In the already familiar manner, the index of growth of industrial production and the index of
divergence of industrial trade started downhill in the middle of
1960. Economic policy did not take account of that and, as the annual plans of the period show, there was a failure to grasp what
was in fact the matter: thus, in the midst of those downward movements, at the beginning of 1961, the most radical reform since
1950-1952 was inaugurated. A special study has been written of

what was done, and what the consequences were, so we need only
recapitulate here some of the more important conclusions. (9)
Three reforms were carried out simultaneously: in banking, in the
sphere of income distribution, and in foreign exchange. Those reforms were not well prepared, nor were they mutually compatible.
The liberalization of the distribution of the income of economic
organizations was intended to encourage work collectives to raise
production, increase labor productivity, conduct business activity
more rationally, etc. As it happened, however, economic organizations "... lost much time in discussions and attempts to adjust
to the changed conditions of their income distribution, and when
those were completed, the result diverged significantly from expectations. Namely, in not a few cases, adjustment to the changed
conditions meant the discovery of ways to achieve a better financial result without an increase in production...." (10) The increase
of the rate of exchange to 750 dinars to the dollar reduced the existing divergences of individual exchange rates in international
trade, and that, together with an orientation toward tariffs, was
necessary to liquidate the system of multiple exchange rates and
to make possible freer trade relations. Liberalization of the foreign trade regulations was required to hasten the inclusion of the
Yugoslav economy in international trade, and toward that end, foreign credits were secured. However, "... extensive utilization of
foreign capital made it possible to attain a significant increase in
imports along with the stagnation of exports, but the corresponding changes in the activity of economic organizations were not
forthcoming. Nor was the planned increase of foreign exchange
reserves achieved." (11) But the most serious disturbances origi-
nated in the sphere of credit policy. It was precisely 1961 that
was chosen for the introduction of order and discipline in that
sphere. Credit was limited to the covering of short-run needs for
working capital. Longer-term additions to working capital, as
well as investment in fixed capital, had to be covered by the enterprises' own funds or by loans from the social investment funds.
"However, the mechanism of financing durable investments was
not adjusted to this reorientation of credit policy.... Furthermore, the more uneven arrangement of accumulation and the com-
mitment of funds determined earlier had the consequence of reducing the possibility of reorienting economic organizations significantly more than is apparent from overall assessments. The
speculation of economic organizations that they would not be held

to carrying out the goals set for credit policy also operated in the same way. Thus, economic organizations did not reduce their investments in fixed capital so that there were additions to working capital, as was expected, but continued to spend, to all appearances, as they had before." (12) The result was a shortage of working capital, then mutual indebtedness, and finally complete illiquidity of the economy, which led to a sharp slowing down of production.

All these short-run effects were added to the consequences of structural disproportions, price disparities, and an inadequate system of planning. "Structural disproportions...are not perceived completely or in time, and problems have not been subjected to fundamental research. Our system of planning, including here the implementation of plans as well, has not been worked out either conceptually or methodologically. Pragmatism in working out plans, the slow introduction and neglect of scientific methods of analysis, and consequently a certain subjectivism and arbitrariness in the construction of the basic proportions of production and distribution, have constantly introduced elements of incongruity into the economy." (13)

In such conditions the rate of growth was quickly halved, and the trough of the cycle fell lower than before and lasted longer. The lowest point was reached at the beginning of 1962. "Then rather worrisome phenomena were established in our economic life," says Boris Kraigher in his exposé. "There occurred relative stagnation in economic development, a large deficit in the balance of payments, and a rapid increase in the Federal budgetary deficit. There occurred the phenomenon of irresponsible distribution of income to personal incomes, which was expressed in excessively wide spans. Some sort of inertia prevailed in the business activity of economic organizations, and there began to be an excess of all forms of consumption, instability in the market, and large oscillations in prices." (14) In order to return the economy to the path of the upswing, there were discharges of mutual debts, pumping of credits, pressing of exports, and reduction of legal and organizational changes. In addition to all these usual measures there was also a political mobilization, and the Yugoslav economy quickly found again its normal path of rapid expansion.

5. Economic reform. The lessons of the experience with the last cycles were unfortunately not learned, and the relatively quiet year of 1963 was not used to prepare a program of system-

atic action for 1965 and the following years that would be oriented toward scientifically studying the building of the system and adapting economic policy to new conditions. Prices began to increase at the beginning of 1964. The earlier disparities accumulated to the extent that stabilization was no longer possible by simple price control and deflationary policy. In the course of 1964, along with a significant increase in prices of agricultural products and some intermediate goods, prices for coal increased by 10% and by 40% for electrical energy. (15) The adoption of deflationary credit policy slowed the relative growth of the money supply, but remained totally incapable of harmonizing the volume and structure of supply and demand. (16) Economic instability increased still further. In 1965 two drastic interventions, which were mutually determined, were carried out: administrative freezing of prices and administrative correction of disparities at a higher price level. That necessitated a new rate of exchange, which was significantly increased from 750 to 1250 dinars for a dollar. The increased costs of imported intermediate goods, along with the fixing of prices, had to induce deflation. Internal demand fell, exports increased, and the balance of payments deficit temporarily disappeared (17), but at the price of reducing the potential social product in keeping with the standard explanation given in the analysis of Graph 11.1. Enterprise income was freed of various tax burdens that had accumulated in the course of time. Subsidies were reduced. Reduction of tax contributions of various forms necessitated adaptation of the government budget. Elimination of inflationary pressures required reduction of aggregate demand. But global reduction of demand does not have the structure which corresponds to the possibilities of supply. Capacities remain unutilized. Some branches of investment goods industries found themselves in an especially difficult situation. Unprepared for a greater breach of the foreign market, with a dried-up domestic market and very small possibilities for credit, those branches at times did not use 50% of their capacity, which increased costs and made the situation still more difficult. That entire complicated action was begun after mid-1964, when the economic upswing once again turned downward. It could be expected that the effects on retardation would be similar to the earlier effects, and that the new depression would not be of lesser magnitude than the preceding one.

"Here the historical analysis is interrupted," we wrote in the original text of this study at the beginning of 1966, "for we have arrived at the last available data. The question naturally arises as to how the next cycle will appear. The answer to this question depends on the extent to which economic policy makes use of the lessons of past experience and of the results of economic theory. Provided nothing essential changes, we can expect that the current cycle will reach the minimum somewhere in the second or third quarter of 1966, and the maximum in the middle of 1968." (18) Events have shown that the forecast of the turning of the cycle in the second or third quarter was not realized. Does that mean that it was a matter of a mistaken forecast, a forecast founded on a mistaken theory? Sometimes unfulfilled forecasts make possible a more fruitful empirical analysis than fulfilled ones. It appears that this is what has actually happened. We need only recall the fragments of analysis of events in 1966 that are scattered in various chapters of this study to convince ourselves of this.

A look at Graph 7.1 will establish that the fall of industrial production stopped at the end of 1965 and then was held on a plateau at the index 105 until the third quarter of 1966. Industrial production of the developed regions, which usually pulls along total industrial production, shows an acceleration trend from the third quarter of 1965 to the third quarter of 1966. The construction cycle turned upward in the first quarter of 1966, and investment expenditures did the same a quarter earlier (Graph 5.5). The growth of industrial inventories slowed down from the first to the third quarter of 1966, as did accounts payable; deflated sales of the economy accelerated until the third quarter and, similarly, the liquidity of the economy increased until the third quarter of 1966 (Graphs 9.3, 10.2, 10.3). Thus, according to all the key movements, the Yugoslav economy was ready for a new upswing in the middle of 1966. Why did that upswing not occur? The following fragments from the annual report of the National Bank gives a condensed, though not complete, answer to that question (19):

> The stock of money grew in 1966 by 5%, and total liquid resources by 6%. Short-term bank credits increased 3%. Bearing in mind that at the same time the social product in current prices increased by nearly 24%, it is obvious that the goal of monetary-credit policy to have the money supply grow slower than the increase in the social product was fully realized. In order to realize such a movement of the money supply and credit, severe restrictive measures were adopted

in the course of 1966, <u>especially in the second half of 1966</u> (my emphasis — B.H.).

The falling rate of growth of industrial production, reduction of construction, and the <u>low rate of economic activity in general constituted one of the most significant components by which monetary-credit policy contributed to the realization of stabilization goals</u> (my emphasis — B.H.).

Distinguishing the question of whether credit policy can operate more restrictively from the question as to whether it has operated restrictively enough, it can be said that it is difficult to assume that the credit policy measures could be essentially more restrictive, but also that their restrictive effect was not sufficient, especially in the field of the balance of payments ... the conclusion is that <u>it is necessary to continue with restrictive measures</u>, especially having in view the effect in the field of foreign trade ... (my emphasis — B.H.).

And thus under monetary-credit pressures in the second half of 1966, everything again turned downward instead of there being an upswing: in just one year expansion of industrial production fell from +5% to −1%, investment began to fall absolutely, the growth of inventories quickened, illiquidity reached the proportions of 1961, and the growth of labor productivity quickly fell to zero. And after all that the National Bank found it necessary to apologize for the fact that credit restriction was not still more severe! And to conclude that it was necessary to continue with the same policy!

Therefore, the theory on which the forecast was founded was not mistaken. The dramatic struggle of industry — and of the whole economy — to start to rise again from the level of 105 toward the normal rates of growth for Yugoslav conditions lasted the entire year. The word "dramatic" has not been chosen haphazardly; it exactly describes what happened in many collectives. With a little help on the part of economic policy, that struggle could have been terminated successfully. However, economic policy was rigid and altogether inadequate. In that respect, naturally, it is not a question solely of the measures which the National Bank was obliged to carry out. The assumption of the forecast, "to the extent that nothing essential changes," obviously was not realized, for much that was essential changed, work collectives finally broke under unbearable pressure, and the economy fell still another flight of steps lower in its path of growth. That flight represents a difference in the rate of growth of some 6%, which in relation to a social product (excluding agriculture) of 7,200 billion old dinars represents a loss of 430 billion in the course of one year. The loss is further increased when one takes into account that, instead of retardation in the course of that year, there could have been an initial acceleration of growth of 5%.

In mid-1967 production lagged at the index 98-99. A new plateau of several quarters' duration was formed. According to all indications the economy was again ready for an upswing. Whether the upswing would come and at what tempo — or whether there would be still another step lower — would depend exclusively on economic policy, on the extent to which economic policy utilized the lessons of previous experience and the results of economic theory. This time monetary policy did not prevent the upswing from beginning. Growth accelerated during 1968 and developed into a boom in 1969.

The five cycles analyzed are distinguished from each other by the reasons for their appearance. The first, fourth and fifth were conditioned by economic reforms; the second, by the remedy for inflation; the third, by uncontrolled expansion of imports. However, two characteristics are common to all: every cycle was set in motion by difficulties in international trade and in every cycle the depression was deepened by reforms that were initiated in the retardation phase, i.e., when it was not the time for them. One must exclude from this statement the first cycle, which was in every respect exceptional; that cycle began in the search for a new economic system, when solutions objectively could not be known, and when in fact it was a question of Yugoslavia's struggle for existence. But with respect to the other cycles, I believe that one can speak of the bad timing of the reforms: the second cycle began with the investment reform, the third with the reform in income distribution, the fourth with three simultaneous reforms, and the fifth with a complex of reforms called "the economic reform." With reference to these facts, the beginnings of business cycles in Yugoslavia must be sought in the retardation phase, and not in the accelerative phase, and the determination of timing and content must be carried out according to the key reform actions that have been implemented to date. This picture is obtained:

186

Cycle I: New economic system (1), III/1949-III/1955
Cycle II: Transition to the second five-year plan, III/1955-II/1958
Cycle III: New system of income distribution, II/1958-IV/1960
Cycle IV: New economic system (2), IV/1960-I/1965
Cycle V: Economic reform, I/1965-?

In that way Yugoslav cycles — until now purely statistically determined — have received their names and their economic content.

12.3 Frequency of Legal Regulations and the Rate of Economic Growth

Now we are finally in a position to answer the question of the causal connection between the number of normative acts of state bodies and economic fluctuations. It follows rather unambiguously that the waves of legal regulations intensified economic fluctuations. If there were fewer regulations in general, if they were better prepared, and if, particularly, there were fewer regulations adopted in the downswing phases, the growth of production would have been more even and therefore the average rate of growth would have been higher. The connection between the quarterly number of regulations (moving averages) and the indices of growth of industrial and of IFC production is shown on the scatter diagram (Graph 12.2).

We obtain the following two regression equations:

$$\text{Industry:} \quad y = -0.39x + 125.7 \quad r = -0.47$$
$$\text{Production:} \quad y = -0.46x + 126.6 \quad r = -0.50$$

where x represents the number of economic regulations in the quarter, and y the corresponding index of annual growth of production. It turns out that for every additional regulation in the course of a month (i.e., three additional regulations quarterly), the rate of economic growth falls by over 1%. The larger coefficient of the trend of IFC production shows that it is even more sensitive to an increase in regulations than is industrial production. At a level of social product (excluding agriculture) of 7,000 billion old dinars, one excess regulation monthly costs the Yugoslav economy about 100 billion old dinars annually, on the average.

The analysis is not concluded with that. The lower part of Graph 12.2 shows a rather large scatter of points about the re-

Graph 12.2 CONNECTION BETWEEN THE NUMBER OF ECONOMIC
REGULATIONS AND THE INDEX OF GROWTH OF INDUSTRY
AND PRODUCTION
(EXCLUDING AGRICULTURE)

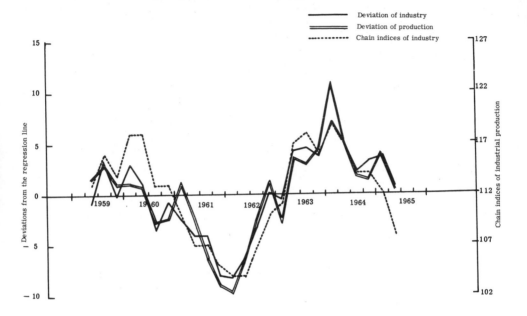

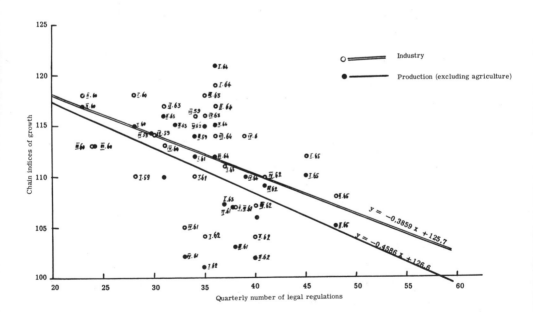

gression lines. Is that scatter without any order, or is there something systematic there? To ascertain if the deviations from the regression line are consistent over time, we introduce a special graph, which is worked out in the upper part of Graph 12.2. The result is surprising: again a cycle! And it is not just any cycle, but one which entirely corresponds to the industrial cycle; this can be seen when the latter is also drawn on the same graph. The coefficient of correlation between these two series — between the deviations from the industrial regression line and the industrial chain indices of growth — is very high and amounts to 0.88. Accordingly, we have worked out the explanation of the connection between industrial growth and the number of legal regulations in two stages. In the first stage $0.47^2 = 21\%$ of the total variance is explained by the regression line. In the second stage $0.88^2 = 77\%$ of the remaining variance is explained. In that way about four-fifths of the total variations are explained in both stages.

It remains for us to interpret the results, especially for the second stage. It is obvious that the effects of legal regulations on the rate of growth are not the same in all phases of the cycle, and that they essentially depend on the point of the cycle where the economy is at the moment. In the first stage we determine the effect from the equation $y = 0.39x + 126$, which means that one additional regulation quarterly reduces the annual rate of growth by 0.39%, on the average. If the economy is at that moment just on the trend line, which in our case means at the beginning or at the end of the cycle, then there is no deviation of the current rate from the average rate and the equation of the first stage completely determines the effect. If, however, the economy is somewhere within the cycle, then it is necessary to add to or subtract from the effect of the first stage — depending on whether the economy is above or below the trend — the effects from the equation of the second stage, $z = 0.77u + 0.02$, where z represents the deviation of the rate of growth from the regression line, and u the deviation of the rate of growth from the average rate of industrial growth. It follows that the negative effects of additional regulations are stronger than the average in phases of the cycle below the trend and weaker than the average in phases above the trend. In other words, administrative interventions in phases of depression and revival reduce the rate of growth more than in phases of boom and recession. What is more, during the lowering below the trend, i.e., the entry into depression, the negative effects of regulations become all the stronger, reach a culmination at the bottom of the cycle, and begin to weaken at the emergence from depression. From the historical survey we saw that <u>far-reaching reorganizations and reforms were carried out precisely in the phases when the economy rose to below the level of the trend</u>, and that the boom phase remained unrealized. In that way the negative effects were increased unnecessarily.

Perhaps this is the place to emphasize one fact. The present Yugoslav economy is truly a market economy and very different from the rigid, semi-administrative economy of ten years ago, not to mention earlier periods. But it appears that this has not been noted, and old conceptions, bureaucratic approaches, intuitive and ad hoc solutions, short-run pragmatism, and neglect of scientific economic research continue to burden Yugoslav economic policy. A market economy is like a precious machine, highly productive but sensitive. A skilled worker can attain exceptional results with it. When there is inept leadership, waste and breakdowns occur.

Notes

1) A second possible method would be to measure the degree of bureaucratic control and interference in the business activity of economic organizations on the part of the state apparatus, the banks (as exponents of that apparatus), the Social Accounting Service, the price bureau, and other such bodies. What happens in that sphere is illustrated by the notes of Ž. Šurjak in Vjesnik u srijedu, May 4, 1966: "A Zagreb import firm imports these days from West Germany five spare electric bulbs at a value of 7.5 DM, which are necessary for a machine (value about 30,000 DM) to be able to run for the next five years. The importing of these bulbs requires: an application for approval of import (to Yugobank) in three copies; a report on the final transaction (to the National Bank) in 12 copies; a payment order (to the National Bank) in 8 copies; a dinar transfer (to the National Bank) in 4 copies. That is, a total of 30 copies of forms or documents which must be calculated, written out, signed, and verified. The National Bank, in order to complete the allotment of foreign exchange, collects on the form of the 'payment order' — which the importer fills out — six stamps so that the payment abroad may be approved." This sketch explains at once why industrial imports continue to accel-

erate even after the economic upswing has already long turned downhill. It would be useful to examine and quantify the effects of this type of administrative intervention. Until that is done it appears to me justified to assume that they are closely correlated with the phenomena examined in the text.

2) For example, in the report of the Social Accounting Service's central office for Croatia, it is stated: "In the course of 1965, in only 24 bulletins of official interpretations of the Federal Secretariat for Finance there appeared 260 interpretations of the turnover tax and rates..." (Borba, May 15, 1966).

3) M. Popović, Društveno-ekonomski sistem (Belgrade: Kultura, 1964), pp. 160-61.

4) Narodna Banka, Godišnji izvještaj 1956, p. 29.

5) Credit increased by 178 billion dinars in 1954, 97 billion in 1955, 307 billion in 1956 (ibid., p. 65).

6) The structure of gross economic investments in fixed capital was as follows:

	1953-1956	1957-1960
Industry	59.1	43.8
Agriculture	7.0	15.8
Transportation	22.9	27.4

(B. Horvat, "O karakteristikama našeg privrednog razvoja," Naša stvarnost, 1961, No. 1, p. 13).

7) Total imports grew in 1957 by 31%, and exports by 18%; the trade deficit amounted to 80 billion dinars, and the payments deficit was 59 billion dinars ($1 = 300 d.). See SZS, Jugoslavija 1945-1964, pp. 86, 197, 198.

8) See V. Zeković and S. Novaković, Ekonomika Jugoslavije (Belgrade: Rad, 1962), pp. 186-190.

9) B. Horvat et al., Uzroci i karakteristika privrednih kretanja u 1961. i 1962. godini, SZPP, DAM-7 (Belgrade, 1962).

10) Ibid., p. 175.

11) Loc. cit.

12) Ibid., p. 174.

13) Ibid., p. 169.

14) Razvoj i problemi društvenog i privrednog života Jugoslavije (Belgrade: Komunist, 1963), p. 59.

15) Narodna Banka Jugoslavije, Godišnji izvještaj, 1964, p. 29.

16) By the first half of 1964 the further development of events could already be accurately predicted, i.e., the development of a

classical business cycle. In the middle of that year, in a shorter essay ("Lessons of 1961 and 1964") which Komunist, for which it was written, did not publish because the forecasts were too unpopular, but which was later published in Vjesnik (November 11 and 12, 1964), I warned that the country had entered a cyclical boom which is followed by a recession. See B. Horvat, Ekonomska nauka i narodna privreda (Zagreb: Naprijed, 1968), Part I.

17) It is necessary to emphasize, however, that total payments were settled in a way that compensated for a deficit of convertible currencies by a surplus in clearing accounts. Since these two are not comparable amounts, the payments deficit in fact was not eliminated.

18) In 1965 the volume of investment was reduced by 12-14%, which represents a stronger contraction than in 1956. See SPK, Neki problemi proizvodnje i tržišta u 1966. godini (Belgrade, April 1, 1966), p. 3.

19) B. Horvat, Ekonomska nauka i narodna privreda.

20) Narodna Banka Jugoslavije, Godišnji izveštaj 1966, pp. 4, 39, 40.

Chapter 13

INTERNATIONAL COMPARISONS

In order to ascertain the efficacy of Yugoslav economic policy with regard to economic fluctuations, we must carry out an international comparative analysis. Let us begin with the hypothesis that economic instability increases with the stage of growth and that it is different in various institutional systems. We shall therefore choose countries with high growth rates to obtain comparability with the Yugoslav economy, and divide them into two groups: countries with capitalist markets and countries with central planning. Since quarterly data do not exist for all the countries chosen, we will use annual data. Time series of fourteen years cover the period of normal postwar development and are sufficiently long to draw definite conclusions with respect to the characteristics of economic movements in that period. Movements of the social product and industrial production of the eleven countries that we are comparing are shown on Graph 13.1 by chain indices.

Construction of instruments for measuring the intensity of economic fluctuations represents a special problem. The average deviation of empirical values in relation to the arithmetic mean would give a biased estimate for, as can be seen on the graph, in every case the fluctuations occur about some trend of annual growth rates, and not about some average rate of growth. For the same reason the usual statistical coefficient of variation would also give a biased estimate. Parenthetically, I would note that this is still another illustration of the need to carry out the analysis on the basis of changes in rates of growth, and not on the basis of changes of absolute magnitudes, as is customary. In the latter case the effects of changes in growth rates would remain

193

Graph 13.1 CHAIN INDICES OF ANNUAL GROWTH OF SOCIAL PRODUCT

AND INDUSTRIAL PRODUCTION IN ELEVEN COUNTRIES

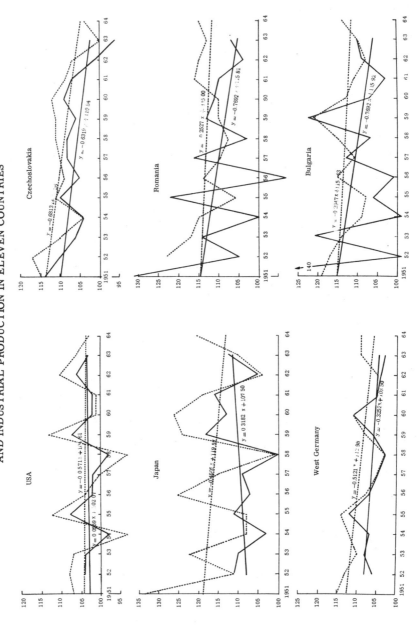

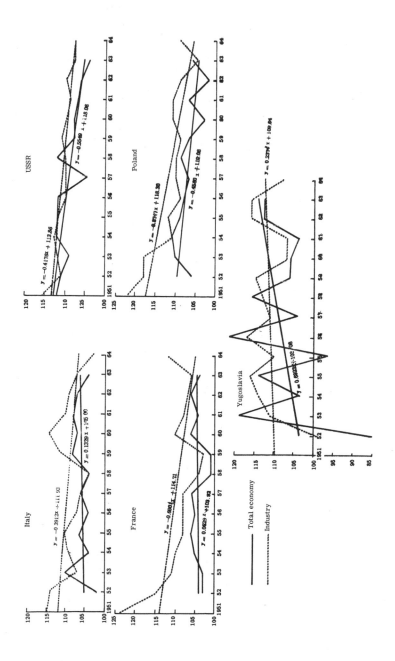

unaccounted for by the measure, and the result would be biased. Selection of a definite mathematical function for expressing the trend is always arbitrary to a certain degree. Our graph shows that in some cases a straight line is entirely efficient, while other configurations of empirical values conform better to a quadratic or cubic parabola or even some oscillatory curve. Does that mean that for every case it is necessary to choose a corresponding curve? I think that this would be mistaken in terms of the goal of the analysis. A parabola of the second or third degree and oscillatory curves would mean that in the course of 14 years the economy passed from the phase of acceleration (deceleration) to the phase of deceleration (acceleration) one, two, or more times. But passing from accelerated to decelerated growth and the reverse in a relatively short time period also represents a type of economic fluctuation, and it would not be necessary to eliminate that effect. Therefore we will interpolate a linear trend in all cases. As an instrument for measuring the intensity of fluctuations I will use the average of absolute values of relative deviations from the trend, which I will call the coefficient of fluctuation (1):

$$\left| \frac{1}{N} \sum \frac{\text{trend} - \text{empirical value}}{\text{trend} - 100} \right|$$

This coefficient measures the proportion of deviations from the trend — of rates of growth. In this form both the trend of values and the empirical values represent chain indices.

Of the eleven countries cited, only the USA, Italy, Czechoslovakia and France are not among the twelve countries with the most expansive economies in the world. (2) For the sake of homogeneity — and, through that, comparability — of groups, the USA is separated from the capitalist group and Czechoslovakia is separated from the centrally planned group. Those two countries have the most unstable economies within their groups, and they achieve the lowest rates of growth. Therefore they obviously represent special cases, and it would be interesting to establish the reason for this. Perhaps this hypothesis is plausible. Of the five capitalist countries the USA lagged the most in planned regulation of its economy, and at the same time it is the most developed and complex economy in the world. The U.S. lag in the construction of an adequate mechanism of economic coordination results in hypertrophic fluctuations in that country. It is interesting that

Table 13.1

Intensity of Economic Fluctuations in Eleven Countries in the Period 1950-1964

Country	Social Product 1951-1963				Industrial Production 1950-1964			
	Rate of Growth		Coefficient Fluctuation		Rate of Growth		Coefficient Fluctuation	
	%	Rank	Coefficient	Rank	%	Rank	Coefficient	Rank
1. USA	2.9	–	0.80	–	3.9	–	1.15	–
2. Japan	9.5	1	0.41	1	15.9	1	0.50	1
3. West Germany	6.4	2	0.28	4	9.0	4	0.30	4
4. Italy	5.7	3	0.31	2	9.0	3	0.31	3
5. France	4.3	4	0.31	3	9.5	2	0.35	2
Average* 2-5	6.5	–	0.33	–	10.9	–	0.39	–
6. Czechoslovakia	6.0°	–	0.60°	–	9.3	–	0.30	–
7. Romania	9.6°	1	0.68°	2	12.8°°	2	0.26°°	1
8. Bulgaria	9.6°	2	0.73°	1	13.1	1	0.22	2
9. USSR	9.1°	3	0.15°	4	10.8	4	0.08	4
10. Poland	7.2	4	0.25	3	11.6	3	0.21	3
Average* 7-10	8.9	–	0.45	–	12.1	–	0.19	–
11. Yugoslavia	7.4°°	–	1.25°°	–	11.3°°°	–	0.34°°°	–

*Unweighted arithmetic mean.   ° 1950-1963   °° 1951-1964   °° 1951-1964   °°° 1951-1965

Czechoslovakia is also the most developed country in its group, but contrary to the American case, it was probably hindered by having a rigid centrally planned economy like the others in the group. Rigid centralized planning in such a complex economy as that of Czechoslovakia stifles economic expansion and leads to disproportions and refractions. (3)

In analyzing Table 13.1 we observe, first of all, that the hypothesis of the determination of instability in the rate of growth appears entirely correct: in almost all cases the rank of the rate of growth corresponds to the rank of the coefficient of fluctuation. Furthermore, and this is probably a surprise, the economic instability of the socialist countries is 36% greater than that of the capitalist countries; the index of fluctuation is 0.45, compared to 0.33 in the capitalist group on the basis of social product. That information cannot be left without interpretation. The difference can be explained at least partially by the following three factors: (1) the rate of growth in the socialist group is greater than in the capitalist countries; (2) the socialist group includes less developed countries (especially Bulgaria and Romania) in which agriculture, and therefore fluctuations of agricultural production, have much greater significance; and (3) the social product in the first group includes services whose volume fluctuates less than the volume of material production, which comprises the national income of the second group. Elimination of these factors would require substantial work, and therefore we will carry out the group comparisons on the basis of an aggregate which permits more direct comparability. That is worked out in the second part of the table, where fluctuations of industrial production are measured. It can be seen that the socialist group has, along with a higher rate of growth, significantly smoother industrial expansion. This gives us an indication that planning accelerates growth and reduces fluctuations. However, it is necessary to have in mind that while the first index is biased to the advantage of market economies, the industrial index of fluctuation is biased to the advantage of centrally planned economies, where industry is the object of special attention and industrial stability is achieved at the expense of instability in other sectors. Therefore an unbiased measure of relative instability is somewhere between our two indices. It is also necessary to bear in mind that our index is constructed so that it moderates fluctuations of economies with high growth rates in relation to those with low rates, i.e., it reduces the fluctuations of the centrally planned group in comparison to the capitalist group. Had the index been constructed in such a way that the relative deviations from the corresponding trend of production were used — instead of the trend of growth rates — that index would correspond to the average of absolute, and not relative, deviations from the trend of the rate of growth. This would increase fluctuations in the centrally planned group. In other words, the index of fluctuation on the basis of changes in rates of growth (of chain indices) is more favorable to the centrally planned group (and Yugoslavia) than the index of fluctuation on the basis of changes of production. (4)

These considerations offer criteria for judging Yugoslav economic movements. The coefficient of fluctuation on the basis of social product is 1.25. That means that on the average the deviations amount to 125% of the trend of growth rates. In that respect the Yugoslav economy was significantly more unstable than any of the ten economies cited, including the U.S. The basic reason for that extreme instability must be sought, as we saw earlier, in agriculture. Since agricultural fluctuations have been reduced in recent years, and the share of agriculture in total production has fallen, we can expect less instability in the future with respect to this factor. Economic instability as measured by industrial fluctuations is somewhat less than in capitalist countries, but it is 79% greater than in countries of the socialist group. That is a very significant piece of information, and it supplements our earlier analysis of the conditioning and effects of business cycles in Yugoslavia.

We must still examine the question of whether there is some connection between the economic fluctuations of various countries. Graph 13.1 shows that there is no connection whatever between the economic fluctuations of the socialist countries, although they proclaimed firm economic cooperation through COMECON. In the capitalist countries there is a certain synchronization of economic movements, especially if the USA is excluded. Thus, in 1954 all the countries except France (and there, too, with respect to industry) experienced a retardation of total production, while in the following year in every one, without exception, the index of social product attained a local maximum. In 1958 all the countries experienced a pronounced retardation in both total and industrial production. In 1960 all the countries except the USA attained a maximum in industrial production. This was followed by a drop, which ended in Japan in 1962, and in France and West Germany in 1963; and in all countries except Italy industry was again in an upswing in 1964.

In connection with the ever-greater opening up of the Yugoslav economy to international trade, the synchronization established is very important — and dangerous. To the extent that a corresponding protective mechanism is not constructed, fluctuations in the world market will be transmitted to the Yugoslav economy and, if that catches the Yugoslavs unprepared, they will again have waves of administrative interventions, with all the consequences which follow from that. As far as I can ascertain, the first case occurred with the cycle of 1958. Reduced opportunities on the world market hit Yugoslav exports, and the index of divergence reached a maximum, which we have discussed (5) (see Graph 11.2). There were other instances of synchronization, but I assume that they are random.

Finally, let us use another item of information from our graph, one that takes account of the trends of changes in growth rates. Since the time series is relatively short, selecting beginning and final years can have a strong influence on the slope of the trend. For Yugoslavia I chose 1952 and 1965 for the beginning and final years for industry, since in both years there was a slowing of industrial growth; for the social product I used 1952 and 1964, which is not entirely satisfactory. Data for 1965 were still not available, while extending the series backwards would increase the already large coefficient of fluctuation, and in 1964 agricultural production increased 6%, while in 1952 it fell 31%. The result is that the trend shows an unrealistically high rise. For other countries I was guided by the need to obtain a longer time series but, at the same time, one that would cover only normal development. Since postwar reconstruction was completed in all the countries considered between 1950-1952, that determined the choice of the beginning of the series. Given these limits, let us now look at what the graph tells us. The data are summarized in Table 13.2.

The socialist countries began the period with high rates of growth. From then on general economic and industrial expansion slowed down in all these countries (6) (negative slope). It can be surmised that this deceleration evoked the reforms toward decentralization in those countries in recent years. At the end of the period the trend rates of growth in the socialist countries fell to the level of the capitalist group. A slowing of industrial growth

Table 13.2

Characteristics of Trends of Growth Rates of Eleven Countries, 1950-1964*

	Social Product			Industry		
	Coefficient of Trend	Calculated Rate of Growth**		Coefficient of Trend	Calculated Rate of Growth**	
		Initial	Final		Initial	Final
1. USA	0.06	2.7	3.3	-0.06	4.5	3.8
2. Japan	0.32	7.8	11.3	-0.45	19.1	13.3
3. West Germany	-0.33	8.2	4.6	-0.51	12.4	5.7
4. Italy	0.13	5.1	6.6	-0.39	11.5	6.5
5. France	0.06	4.0	4.7	-0.69	14.1	5.1
Average 1-5	0.05	5.6	6.1	-0.42	12.3	6.9
6. Czechoslovakia	-0.63	9.9	2.4	-0.68	13.7	4.9
7. Romania	-0.77	14.5	5.3	-0.25	14.7	11.7
8. Bulgaria	-0.77	15.2	5.9	-0.30	15.1	11.3
9. USSR	-0.55	12.6	5.9	-0.42	13.4	8.0
10. Poland	-0.46	9.6	4.6	-0.88	17.4	6.0
Average 6-10	-0.63	12.4	4.8	-0.51	14.8	8.4
11. Yugoslavia	0.69	3.8	12.1	0.24	9.9	13.0

*Note same as for Table 10.3.

**Initial and final rates represent the trend values at the beginning and end of the period.

took place in the capitalist group at approximately the same tempo as in the socialist group. The USA represents the exception: the slope is so small that it can be concluded that the rate of growth in the USA did not change; the social product fluctuated at about a rate of 3%, and industrial production at about 4.2%. The rate of growth of the social product fell in West Germany, stagnated in France, and increased in Italy and Japan. Economic movements in Yugoslavia deviate from this picture. In Yugoslavia both industrial and general economic expansion accelerated. Therefore the final rates were significantly higher than the beginning ones, and at the end of the period the rate of growth equaled that of Japan (see Graph 13.1). Those are very favorable movements. They indicate that the developmental potential created by the great social reform of 1950-1952 is not exhausted. However, if we also included the last two or three years, 1965-1967, in the calculation, this would perceptibly turn the trend downward. Whether and to what extent the potential will be utilized, whether and to what extent the satisfactory trend will be continued, whether and to what extent business cycles will be eliminated — all depend on the efficacy of economic policy in the coming years.

In the meantime, however, it will be of interest to renew the discussion of secular cycles on the basis of the material just presented. Graph 13.1 and Table 13.2 show: (a) that from 1950 on, industrial expansion constantly markedly slowed down in the ten countries which have the greatest part of the world's industrial potential, and (b) the rate of growth of the social product was maintained in the capitalist group but fell markedly in the socialist group (7), so that there was an overall decline. Don't these movements indicate the downward phase of a secular Kondratiev cycle?

The last Kondratiev began, according to Schumpeter, at the end of the 1890s, and its trough was reached at the time of the world economic crisis of 1929-1933. Insofar as that theory truly expresses some secular law and secular cycles last about half a century, then the third Kondratiev ends its revival phase at the beginning of the Second World War. During the war a new, fourth Kondratiev begins, which has its culmination in the postwar reconstruction. After that follows the recession phase, which our twenty series reflect. That recession — in the absence of artificial activators of expansion such as wars and armaments races — may develop into an acute world crisis. Schumpeter gives the following dates for the three most severe world economic crises: 1825-1830, 1873-1878, 1929-1934. All three crises occurred in the troughs of the corresponding three Kondratiev waves. The intervals between those troughs are 48 and 56 years. If that periodicity continues, the next world crisis ought to break out at the end of the 1970s.

However, our knowledge of these secular mechanisms is so insignificant that nothing more serious can be said ex ante. Guesses are possible, but not forecasts. It may be said eventually that in the meantime we have at least learned to crudely control cumulations in economic movements, so that a crisis can no longer widen so spontaneously as in the past. It may be said that the centrally planned economies represent a qualitatively different type of economy as compared to the capitalist economies of former days. Schumpeter would probably accept that thesis without further argument with respect to his theory of waves of innovative activity of capitalist entrepreneurs as generators of cycles. But, on the other hand, the data we have cited show that in a complex modern economy central planning is not so efficient as was formerly thought. The fact is that economic expansion in the most important countries of the world — capitalist and centrally planned alike — is slowing down, and although we cannot maintain that this deceleration will continue, we cannot be sure that it will end quickly. In connection with the fact that the Yugoslav economy is beginning to open up to the world, we must take these facts into account very seriously.

Notes

1) We could also use as a statistical measure the so-called relative standard error of estimate. But the "coefficient of fluctuation" is more easily calculated and has more direct meaning intuitively. That coefficient is similar to the coefficient of the average relative intensity of cyclical variation, which A. Dobrić discusses in his textbook Statistika u oblasti analiza cijena (Sveučilište u Zagrebu: Zagreb, 1956), p. 148.

2) See Z. Popov, op. cit., p. 117.

3) The Czech economist Goldmann also gives a similar explanation. See his article "Fluctuations and Trend in the Rate of Economic Growth in Some Socialist Countries," Economics of Planning, 1964, No. 2, pp. 88-98.

4) G. Staller carried out a similar comparative study of fluctuations of market and planned economies for the period 1950-1960 ("Fluctuations in Economic Activity: Planned and Free-Market Economies, 1950-1960," American Economic Review, June 1964, pp. 385-395). Staller uses as one of the indicators the "standard error of the least-squares fit of the series y_t/y_{t-1} to time...; it [the indicator] expresses the fluctuations in percentage points measured from the trendline fit to yearly growth rates." The results are as follows:

	Social Product	Agri- culture	Industry	Construc- tion
Planned econo- mies*	6.5	12.3	4.2	11.9
Market econo- mies, all**	3.0 (3.8)°	7.4	4.1	8.1
Market econo- mies, less de- veloped***	3.4 (4.3)°	8.2	3.9	9.9

*)Bulgaria, Czechoslovakia, East Germany, Hungary, Poland, Romania, USSR, Yugoslavia

**)Austria, Belgium, Canada, Denmark, France, West Germany, Greece, Iceland, Ireland, Italy, Luxemburg, Netherlands, Norway, Portugal, Sweden, Turkey, England, USA

***)Austria, West Germany, Greece, Ireland, Italy, Netherlands, Portugal, Turkey

°)The figures in parentheses are related to domestic material product in factor prices, which is comparable to the social product as calculated in East European countries.

Staller concludes that fluctuations are greater in the planned group than in the market group. The countries that have the least fluctuations of social product (on the basis of the comparable definition) are the USSR (1.9) and Norway (1.8); the countries that have the greatest fluctuations are Yugoslavia (11.8), Romania (11.6), Bulgaria (10.4) and Turkey (7.5). In agriculture the extremes are Poland (4.0), Czechoslovakia (4.6), England (2.7), Sweden (4.3) and the USA (4.5), on the one hand, and Yugoslavia (25.6), Bulgaria (18.4), Romania (17.6) and Canada (20.2) on the other. Industrial production fluctuates least in the USSR (1.4) and most in the USA (7.5). Construction expands evenly in the USSR

(4.7), France (4.4) and England (3.7), and with large fluctuations in Bulgaria (18.5), Romania (17.4), Turkey (17.1), and Yugoslavia (16.0, but calculated on the basis of actual working time in hours, rather than value of production as in other countries). It follows that during 1950-1960, among the 26 economies considered, the Soviet was the most stable and the Yugoslav, Romanian and Bulgarian economies were the most unstable.

5) In 1958 world exports fell by 5%. In this connection the National Bank's <u>Annual</u> Report for 1958 states: "...the growth of the volume of trade was less than in earlier years, which to a large degree can be attributed to the situation on the world market" (p. 97).

6) Goldmann, studying the same period with the aid of 7-year averages, also noticed the long-term slowing down of the industrial rate of growth in the socialist countries (Czechoslovakia, Poland, Hungary and East Germany (op. cit., pp. 95-97).

7) It is necessary to mention, however, that the statistics in some countries in that group were unreliable in earlier years, and the deceleration is probably misleadingly overemphasized.

Chapter 14

LONG CYCLES

The relatively short period accessible to analysis makes it very difficult to establish regularity with respect to the lengths and amplitudes of cycles. It is especially difficult to establish whether alongside short cycles, which we have analyzed in detail, there are also longer cycles. In this chapter we will use the most advanced statistical techniques developed to date to squeeze out maximum information from the available data. We will avail ourselves, therefore, of the following methods of analysis: correlogram, periodogram, autoregression scheme, and moving averages.

14.1 Correlogram

Insofar as there is some regularity in economic fluctuations, we can expect serial correlation of the data. Correlation will be greatest for those time intervals which correspond to some distinct period of fluctuation. Therein lies the sense of correlogram analysis. Moreover, a correlogram also enables one, at least theoretically (i.e., for infinite series), to establish the nature of an empirical series, namely, whether what we have are moving averages of random disturbances, harmonic movements, or autoregression. Let us begin with that analysis. (1)

Let us take moving averages of random disturbances as our index:

$$y_t = a_1 \varepsilon_t + a_2 \varepsilon_{t+1} + \cdots + a_m \varepsilon_{t+m-1} \qquad (14.1)$$

We assume that $E(\varepsilon_t) = 0$, from which it follows that $E(y_t) = 0$. Then if $\underline{k}$ is the order of the correlation, and $\underline{m}$ the number of terms of the moving average, for $m > k$ it holds that

$$E(y_t y_{t+k}) = E(a_1\varepsilon_t + \cdots a_m\varepsilon_{t+m-1})\,(a_1\varepsilon_{t+k} + \cdots + a_m\varepsilon_{t+k+m-1}) =$$
$$= (a_1 a_{k+1} + a_2 a_{k+2} + \cdots + a_{m-k}a_m)v \tag{14.2}$$

since owing to the assumed randomness,

$$E(\varepsilon_t\,\varepsilon_{t+k}) = \begin{cases} 0, & \text{za } k \neq 0 \\ v, & \text{za } k = 0 \end{cases} \tag{14.3}$$

insofar as $k \geqslant m$ holds, naturally,

$$E(y_t\,y_{t+k}) = 0 \tag{14.4}$$

Accordingly, for infinite series originating from moving averages of random disturbances, serial correlation disappears for $k \geqslant m$ and from that point the correlogram overlaps the abscissa. Let us assume now that it is a matter of a harmonic movement:

$$y_t = A\sin\,\theta t + \varepsilon_t \tag{14.5}$$

and, as before, we can assume that $E(y_t) = 0$, and therefore

$$\begin{aligned}
E(y_t\,y_{t+k}) &= E\,[A\sin\,\theta t + \varepsilon_t]\,[A\sin\theta\,(t+k) + \varepsilon_{t+k}] \\
&= A^2 E\,[\sin\,\theta t\,\sin\,\theta\,(t+k)] \\
&= \frac{A^2}{n}\sum_{t=1}^{n}\,\sin\,\theta t\,\sin\,\theta\,(t+k) \\
&= \frac{A^2}{2n}\sum_{t=1}^{n}\,[\cos\,\theta\,k - \cos\,\theta\,(2t+k)] \\
&= \frac{A^2}{2}\cos\,\theta k - \frac{A^2}{2n}\frac{\cos\,\theta\,(k+n+1)\,\sin\,n\theta}{\sin\,\theta}
\end{aligned} \tag{14.6}$$

Insofar as $\underline{n}$ is large, and θ is not very small, the covariance is reduced to:

$$E(y_t\,y_{t+k}) = \frac{A^2}{2}\cos\,\theta k \tag{14.7}$$

Similarly, the variance is found:

$$E(y^2_t) = \frac{A^2}{2} + \text{var } \varepsilon \tag{14.8}$$

From this it follows that

$$r_k = B \cos \theta k, \quad B = \frac{A^2/2}{A^2/2 + \text{var } \varepsilon}, \quad k > 0 \tag{14.9}$$

An infinite series of harmonic terms thus forms a correlogram that is also harmonic with the period of the original components. If the terms of the empirical series are composed of higher harmonic components, the period will be different but the oscillations continue infinitely.

Finally, let us take an autoregression equation of the second degree:

$$y_{t+2} + a\, y_{t+1} + b y_t = \varepsilon_{t+2} \tag{14.10}$$

Insofar as $4b > a^2$, the characteristic equation has complex roots and the general solution runs:

$$y_t = A p^t \cos (\theta t + \varphi) + B \tag{14.11}$$

The period is $\frac{2\pi}{\theta}$, where θ is determined from $\cos \theta = -a/2p$, $p = \sqrt{b}$. Insofar as $b < 1$, the oscillations are damped, which we take as the typical case. By certain transformations we obtain a correlogram of this form:

$$r_k = \frac{p^k \sin (k\theta + \psi)}{\sin \psi}, \quad k \geq 0 \tag{14.12}$$

in which the same factor of damping $p < 1$ appears as well as the same autoregressive period $\frac{2\pi}{\theta}$ as in the autoregression equation. It is necessary to have in mind, however, that this period is not necessarily equal to the average period of fluctuation of the empirical series.

Let us look now at our empirical correlogram on Graph 14.1. Not one curve coincides with the axis of the abscissa, so that it is probably not a matter of moving averages of random disturbances. Two of the three curves show damping, which indicates the autoregressive character of the movements. But the most interesting feature is the information with respect to the length of the cycle.

The correlogram of the industrial indices for the period 1953-

Graph 14.1 CORRELOGRAM OF THE INDEX OF INDUSTRIAL PRODUCTION AND EXPORTS

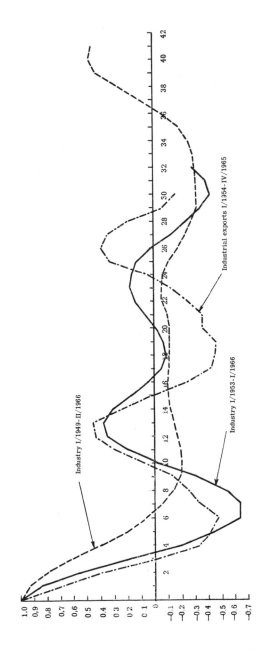

1965 shows exceptional regularity for an empirical series. Peaks
appear for $k = 13$ and 23, and troughs for $k = 7.18$ and 30. The period of fluctuation is therefore between 10 and 12 quarters. It is
worth observing that industrial exports show still more regular
fluctuations, which, in addition, agree with the fluctuations of industrial production. For export peaks appear at $k = 13$ and 26, and
troughs at $k = 6$ and 19, which indicates a period of about 13 quarters. Since both series are relatively short, it would be useful to
extend at least one series to obtain additional information. That
is done for the series of industrial production, which is extended
back to the beginning of 1949 by interpolating quarterly data between the known annual data. As a result we obtain a correlogram
with an entirely different shape, from which neither peaks nor
troughs can be established with certainty. That extension does
not enable us to establish the existence or nonexistence of long
cycles, but it can be interpreted, I think, as an indication that the
periods up to 1953 and after 1953 are essentially different and
therefore that a regularity which holds equally for both periods
probably cannot be found.

14.2 Periodogram

The correlogram is not suitable for discovering the simultaneous existence of several different cycles in some given empirical movement. For that purpose a periodogram is constructed.

Two rows are taken that, with the exception of the terms in
front of the summation sign, represent the covariance: (2)

$$A = \frac{2}{n} \sum_{t=1}^{n} u_t \cos \frac{2\pi t}{\mu} \qquad (14.13)$$

$$B = \frac{2}{n} \sum_{t=1}^{n} u_t \sin \frac{2\pi t}{\mu} \qquad (14.14)$$

and let

$$S^2 = A^2 + B^2 \qquad (14.15)$$

We assume that the terms of the actual statistical series are given
by this expression:

$$u_t = a \sin \frac{2\pi t}{\lambda} + b_t \qquad (14.16)$$

210

Accordingly,

$$A \frac{2a}{n} \sum_{t=1}^{n} \left(\sin \frac{2\pi t}{\lambda} \cos \frac{2\pi t}{\mu} \right) + \frac{2}{n} \sum_{t=1}^{n} b_t \cos \frac{2\pi t}{\mu}$$

where the second summation is equal to zero for b_t and $\cos \frac{2\pi t}{\mu}$ are not correlated. If we write $\alpha = \frac{2\pi}{\lambda}$, $\beta = \frac{2\pi}{\mu}$, we will obtain

$$A - \frac{2a}{n} \sum_{t=1}^{n} \sin \alpha t \cos \beta t - \frac{a}{n} \sum [\sin (\alpha - \beta) t + \sin (\alpha + \beta) t]$$

$$- \frac{a}{n} \left[\frac{\sin [\frac{1}{2}(\alpha - \beta) n] \sin \frac{1}{2}(\alpha - \beta)(n+1)]}{\sin \frac{1}{2}(\alpha - \beta)} + \frac{\sin [\frac{1}{2}(\alpha + \beta n] \sin[\frac{1}{2}(\alpha + \beta)(n+1)]}{\sin \frac{1}{2}(\alpha + \beta)} \right]$$

$$(14.17)$$

For large $\underline{n}$ the second summation tends to zero, and if $\alpha \rightarrow \beta$ it holds that $\sin 1/2 \ (\alpha - \beta) \ n \doteq 1/2 \ (\alpha - \beta) \ n$ and thus, as a final result, we obtain

$$A \doteq a \sin \frac{1}{2} (\alpha - \beta)(n+1) \qquad (14.18)$$

$$B \doteq a \cos \frac{1}{2} (\alpha - \beta)(n+1) \qquad (14.19)$$

$$S^2 = A^2 + B^2 = a^2 \qquad (14.20)$$

However, the condition $\alpha \rightarrow \beta$ means that the tentative period μ approaches the actual period λ. Therefore, when these two periods approximately agree, the intensity S^2 is equal to the square of the amplitude of the original movement. If the tentative and actual period diverge, S^2 will be small because of the division of the square brackets into the expressions A and B with $\underline{n}$. For this result to hold it is obviously necessary that $\underline{n}$, the number of terms in the statistical series, be sufficiently large.

Graph 14.2 contains the periodogram of the deviations of the rate of growth of industrial production from the average rates determined in the period from the beginning of 1949 to the end of 1966. In order to obtain a sufficiently large $\underline{n}$, the period is extended backward by interpolations and forward by forecasts. Thus 72 quarters are obtained. However, the graph shows that this was still not a sufficient number of statistical observations, for $\mu > 35$ quarters, i.e., when the entire period permits only one cycle of that length to develop fully, the periodogram begins to behave very oddly.

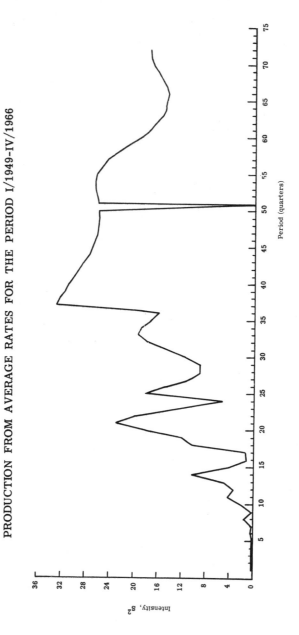

Graph 14.2 PERIODOGRAM OF DEVIATIONS OF GROWTH RATES OF INDUSTRIAL
PRODUCTION FROM AVERAGE RATES FOR THE PERIOD I/1949–IV/1966

Analysis of the periodogram indicates the possibility of the existence of the following five periods:

Period (quarters) μ	Corrected Intensity $S^2 = \dfrac{N(A^2+B^2)}{72}$	$k = \dfrac{S^2}{15.77}$	$k = \dfrac{S^2}{8.87}$
14	10.23	0.65	1.16
21	22.81	1.45	2.58
33	19.30	1.23	2.18
37	32.71	2.08	–
54	26.68	1.70	–

What is the significance of these periods? Obviously it would be necessary to test the significance of the individual periods. Satisfactory tests have not yet been developed. The most suitable existing test, Schuster's, has this meaning.

We take $u_1 \ldots u_n$ random elements from a normal population with variance σ^2. Then

$$A = \frac{1}{n} \sum_{t=1}^{n} u_t \cos \frac{2\pi t}{\mu} \qquad (14.21)$$

is normally distributed with

$$\text{var } A = \frac{4\sigma^2}{n^2} \sum_{t=1}^{n} \cos^2 \frac{2\pi t}{\mu} = \frac{2\sigma^2}{n} \qquad (14.22)$$

and similarly

$$\text{var } B = \frac{2\sigma^2}{n} \qquad (14.23)$$

Furthermore, cov $(A,B) = 0$ and A and B are independent. Therefore their joint distribution, taking into account that $A^2 + B^2 = S^2$, is given by the expression

$$dF = \frac{n}{4\pi\sigma^2} \exp\left(-\frac{n}{4\sigma^2} S^2\right) dS^2 \qquad (14.24)$$

and the mean value of S^2 is

$$E\,(S^2) = \frac{4\sigma^2}{n} \qquad\qquad (14.25)$$

It follows that the probability that S^2 exceeds the value $\frac{4\sigma^2 k}{n}$ is e^{-k}. We continue from this point with Walker's supplement. If e^{-k} is small, the probability that none of $\underline{m}$ independent values of S^2 exceeds $\frac{4\sigma^2 k}{n}$ is $(1-e^{-k})^m$. Accordingly, the probability that at least one S^2 exceeds $\frac{4\sigma^2 k}{n}$ is

$$1-(1-e^{-k})^m \qquad\qquad (14.26)$$

This test, as well as all the others, is based on the assumption of random normal variation of the original series, which, however, we think is not random. Nevertheless the test makes some sense. If S^2 is not significant on the basis of the assumption of random variation, it probably is also not significant when the series is systematic.

In our case the mean value of the intensity $E(S^2) = \frac{4\sigma^2}{n} = 15.77$ for all values, and $E(S^2) = 8.87$ for the first 35 values of S^2. If we express the values of $\underline{k}$ as ratios of actual and mean intensities, we obtain the data that are presented in the second part of the table on page 213. We must still establish, on the basis of formula (14.26), the probability that at least one of the 71 or of the 35 independent values of $\underline{k}$ exceeds the given values:

k	P_{71}	Probability	P_{35}
2	0.999		0.993
4	0.731		0.477
6	0.164		0.085
8	0.022		0.011

It follows that <u>not one of the periods found is significant.</u> The one that comes closest to significance is the period of 21 quarters. But in that case also the probability is almost 50% that some other period has greater intensity.

Therefore our final result is negative. Insofar as there are longer periods, the periodogram has not even made it possible to establish with some certainty the existence of some shorter period of fluctuation. The reason for that must be sought in part in the shortness of the series. Probably more important, the reason must also be sought in the peculiarities of the mathematical model of the periodogram. That model requires that peaks and troughs appear at regular intervals, while we know that this was not the case in the period considered. Therefore, just as with the correlogram, we can nevertheless draw one important conclusion: the 1949-1966 period is too heterogeneous for us to be able to consider it as a whole. The first fourth is especially different from the remaining three-fourths of that period. Therefore in the next section we will ignore that first — administrative — period and we will divide the remainder of the period into cycles.

14.3 Autoregression Scheme

The next step in our analysis consists of the approximation of economic movements by autoregression equations. For reasons which will immediately be clear, we will use difference equations of the second and fourth order. The four equations used with the empirical values of the parameters are given in the following table, where y_t is the chain index of industrial production in quarters $\underline{t}$, obtained on the basis of 4-quarter moving averages:

Equations	Correlation Coefficients for the Period		
	III/1953 –II/1965	III/1953 –IV/1960	I/1959 –II/1965
1. $\Delta^2 y_t = a y_{t+1} + c$ $y_{t+2} = (a+2) y_{t+1} - y_t + c$	0.54	. . .	0.64
2. $y_{t+2} = a y_{t+1} + b y_t + c$ $a_1 = 1{,}1677 \quad a_2 = 1.5218$ $b_1 = -0{,}5363 \quad b_2 = -0.6674$ $c_1 = 41{,}7514 \quad c_2 = 16{,}1694$	0.91	0.83	0.95
3. $\Delta^4 y_t = a \Delta^2 y_{t+1} + b y_{t+2} + c$ $y_{t+4} = (a+4) y_{t+3} - (2a-b+6) y_{t+2} + (a+4) y_{t+1} - y_t + c$ $a_1 = -3{,}7182 \quad a_2 = -3{,}2121$ $b_1 = -1{,}2507 \quad b_2 = -0{,}4719$ $c_1 = 141{,}0648 \quad c_2 = 52{,}2933$	0.95	0.98	0.98

4. $y_{t+4} = ay_{t+3} + by_{t+2} + cy_{t+1} + dy_t + e$ 0.93   0.93   0.98

$a_1 = 0,6450$ $a_2 = 1,1055$

$b_1 = 0$ $b_2 = 0$

$c_1 = 0$ $c_2 = 0$

$d_1 = -0,4901$ $d_2 = -0,3933$

$e_1 = 95,4067$ $e_2 = 32,0724$

On the basis of the results obtained in the earlier analysis, we now do not take into account the period before 1953. Since two of the three cycles in the 1953-1965 period were short, and one was somewhat longer, this period is also not treated as a unit; it is divided into two subperiods which partially overlap, namely, into the periods III/1953-IV/1960 and I/1959-II/1965. In the table on pages 215-216 the first column of coefficients relates to the first period, the second column to the latter. That the division into two periods was justified can be seen from the fact that the coefficients of multiple correlation are greater for movements in the second subperiod, which means that the last cycle was more regular than the earlier two. Also, the empirical values of the parameters are somewhat different for each of the subperiods.

The first equation contains the condition that the amplitude does not change, i.e., we have a true harmonic movement. The relatively low coefficients of correlation show that this equation provides a poor description of the economic movements and the parameters are not calculated.

In the second equation the limiting condition is abandoned and a completely general difference equation of the second order is adopted. The correlation increases significantly, and from the regression coefficients we can calculate the parameters which interest us most, the factor of damping $\underline{p}$ and the period of fluctuation P:

$$P_1 = \sqrt{0,5363} = 0,73, \cos\theta = \frac{1,1677}{2 \cdot 0,73} = 0,80, \theta = 36°50', P_1 = \frac{360}{36,83} = 9,8$$

$$P_2 = \sqrt{0,6674} = 0,81, \quad \cos\theta = \frac{1,5218}{2 \cdot 0,81} = 0,94, \theta = 20°, P_2 = \frac{360}{20} =$$

As we expected, the period of fluctuation in the second subperiod is prolonged to 4.5 years. The damping is rather large, so that the fluctuations degenerate very quickly into a horizontal line. A glance at Graph 14.3 reveals that this equation also does not describe the fluctuations of industrial production in a satisfactory way. (3)

The third and fourth equations have equal coefficients of multiple correlation and describe industrial movements equally well, as can be seen from the graph. The third equation includes the restraint that the amplitudes of the components of the sine wave are constant (see the Mathematical Appendix), while the fourth equation is completely general. It can be seen that removing the restraint does not improve the results perceptibly, so that the third equation, which is mathematically simpler, is entirely adequate for the analysis. In the fourth equation the regression coefficients $\underline{b}$ and $\underline{e}$ are insignificant at the 10% level, so they are ignored and the remaining coefficients are calculated anew. The new coefficients, as well as all coefficients in the other equations, are highly significant. Introducing the fifth and sixth terms in the equation gave insignificant coefficients for these terms and it can therefore be concluded that the difference equation of the fourth degree describes the empirical movements in the best possible way.

For the third equation the roots of the auxiliary equation have these values for subperiods I and II:

$$\text{I } m_{1,2} = 0,8130 \pm 0,5823 \text{ i,} \qquad m_{3,4} = -0,6721 \pm 0$$
$$\text{II } m_{1,2} = 0,9239 \pm 0,3827 \text{ i,} \qquad m_{3,4} = -0,5499 \pm 0$$

As we have already mentioned, $p_1 = p_2 = 1$; and the period of oscillation looks like this:

$$\text{I } \cos \theta_1 = 0,8130, \qquad \theta_1 = 35°40', \qquad P_1 = \frac{360}{35,67} = 10,1$$

$$\cos \theta_2 = -0,6721 \qquad \theta_2 = 180° - 47°50', \qquad P_2 = \frac{360}{132,17} = 2,7$$

$$\text{II } \cos \theta_1 = 0,9239, \qquad \theta_1 = 22°30' \qquad P_1 = \frac{360}{22,5} = 16,0$$

$$\cos \theta_2 = -0,5499, \qquad \theta_2 = 180° - 56°40' \qquad P_2 = \frac{360}{123,33} = 2,92$$

In order to be able to interpret these results, it would be useful also to solve the general, fourth equation. The roots of the auxiliary equation are easily calculated on an electronic computer.

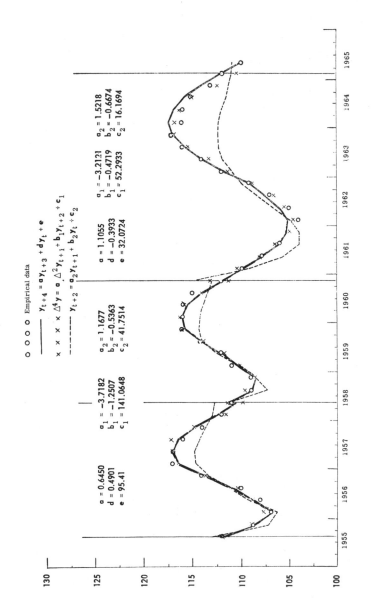

Graph 14.3 Approximation of Industrial Cycles by Autoregression Equations

For the two periods considered, these factors of damping ($\underline{p}$) and of length of period (P) are obtained in quarters:

$$\text{I} \quad p_1 = 0.96 \qquad P_1 = 10.4$$
$$p_2 = 0.73 \qquad P_2 = 9.3$$
$$\text{II} \quad p_1 = 0.99 \qquad P_1 = 17.0$$
$$p_2 = 0.63 \qquad P_2 = \underline{6.7}$$

The results are very informative. The periods of oscillation are prolonged from 10.1-10.4 quarters in the period III/1953-IV/1960 to 16-17 quarters in the period I/1959-II/1965. For the wavy movements compounded of two or more sine waves, the periods of the components of the movements cannot be ascertained by the naked eye. Mathematical analysis shows that Yugoslav industrial cycles consist, in all, of two sine wave components, since testing of the hypothesis of a larger number of components gave statistically very convincing negative results. The component cycles are such that one has a longer period and the other has a shorter period. The longer periods are equal for the third and fourth equations and correspond to the periods that we established earlier for industrial cycles directly (11 and 10 quarters in the first two cycles and 17 quarters in the following — see Table 5.2). Short periods are significantly different. Furthermore, for the longer components of the cycles the factor of damping is approximately equal to one (which was used as an assumption in equation three) and the oscillations are therefore regular. For shorter cycles we have pronounced damping. We may therefore conclude that industrial cycles in Yugoslavia can be described in a satisfactory way by the sum of two sine waves. The period of the longer sine wave corresponds to the visible period of the cycle of empirical magnitudes, and the amplitude is constant. Therefore the longer sine wave can be understood as the basic wave, which moves regularly. On this basic wave are then superimposed irregular shorter waves with periods of some 3-9 quarters and with significant damping. The regular basic wave can be interpreted economically as periodic structural refractions, and the superimposed short fluctuations — as stochastic shocks (disturbances) which constantly occur in every real economy. It is necessary to add that the coefficient of multiple correlation for both equations is exceptionally high: $R = 0.93-0.98$. And the deviation of the calculated from the empirical values in the entire period considered is 0.5% for the third equation and is further reduced to 0.4% for the fourth equation. Accordingly, the sum of the two sine waves presents a practically perfect description of the empirical industrial cycles.

Since we are not dealing with acoustics or light, this harmonic analysis must not be interpreted mechanically. We still know almost nothing about the systematic characteristics of the economy, and therefore we do not know either to what extent the result obtained is pure mathematical fitting of a curve, or to what extent there is presupposed economic content. Under the circumstances it is best that we conceive it as additional information about the behavioral characteristics of the Yugoslav economy. The information indicates the possibility that, in addition to the already-known short cycles of 3-4 years, there also may be ultrashort cycles of about 3 to 9 quarters. The existence of longer cycles was not uncovered by this technique.

14.4 Moving Averages

In the introductory methodological discussion we established the fact that moving averages hide oscillatory effects. Generally, short variations are overemphasized at the expense of longer ones, and fictitious oscillations are introduced by summation of random influences. Therefore, when moving averages are adopted it is necessary to take these effects into account, and calculations must be carried out so that they are minimized. It also follows from the earlier discussion that the effect is minimized for harmonic components by equalizing the path of the moving average with the period of oscillation of the components. This is, after all, intuitively obvious. If we wish to determine the trend, and we know that there are "seasonal fluctuations," then the smoothing of these fluctuations requires that the path of the moving average be made equal to the period of fluctuation. The effect of the random component will be minimal if the sum of the squared weights is minimized, i.e., if a simple moving average is adopted. We will adopt only such moving averages in this study.

Since we are now interested in longer cycles, quarterly data are no longer necessary and it is sufficient to use annual data, by which the series is extended. We will consider the following strategic economic series: the economy, agriculture, total investment, total exports, industry, industrial investment, and industrial exports. Six-year moving averages were used for the economy and industry until 1957, and four-year averages were used from then on. That was done because the first cycle was atypical (six years) and because adoption of the six-year and four-year moving averages for the entire series shows the same values on the boundary of 1956 and 1957, so that the six-year curve directly passes over to the four-year curve. Agriculture has two-year cycles until 1960, and four-year cycles after that, and therefore four-year moving averages must correspond to that series. As for the other series, we know that after 1953 they follow industrial production on the whole, so four-year moving averages are also adopted for them. All these movements are shown on Graph 14.4. For the sake of comparability, fluctuations of quarterly industrial production are also shown.

We can read the following message from Graph 14.4 All the series, with the exception of industrial investment, reach a minimum in 1951. All the series, except total and industrial exports, reach a maximum in 1959. Both export series reach a maximum somewhat earlier. Exports show a decline beginning in 1956, and the other series fall from 1959. The retardation of exports led to well-known difficulties, and efforts were made from 1961 to accelerate exports again. These efforts produced definite results after two years, but the expansion of exports began to slow down after 1964 and devaluation failed to change that tendency. Industrial investment gives a series that is in complete disharmony with all other series. That indicates two things. First, industrial investment was subjected to exceptional administrative shocks, and second, the trough in the three-year period 1955-1957 is probably responsible for certain structural disproportions (especially as regards energy and ferrous metallurgy) which expressed themselves later. Huge oscillations in industrial investment generally must have a pernicious influence on the stability and intensity of industrial expansion. Agricultural production alone, of seven aggregates considered, gives some optimistic indications. Agricultural expansion accelerated from 1962 on, and that may have aided the upturn of the other economic movements. Also, although the rate of growth of exports fall, it is still always greater than the rate of growth of production. In that way the share of exports in production grows, which creates the preconditions for widening the basic bottleneck of Yugoslav economic expansion.

As we could have expected, our series do not show any special

Graph 14.4 CHAIN INDICES OF ECONOMIC MOVEMENTS IN YUGOSLAVIA, 1949-1967

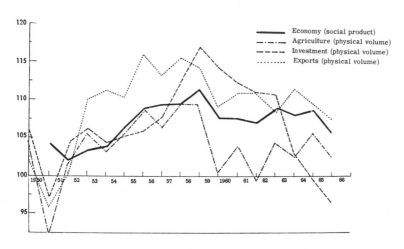

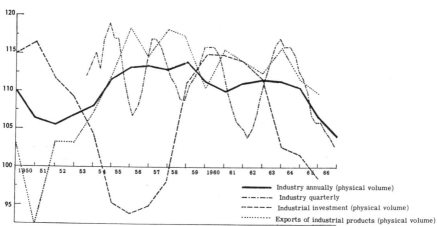

Note: For "economy" and "industry annually," six-year averages are used until 1957 and four-year averages from 1957 on. Four-year averages are used for the other series.

roundness in the movements. However, they show a high degree of synchronization in the movements, and especially synchronization with the movements of industrial production. This enables us to observe the rhythm of general economic movements through the movement of industrial production. And there we notice an acceleration from 1951 to 1959, and after that a retardation up to the end of 1966, when the last data for moving averages are reached. Accordingly, it is a matter of a cycle of at least 15 years. Whether that cycle will last longer than 15 years is something that cannot be forecasted now with certainty, but it is very probable on the basis of the indications available at this moment. The worrisome thing about industrial production is the movements after 1959. The reform of 1961 evoked retardation in steps, after which there was a tendency to return to the earlier level. That level was not reached; the reform of 1965 pushed the industrial curve yet another step lower, and the industrial trough in 1967 was lower than in 1952. A similar phenomenon can reappear, and that would significantly prolong the retardation phase of the long cycle, decelerate growth, and prolong the cycle to a total of 18-20 years. We are reminded of the earlier statement concerning the greater frequency of cycles of that length in other countries.

We can, it seems to me, conclude with this remark. Besides the existence of short cycles, we have also established the existence of cycles in the longer-run trends of economic movements. The shortness of the time series does not permit the determination of those longer cycles more precisely. But in interpreting those cycles it is necessary to have in mind that there is nothing mechanical and absolutely unavoidable about them. Whether the present phase will continue and be prolonged depends almost entirely on the efficacy of the work of economic policy bodies.

The retardation of economic growth after 1959 coincides with the acceleration of the decentralization and democratization of the Yugoslav economy and society. Because of the contemporaneousness of those two processes it may be thought that they stand in a relationship of effect and cause. It is well known that such a conclusion is in fact drawn. I have repeatedly, in this study and elsewhere (4), tried to give an alternative explanation which, to me, seems incomparably closer to the truth. The problem is that the building up of Yugoslav society has lagged behind the development of the material base, that administrative and political bodies

are not prepared and able to manage an economy as complicated
as the present Yugoslav economy, that pragmatism and neglect of
theory result in totally unnecessary losses and failures, and that
the potentialities of the Yugoslav social system are significantly
greater than the actual achievements of the last years. Can these
theses be proved? Or are they only the expression of a personal
belief? Insofar as a classical fundamental proof is sought in the
sense of an experiment, then such a proof can be given only ex
post, through the results of future development. But the scientific
substantiation of economic policy would have the role of an experiment that would draw all the necessary conclusions from development up to the present time.

However, it can hardly be doubted that a high degree of plausi-
bility of the conclusions — whether positive or negative with respect to the stated hypothesis — can also be attained by ex ante
analysis. This study offers many elements for such an analysis,
but does not verify the hypotheses. Verification would require an
entirely different study which, to be sure, logically begins with
the present, but is not oriented toward an analysis of what has
happened, but rather toward what might and must happen. In other
words, it would be necessary to turn from analysis of business
cycles and the functioning of the economic mechanism to the elab-
oration of an economic stabilization policy and the establishment
of ways of more fully utilizing existing potentials.

At this moment we can only guess at what those potentials are.
It appears to me, however, that it is now already possible to mention a more serious indication. Long cycles (Graph 14.4), deviations from the trend (Graph 5.3), average rates of growth within
individual cycles (Table 5.3), and other indicators show that actual economic growth accelerated until 1960, and that after that
year they slowed down. But actual growth is not identical with
potential growth. The precise establishment of potential growth
is, of course, very difficult. In that respect we return right to the
problem emphasized at the beginning of this study. We will therefore attempt to solve a similar problem in a similar way.

When the retardation phase in the depression reaches the trough
of the cycle, it can be assumed that the basic obstacles to more
rapid growth have been removed, that the economic structure is
better proportioned, and that the institutional system has been
brought up to date in relation to the needs of the economy by the
implementation of a reform. Accordingly, the rate of growth

realized in the conditions after the lower turning point corresponds in principle to growth in a well-balanced economy. However, because of unutilized capacities and large inventories, the material conditions for rapid growth are more satisfactory than in a normal situation in which the factors of production are fully utilized. For that reason the rates of growth in the accelerative phase of the cycle must be adjusted downward. The correction can, naturally, be carried out in various ways. In the absence of further information, correction with the aid of the average rate of growth in the course of the cycle (measured from peak to peak) seems to me to be most suitable. We will therefore use, as indicators of potential expansion, the arithmetic mean of average rates of growth and the rate of growth realized in the accelerative phases of the cycles. This picture is obtained (rates of growth of the social product, excluding agriculture; data are annual, for quarterly data do not exist for this aggregate):

1952-1955	11.0%
1955-1957	12.0%
1957-1960	12.1%
1960-1964	13.7%

The last cycle, which began with the reform, still does not have an accelerative phase, and therefore it is not possible to calculate the rate-indicator. It can be seen that the rates of potential expansion rise. They rise, and significantly, even after 1960. Although these data are entirely unsatisfactory for a firm conclusion, I assume, nevertheless, that they give a strong indication of the justification for stating the following thesis: institutional changes after 1960 and the general development of Yugoslav society freed social forces and developed initiatives which offered the possibility of achieving an even more rapid economic expansion than that which until now has been considered exceptional both among Yugoslavs and in the rest of the world. It is up to the Yugoslavs to transform that possibility into reality.

Notes

1) Worked out according to M. G. Kendall, The Advanced Theory of Statistics (London: Griffen, 1959), II, Ch. 30.

2) According to Kendall, op. cit.

3) Graph 14.3 is divided into three parts that correspond to the

three cycles. Fitting of the curve in each part is carried out in such a way that the constants of the corresponding equations are found by the method of least squares (see the Mathematical Appendix). Because of that procedure the ends of the preceding cycles and the beginnings of the following cycles do not entirely overlap on the boundaries of the cycles.

4) See B. Horvat, Ekonomska nauka i narodna privreda (Zagreb: Naprijed, 1968).

Chapter 15

CONCLUSIONS: THE MECHANISM OF MOVEMENTS IN THE YUGOSLAV ECONOMY

Methodological Problems

1. An economy should be regarded as a large system. Research shows that this system is unstable by nature. Insofar as suitable measures for regulating and directing the system are not under-taken, and efficient self-regulating institutions are not built into it, fluctuations are unavoidable. These fluctuations reduce the rate of growth and result in losses of production. The estimate we have made shows that in the fifteen-year period 1952-1967 probably about one-fourth of the social product was lost because of uneven development and reduction of the potential rate of growth.

2. In the statistical analysis of economic fluctuations in the Yugoslav economy we start with the following model. It is assumed that the economy moves along some long-run trend with a constant rate of growth $(a-1)$. It follows that the trend values of the social product will be determined by the equation

$$\bar{y}_t = a^t \qquad (15.1)$$

Let us assume, furthermore, that in the short run the economy oscillates about that trend, but in such a way that the amplitudes of deviations are proportional to the values of the trend in the period $\underline{t}$. What we are assuming, then, is that with the expansion of production, fluctuations increase absolutely but remain rela-tively constant, i.e., deviations from the trend represent equal proportions of the trend values of production in the respective periods. The factor of proportionality is designated by k̲, and deviations from the trend are determined by the expression

$$y_t^* = k \, a^t \cos t \qquad (15.2)$$

If now the trend values, which represent equilibrium growth of production, and deviations from the trend, which reflect fluctuations, are summed we obtain our model

$$y_t = \bar{y}_t + y_t^* = a^t \, (1 + k \cos t) \qquad (15.3)$$

3. In studying economic fluctuations one can consider: (a) absolute deviations from the trend, (b) relative deviations from the trend, and (c) movements of growth rates. In expansive economies such as the Yugoslav, approach (a) lacks analytic value. Approach (b) is inconvenient from the point of view of statistical calculation. Approach (c) is chosen as most efficient. In comparing movements (a) and (b) with (c) it is necessary to have in mind that the turning points of the path of growth rates precede the turning points of the path of relative and absolute deviations from the trend by one-fourth of the period. That means that the deviation from the trend attains a maximum when the rate of growth has already fallen to the average; production returns to the trend value when the rate of growth has fallen to the minimum and falls below the trend when the rate of growth begins to increase. Instead of annual rates of growth, chain indices can be used to avoid calculation of negative values when, occasionally, contractions occur in economic movements. Seasonal fluctuations are eliminated by a method that uses quarterly changes of annual rates of growth, measured by calculating ratios of the same quarters of successive years.

Industry

4. Chain indices of economic movements, corrected for seasonal fluctuations, reveal the existence of business cycles in Yugoslavia. These cycles last three to four years and have a tendency to become prolonged and deeper. In industry the amplitudes of the cycles are 10-20 percentage points. This means that, at the peaks of the cycles, industry expands at a rate close to 20%, while in the troughs of the cycles it is stagnant. Because of the dominant position of industry in the Yugoslav economy, industrial

cycles predetermine cycles in all other economic movements with the exception of agriculture. The periodicity of Yugoslav business cycles is exceptionally regular. Given the complexity of economic movements, it is surprising how precisely industrial cycles can be described by the sum of two sine waves: for the period 1953-1965 the coefficient of correlation between the empirical and calculated movements is $r = 0.93-0.98$, and the empirical path of industrial production deviates from the mathematical (expressed as the sum of two sine waves) in all by 0.4%. It is obvious, therefore, that it is a matter of very systematic movements. It is also obvious that learning the mechanism of those movements can make it possible in the future to subject them to the conscious control of society.

5. All economic sectors of all statistical aggregates do not show the same intensity of cycles. The strongest factors of material instability are agricultural production, construction, and total investment.

Agriculture

6. Agricultural production has its own, exogenously determined cycles which, until 1960, were of two years' duration. Those cycles bring about an absolute reduction of production and have significantly greater amplitudes than the industrial cycles. From 1960 on, the agricultural cycles have toned down; the expansion of production slowed down for several years, but recently it has again shown signs of acceleration. For that reason, and because of the reduction of the share of agriculture in the total social product, agriculture will represent a significantly reduced factor of instability in the future than it has up to now.

Investment

7. Because of a series of unsolved problems, and first of all because of unsolved problems in financing investment and housing construction, the construction industry fluctuates with huge amplitudes and in almost every cycle undergoes a classical depression with negative rates of growth. Rates of growth of construction vary between − 40% in the trough of the second cycle and + 49% at the peak of the first cycle. Even in recent years, with significantly greater volume of construction work, the fluctuations remain intolerably large, from + 28% at the beginning of 1964 to − 16% in

the middle of 1965 (measured by effective working hours; according to the real value of production the fluctuations would be still greater). Since construction fluctuations not only have huge amplitudes, but also coincide with industrial fluctuations, construction represents a dangerous factor of instability in the Yugoslav economy.

8. Investment movements have a special place in the theory of business cycles. The most frequent and thoroughly developed explanations of cycles consist, in effect, of a description of the mechanism of the accelerator-multiplier, because of which retardation (acceleration) of the expansion of aggregate demand leads to an accelerated reduction (increase) of investment demand, and changes in investment magnify variations in aggregate demand. Accordingly, breaks in investment movements turn production cycles upward or downward. It appears that this mechanism does not operate in the Yugoslav economy. If, because there are no quarterly data on real economic investment, the series for construction and machinery production are taken as substitutes, this picture is obtained. The amplitudes of machinery production alone are a little greater than industrial amplitudes, so it is therefore impossible to speak of accelerated instability in the production of equipment. On the other hand, the turning points of the cycles of machinery production lag, especially at the peaks, while the turning points of construction coincide with those of industry; but according to the usual theory they should lead. Therefore, one can rather safely conclude that investment does not provoke breaks in short-run flows of production; on the contrary, acceleration or retardation in production leads to breaks in investment activity.

Inventories

9. After investment in fixed capital, investment in inventories is taken as the most frequent explanation of cyclical turning points. The literature up to now describes two types of inventory fluctuation: one of them corresponds to a capitalist economy, above all the American; the other corresponds to a centrally planned economy, above all the Czechoslovak. In both cases the cycles of inventories and of production coincide; in both cases the cumulation and decumulation of inventories are conditioned by the speculative behavior of producers. In the phase of the cyclical upswing, demand exceeds supply and producers endeavor

to build up inventories to provide for expansion of production; inventories pile up. In recession phases the motivations and movements are the reverse. However, the causes of the discrepancy between supply and demand are very different in the two types of economy. The centrally planned economy is oriented toward production. Consequently, running up against capacity barriers — i.e., insufficient supply in relation to existing demand — results in recession. The capitalist economy is oriented toward consumption. Therefore inadequate demand determines the end of an upswing.

10. In the Yugoslav economy, inventory fluctuations regulate a mechanism that is different from both the capitalist and the centrally-planned. The latter two mechanisms change inventories in accordance with the production cycle and in such a way that changes of inventories absorb a smaller percentage of the increase of production in the accelerative phase and a relatively larger part of the decline in production in the retardation phase. In that way consumption is more stable and fluctuates less than production. In the Yugoslav economy, inventories move inversely to the production cycle — slower in the upswing, faster in the downswing — and thus fluctuations of production are reduced at the expense of greater fluctuations of consumption. As a result of that inverse movement, in accelerative phases of the cycle the investment in total industrial inventories absorbs about 25% of the increase in production; in retardation phases it absorbs the entire increase in industrial production. The latter phenomenon means that in the retardation phase of the Yugoslav industrial cycle an increase in production is possible only if it is exclusively for inventories. And if an attempt is made, by credit restriction, for example, to hamper the formation of a certain volume of inventories, an absolute decline in production will result.

Economic Efficiency and Prices

11. In an economy geared toward rapid expansion of production, high rates of growth are the precondition for full use of capacity. Therefore, in years of expansion the capital coefficients fall perceptibly, and in years of stagnation they increase. Better utilization of capacity and economies of large-scale production reduce costs in accelerative phases of the cycle. Personal incomes act with the same effect: to be sure, they move cyclically synchronized with production, but they have less amplitude and burden

production costs less in the accelerative phases of the cycle than in the retardation phases. As a result of all these movements, pressure on prices will be less at high rates of growth and greater at low rates. Accordingly, contrary to the postulate of the classical theory of supply and demand, in the Yugoslav economy prices will rise more slowly in times of expansion than in recession periods. An empirical test supports that expectation: the correlation between deflated sales of the economy and the general retail price index is $r = -0.62$, which means that the relationship is strong and negative. Thus, prices increase when sales slow down and fall (or rise more slowly) when sales accelerate.

12. For purposes of economic policy it would be of exceptional importance to establish which economic variables control quarterly movements of prices. Research shows that in this respect the Yugoslav economy behaves with unusual regularity: a single variable determines four-fifths of all short-run variations of producers' and retail prices. The factor involved is the movement of personal incomes in relation to the movement of production. When nominal personal incomes grow 6.5% faster than the productivity of labor, producers' prices in industry remain unchanged; prices increase if the excess of personal incomes is greater than this limiting percentage, and they fall if the excess is less. Including credit in the regression equation did not improve the explanation of price variations or even produced a negative coefficient. The latter means that expansion of credit reduces prices. Therefore, contrary to widespread belief, movements of credit do not explain movements of prices. This paradox is easily resolved when one remembers that credit stimulates production, expansion of production lowers costs, lower unit costs put less pressure on prices, and thus it appears statistically that credit lowers prices.

Foreign Trade

13. The large amplitudes of exports (22 percentage points) and, especially, of imports (44 percentage points) in relation to industrial fluctuations (average amplitudes in the period 1952-1957 amounted to 11 percentage points) make foreign trade a dangerous and, as we will see directly, key destabilizer of the Yugoslav economy. In conditions of rapid growth and the practical nonexistence of foreign exchange reserves, the economy is exceptionally sensitive to the acceleration and retardation of imports and exports.

Uncontrolled production expansion near the peak of the production cycle leads to acceleration of imports and an inevitable lag of exports, and that widening of the divergence in growth rates of exports and imports of industrial products becomes the key factor in the turning downward of the industrial path. It has been shown that it is sufficient for the divergence to widen to 6% — i.e., for the chain index of imports to be 6% greater than the chain index of exports — to have breaks in production and cumulative retardation of production. In the depression, export acceleration, which precedes the acceleration of production, helps the revival of production. It is important to note that the index of divergence — which is constructed as an instrument for measuring the speed of separation of import and export flows and is the ratio of the chain index of imports to the chain index of exports multiplied by 100 — has very regular movements. Its cycle, with amplitudes as large as those of imports, corresponds to the industrial cycle with a certain phasal lag. Accordingly, in industrial upswings the divergence in trade widens and at a certain point provokes a production slowdown; in industrial downturns the divergence narrows and at a certain point begins to stimulate the acceleration of production.

The Mechanism of Yugoslav Business Cycles

14. Once the cyclical upswing begins, that is, when there is acceleration of production growth, inventories decline relatively — and at the peaks even absolutely, credit expands by some equilibrium rate of somewhat over 10%, liquidity of the economy increases, and debts are paid. Imports of intermediate goods for industry grow more slowly than industrial production, while industrial exports grow faster than production. The acceleration of production leads to better utilization of capacity and inventories, increases labor productivity, reduces costs and, despite increases of personal incomes and business saving, reduces pressure on prices. The increase of consumption, investment, exports, and demand for intermediate goods stimulates production and, in the absence of effective control and the ex ante coordination of economic movements (planning), the economic machine gradually overheats. Bottlenecks appear that are overcome by intensified importing. Export production slows down, either because it is difficult to accelerate exports further, or because a part of potential exports is absorbed by the expanding domestic market.

The divergence of exports and imports widens rapidly; the discrepancy between imports and exports is covered at first by foreign loans and credits, but soon an explosion of the balance of payments deficit exceeds the possibilities of supplying foreign exchange at reasonable prices, import orders are executed more and more slowly, the supply chains on the internal market begin to break, and the cycle turns downward. Import-oriented enterprises reduce production and new orders to their domestic partners, the internal market begins to disintegrate, inventories accumulate, liquidity is reduced, and the economy becomes indebted by leaps and bounds. The retardation of production reduces imports, the pressure of the balance of payments deficit slackens, and production for inventories prevents a contraction of the internal market. However, personal incomes continue to rise — although more slowly — and since that increase cannot be covered by a rise in labor productivity, business saving falls and prices rise. The drop in investment demand and the rise in prices create new disturbances which delay adjustment of the internal market and check the expansion of exports. Further developments now depend to a large extent on economic policy. Usually at the point great attention is paid to stimulating exports, and credit policy becomes more liberal. As a result, a new acceleration of exports — which precedes the lower turning point of production by about 4-5 months — and an acceleration of inventory accumulation — which continues some 5 months after the turning point — turn the path of the rate of growth upward. A new cyclical upswing begins.

Guiding the Economy

15. The existence of business cycles and their causes were unknown to economic policy bodies and, until a few years ago, even to research workers. This explains the fact that anticyclical policies were not formulated. It also explains why waves of reorganization were begun in the midst of the retardation phases of the cycle, which intensified the slowdown of growth and deepened and widened the troughs of the cycle. Both caused large economic losses which objectively could often have been avoided.

16. In addition to inadequate current economic policy, a significant role in causing instability was played by structural disproportions which were not promptly noted and eliminated. The first

five-year plan was completed with overexpanded basic industries, the second with overexpanded processing industries. The third five-year plan did not succeed in correcting structural disproportions since it was not implemented. Structural disproportions create inflationary and import pressures which cannot be eliminated by price control, credit policy, and short-run financial instruments. If that is attempted, either it has no results or the cycles are deepened with an overall contraction of production; the disproportions remain, but are transformed periodically from a latent to an acute state.

17. In the entire postwar period there were five business cycles, of which the last is still in process. Those cycles were in part set in motion by five important economic reforms, and in part they stimulated the reforms.

We obtain the following picture:

Cycle I	III/1949-III/1955: The New Economic System (1)
Cycle II	III/1955-II/1958: Transition to the Second Five-Year Plan
Cycle III	II/1958-IV/1960: The New System of Income Distribution
Cycle IV	IV/1960-I/1965: The New Economic System (2)
Cycle V	I/1965-?: Economic Reform

Each cycle is thereby not only clearly determined statistically, but it also has a definite economic content.

Regional Cycles

18. Cycles in the developed and underdeveloped regions are synchronized. But the amplitudes of agricultural and industrial fluctuations in the underdeveloped regions are significantly greater than in the developed regions. And the path of the chain indices of industrial production has a much more irregular form for underdeveloped regions. It follows from both factors that the entire economy of the underdeveloped regions is more unstable and requires special attention from economic policy bodies.

Comparisons with Other Economies

19. Of eleven capitalist and socialist countries with high rates

of growth in the period 1951-1965, economic instability was the greatest, by far, in Yugoslavia. One of the main reasons for that was agricultural production, for which, as we have emphasized, we can predict smoother movements in the future. If agriculture is excluded and only industrial fluctuations are considered, the relative instability is reduced, but it is still greater than in any of the five socialist countries. Therefore it is not probable that this instability is inevitable or objectively determined.

Long Cycles

20. From a longer-run point of view, the social product, the physical volume of industrial and agricultural production, industrial and total investment, and industrial and total exports can be taken as strategic economic variables. If we smooth the cyclical fluctuations of the rates of growth of those economic aggregates by four-year moving averages, we obtain a picture of a long business cycle which is not yet completed and which will last longer than 16 years. All the series considered, except total and industrial exports, attained a maximum in 1959. Total and industrial exports attained a maximum somewhat earlier. Exports have shown a downward trend since 1956, and the other series have moved downward since 1959. Not only has economic expansion slowed since 1959-1960, but the instability of the economy has increased. Industrial investment is the only series that is in complete disharmony with all the others. That indicates two things. First, industrial investment was subjected to exceptional administrative blows, and second, the deep trough in the three-year period 1955-1957 is probably responsible for certain structural disproportions (especially in energy and ferrous metallurgy) which appeared later. A similar trough, but this time not only in industrial but also in total investment, began to take shape after 1965, and therefore similar consequences can be expected in the future. In general it can be said that huge oscillations in industrial investment must have an injurious effect on the stability and intensity of industrial expansion and, thereby, on economic growth as a whole. Of seven aggregates considered, agricultural production alone gives some optimistic indications. Agricultural expansion has been accelerating since 1962, and this may help to turn other economic movements upward toward the earlier rapid economic development.

MATHEMATICAL APPENDIX

1. We have a difference equation of the second order

$$\Delta^2 \, y_t = -ay_{t+1} \tag{1}$$

for which

$$\Delta^2 \, y_t = (y_{t+2}-y_{t+1})-(y_{t+1}-y_t) = y_{t+2}-2y_{t+1}+y_t$$

Accordingly, equation (1) in developed form runs

$$y_{t+2}+(a-2) \, y_{t+1}+y_t = 0 \tag{2}$$

and its auxiliary equation

$$m^2 + (a-2)m + 1 = 0$$

has the roots

$$m_{1,2} = \frac{2-a \pm \sqrt{(a-2)^2-4}}{2}$$

which are complex if $(a-2)^2 < 4$, i.e., $0 < a < 4$. The solution of equation (1) then has the form

$$y_t = Ap^t \cos (\theta t-\varphi) \tag{3}$$

where $p=1$, and $\theta = \arccos (1-\frac{a}{2})$. The solution represents a harmonic movement, with amplitude and phase given by the initial conditions.

2. Let us add to equation (1) the constant $\underline{c}$, which can be thought of as the mean value of the stochastic elements:

$$\Delta^2 y_t = ay_{t+1} + c \tag{4}$$

237

The solution for the homogeneous part is given in (3), and the particular solution runs

$$Y_t = B \qquad (5)$$

By insertion in (4) we obtain

$$B + (a-2) B + B = c$$

$$B = \frac{c}{a} \qquad (5.1)$$

and the general solution is accordingly

$$y_t = A \cos (\theta t - \varphi) + \frac{c}{a} \qquad (6)$$

3. Let us consider the general form of the difference equation of the second order

$$y_{t+2} = a\, y_{t+1} + b y_t + c \qquad (7)$$

Its auxiliary equation

$$m^2 - am - b = 0 \qquad (8)$$

has conjugate complex roots

$$m_{1,2} = \frac{a \pm \sqrt{a^2 + 4b}}{2} = p\,(\cos \theta \pm i \sin \theta)$$

if $\left(\dfrac{a}{2}\right)^2 < -b,\ b < 0$. Then the general solution runs

$$y_t = A\, p^t \cos (\theta t - \varphi) + \frac{c}{1-a-b} \qquad (9)$$

where $p = \sqrt{-b}$ a $\theta = \arccos \dfrac{a}{2\sqrt{-b}}$.

4. The difference equation of the fourth order

$$\Delta^2 y_t = a\, \Delta^2 y_{t+1} + b y_{t+2} + c \qquad (10)$$

in its developed form runs

$$y_{t+4} - (a + 4)\, y_{t+3} + (2a - b + 6)\, y_{t+2} - (a+4)\, y_{t+1} + y_t = c \qquad (11)$$

238

and its solution depends on the roots of the auxiliary equation

$$m^4 - (a+4)m^3 + (2a-b+6)m^2 - (a+4)m + 1 = 0 \tag{12}$$

We divide by m^2 and introduce the substitution $u = m + 1/m$ so that we may obtain

$$u^2 - (a+4)u + (2a-b+4) = 0 \tag{13}$$

from which it follows that

$$u_{1,2} = \frac{a+4 \pm \sqrt{a^2+4b}}{2} \tag{14}$$

which is real when $a^2 > -4b$. Then, from the relation determined by the above substitution

$$m^2 - um + 1 = 0 \tag{15}$$

it follows that

$$m_{1,2} = \frac{u_1 \pm \sqrt{u_1^2-4}}{2} = p_1 (\cos \theta_2 \pm i \sin \theta_1) \tag{16}$$

$$m_{3,4} = \frac{u_2 \pm \sqrt{u_2^2-4}}{2} = p_2 (\cos \theta_2 \pm i \sin \theta_2) \tag{17}$$

When

$$u_1^2 < 4 \text{ tj. } a^2 + 4a + 2b + (a+4)\sqrt{a^2+4b} < 0 \tag{18}$$

$$u_2^2 < 4 \text{ tj. } a^2 + 4a + 2b - (a+4)\sqrt{a^2+4b} < 0 \tag{19}$$

From (15) it follows that $p_1 = p_2 = 1$. Particular solution (11) runs

$$Y_t = B \tag{20}$$

from which it follows that

$$B - (a+4)B + (2a-b+6) B - (a+4) B + B = c$$
$$B = -\frac{c}{b} \tag{21}$$

and the general solution is therefore

$$y_t = A_1 \cos (\theta_1 t - \varphi_1) + A_2 \cos (\theta_2 t - \varphi_2) - \frac{c}{b} \tag{22}$$

That solution, besides the constant term, represents the sum of two harmonic movements of constant but different periods, amplitudes, and phasal constants.

5.* The difference equation of the fourth order of the form

$$y_{t+4} = ay_{t+3} + dy_t + e \tag{23}$$

has a solution of the form

$$y_t = (C_1 \cos \alpha t + C_2 \sin \alpha t) \, p_1^t + (C_3 \cos \beta t + C_4 \sin \beta t) \, p_2^t + B. \tag{24}$$

To determine the parameters α, β, p_1 and p_2, we use the auxiliary equation

$$m^4 - am^3 - d = 0 \tag{25}$$

of equation (23).

After estimation of coefficients a, d and e, equation (25) is solved very quickly and effectively by an electronic computer. The roots of that equation are complex conjugate numbers (this follows from the nature of the problem alone, i.e., from calculation of the coefficients a, d, and e) of the form

$$m_{1,2} = p_1 (\cos \alpha \pm i \sin \alpha)$$
$$m_{3,4} = p_2 (\cos \beta \pm i \sin \beta).$$

Coefficient B is obtained as the particular solution of equation (23) in the form $B = e/1 - a - d$.

According to general theory, solution (24) is obtained directly from the difference equations. Depending on the values of the parameters p_1 and p_2, we will have damped or explosive oscillation about the value of $y_t = B$ (if either p_1 or p_2 is greater than one, then explosive oscillations are obtained; if both are less than one, then damped oscillations are obtained; and if they are just equal to one, then we have agreement of the two harmonic oscillations with an amplitude of one and different periods, as in 4).

6. In connection with the fact that in solutions (9), (22), and (24) we have a relatively large number of degrees of freedom, we can attain great accuracy in the approximation of empirical data by

---

*Parts 5 and 6 were worked out by M. Bogdanović, an assistant at the Yugoslav Institute of Economic Studies.

the method of least squares. Even the calculation is carried out in an entirely elementary manner. Here we will demonstrate the approach only to the solution of the form (24), though all these results can be carried over in an analogous way to (9) and (22).

We have solution (24) in the form

$$\bar{y}_t - B = C_1 \, p_1^t \, \cos \alpha \, t + C_2 p_1^t \, \sin \alpha \, t + C_3 \, p_2^t \, \cos \beta \, t + C_4 \, p_2^t \, \sin \beta \, t.$$

We stipulate further that: $y_t - B = Y_t$

$$p_1^t \, \cos \alpha \, t = X_t^{(1)}$$
$$p_1^t \, \sin \alpha \, t = X_t^{(2)}$$
$$p_2^t \, \cos \beta \, t = X_t^{(3)}$$
$$p_2^t \, \sin \beta \, t = X_t^{(4)}$$

Then

$$Y_t = C_1 \, X_t^{(1)} + C_2 \, X_t^{(2)} + C_3 \, X_t^{(3)} + C_4 \, X_t^{(4)} \tag{26}$$

We designate the empirical data by $\hat{y}_t$. Thus we obtain the expression

$$\sum_t (\hat{y}_t - C_1 X_t^{(1)} - C_2 X_t^{(2)} - C_3 X_t^{(3)} - C_4 X_t^{(4)})^2$$

which must be minimized. The further approach is well known. In that way we obtain the values which must take the arbitrary constants C_i (i = 1, 2, 3, 4) to obtain the particular solution of equation (23) that fulfills the conditions of the method of least squares.

GLOSSARY

"Social product" is defined in the Yugoslav national income accounts as the total volume of goods and services produced in industry, mining, agriculture, fishing, forestry, construction, handicrafts, communications, transportation, public utilities, trade, tourism, and catering. It differs from the Western concept in excluding the services of government, defense, health and welfare, insurance, and scientific, cultural, political, and professional organizations.

"The economy" includes only production and services in the sectors included in the definition of "social product."

Helen M. Kramer

TABLES

		Page
1.1.	Social Product Lost Owing to Business Cycles, 1952-1967	3
5.1.	Acceleration and Retardation Phases of Industrial Cycles	45
5.2.	Measured Characteristics of Production Cycles	52
5.3.	Rate of Growth of Industrial Production by Cycles	53
5.4.	Measured Characteristics of Cycles in Industry, Machinery Industry and Construction	62
6.1.	Agricultural Cycles, 1948-1964	67
6.2.	Fluctuations of Agricultural Production and the Balance of Payments Deficit	71
7.1.	Per Capita Social Product and the Rate of Growth of Social Product by Regions, 1952-1965	74
7.2.	Measured Characteristics of Industrial Cycles of Developed and Underdeveloped Regions	78
8.1.	Growth of Productivity of Labor and Employment in Years with Above-average and Below-average Increase in Labor Productivity	82
8.2.	Growth of Productivity of Labor and Efficiency of Capital in Years of Maximum and Minimum Growth of Production	83
9.1.	Inventory Formation in the Yugoslav Economy, 1952-1964	94
9.2.	Structure of Inventories	96
9.3.	Structure of Industrial Inventories	98
9.4.	Cycles of Industrial Production and Inventories	99
9.5.	Nonagricultural Inventories by Economic Sectors	107
9.6.	Turning Points of Industrial Production and Inventories	110
9.7.	Time Lags of Industrial Inventories at the Turning Points of Industrial Production	111
10.1.	Chain Indices of the Social Product	126

		Page
10.2.	Turning Points and Amplitudes of Physical Volume of Production and Deflated Sales	128
10.3.	Rate of Growth of the Social Product, Money Supply, and Cost of Living in Twelve Expanding Economies in the Period 1953-1965	132
10.4.	Value of Production, Supply and Demand for Money, 1958-1967	135
10.5.	Implicit Deflators of Components of the Social Product and Some Price Indices, 1953-1967	137
11.1	Turning Points and Amplitudes of Cycles of Industrial Production, Exports and Imports, and Index of Divergence	162
12.1.	Legal Regulations Governing Relations in the Economy, 1952-1965	171
13.1.	Intensity of Economic Fluctuations in Eleven Countries in the Period 1950-1964	197
13.2.	Characteristics of Trends of Growth Rates of Eleven Countries, 1950-1964	201

GRAPHS

		Page
1.1.	Achieved and Potential Social Product, 1952-1967	5
4.1.	Alternative Representations of Business Cycles	36
5.1.	Industrial Cycles in Yugoslavia	48
5.2.	Business Cycles in Yugoslavia	50
5.3.	Alternative Representations of Industrial Cycles: Chain Indices and Relative Deviations of Industrial Production from the Exponential Trend	54
5.4.	Cycles of Production of Industry, Construction and Gross Investment	56
5.5.	Cycles of Industrial Production, Machinery Production, Construction and Investment Expenditures for Fixed Capital	58
6.1.	Agricultural and Industrial Cycles	68
7.1.	Regional Industrial Cycles	76
8.1.	Cycles of Industrial Production, Employment and Productivity of Labor	84
9.1.	Cycles of Industrial Production and Inventories	100
9.2.	Ratios of Inventories and Production in Industry	104
9.3.	Industrial Production, Inventories, Credits for Working Capital and Indebtedness	108
10.1.	Industry: Nominal and Deflated Sales, Production, Producers' Prices and Relations of Nominal Personal Incomes and Productivity of Labor	120
10.2.	Nominal and Deflated Sales, Retail Prices, Total Personal Incomes and Industrial Production	122
10.3.	Economy: Sales, Credits, Inventories, Demand Deposits, Money Supply and Accounts Payable	124
10.4.	Indices of Producers' Prices	140
11.1.	Establishing Economic Equilibrium	153
11.2.	Cycles of International Trade in Industrial Products	156
11.3.	Cycles of Total Exports and Imports of Goods	158
12.1.	Legal Regulations and Industrial Production	174

245

		Page
12.2.	Connection Between the Number of Economic Regulations and Index of Growth of Industry and Production	188
13.1.	Chain Indices of Annual Growth of Social Product and Industrial Production in Eleven Countries	194
14.1.	Correlogram of the Index of Industrial Production and Exports	209
14.2.	Periodogram of Deviations of Rates of Growth of Industrial Production from Average Rates for the Period I/1949-IV/1966	212
14.3.	Approximations of Industrial Cycles by Auto-regression Equations	218
14.4.	Chain Indices of Economic Movements in Yugoslavia, 1949-1967	222

INDEX

INDEX

Accelerating industrial exports, 11
  agricultural production, 11
  growth, 11
Acceleration, 33, 184, 223
  exports, 161, 232, 233, 234
  growth, 63, 185
  imports, 154, 161, 232
  inventory accumulation, 234
  production, 61, 86, 110, 230, 233
Accelerator, 39, 63
  mechanism, 229
Accumulation, see Saving
Active population, 87
  agricultural, 87
Administrative direction, 17
Administrative measures, 86
  economic, 44
  retardation and stagnation, 4
Agriculture, 2, 4, 11, 34, 41, 48, 67, 68, 81, 82, 87, 91, 92, 95, 106, 126, 167, 198, 199, 220, 221, 229, 236
Allocation of resources, 150
Amortization, 116
Amplitude
  agricultural fluctuations, 235
  curve of growth rates, 39
  exports, 162, 232
  imports, 162, 165, 232

index of divergence, 155
industrial production, 71, 162, 231, 235
inventories, 110
relative deviations, 39
Autoregression model, 23, 27
  economic, 17, 148
  inventory fluctuations, 17
  Klein-Goldberger, 24
  linear oscillator, 23, 27
  moving averages of random disturbances, 27
  servomechanism, 23, 26
  statistical, 35
Autoregression scheme, 206, 215
Averages, 20, 21, 22, 31, 33
  four-term, 32
  moving, 11, 20, 22, 30, 31, 32, 33, 47, 155, 206, 208, 220
  one-term, 22
  simple, 220
  three-month, 33

Balance of payments, 70
  surplus, 154
Bank clearing, 10
Bankruptcy, 10, 143
Base of cycle, 33
Bottlenecks, 24, 93, 233
Boundaries of cycles, 12, 39,

249

40, 45, 52, 207
  IFC production, 60
Budget, 142, 183
  expenses — see Government
    expenditures
  family, 138
Business funds of economic organizations, 129

Capacity, 2
  industrial, 161
Capital, 12
  fixed, 17, 178
  liquid, 127, 129
  working, 102, 116, 127, 146,
    148, 181, 182
Coefficient
  capital, 231
  correlation, 23, 86, 116,
    127, 129, 146, 147, 177,
    189, 215, 216, 229
  elasticity, 133
  fluctuation, 196, 198, 199,
    200
  multiple, 216, 219
  production, 66, 82
  regression, 23, 75, 144, 146,
    216
  serial correlation, 21
  structural, 35
  turnover, 92, 97, 106
  variance, 193
Collectivization, 86
Communal construction, 89,
  229
Comparative advantage, 81, 154
Components
  additive, 31
  cyclical, 13, 14, 23, 41
  harmonic, 205, 220
  oscillatory, 31

  random, 24, 30
  seasonal, 30
  social product, 35
  systematic, 24, 41
  unsystematic, 41
Construction, 2, 12, 49, 61, 63,
  67, 91, 204, 229, 230
Consumer goods, 152, 153
Consumption, 17, 59, 114, 115,
  165
  durable consumer goods, 11
  durable producers' goods, 11
  expected, 17
  government, 153
  intermediate goods, 149
  personal, 149, 152, 153
  public, 149
Contraction, 10, 118, 228
  import, 164
  internal demand, 234
  production, 235
  upswing, 70, 86
Correlogram, 206, 208, 210,
  215
Costs, 113, 142, 145, 147, 183
  fixed, 143
  imported intermediate goods,
    183
  living, 138
  opportunity, 88
  production, 13, 142
  variable, 143
Covariance, 208, 210
Credit, 96, 102, 103, 115, 117,
  129, 130, 134, 136, 144, 146,
  148, 180, 182, 184, 232, 234
  bank, 116
  producers', 116
  restriction, 117, 179, 185,
    231
  short-term, 134, 184

Crisis, 10, 12, 13
  world, 202
Critical decision points, 15
Cycles
  absolute deviations, 39
  administrative, 170
  agricultural, 8, 67, 68, 229
  business, 3, 8, 13, 19, 23,
    32, 40, 43, 44, 47, 48,
    112, 134, 149, 202, 228,
    234
  component, 219
  construction, 12
    twenty-year, 12, 13
    two-year, 13, 139
  construction, 12, 13, 63,
    184
  developed and underdevel-
    oped regions, 235
  empirical, 40
  employment, 82, 83
  English, 42
  foreign trade, 152, 154, 164
  four-year American, 10, 93
  generators of, 203
  German, 42
  growth rates, 38
  housing, 12
  industrial, 12, 34, 43, 44,
    45, 47, 69, 78, 102, 107,
    113, 117, 154, 160, 161,
    219, 220, 228, 229, 231,
    233
  investment, 61, 160
  inventory, 91, 93, 98, 102,
    107, 111, 114, 230
  legal regulations, 170
  long, 9, 13, 31, 206, 234,
    236
  medium-term, 9, 10
  production, 61, 86, 98, 102,
    103, 111, 112, 115, 160,
    231
  productivity of labor, 83, 85
  reference, 32, 34, 111
  regional, 73, 235
  secular, 202
  short, 9, 10, 13, 112, 206,
    220, 223
  sixteen-year, 11
  specific, 32
  typical, 33
    reference, 33
    specific, 33
  ultrashort, 220
  Yugoslav, 10, 44, 228
Cycle-producing mechanism,
  39
Cycles of growth rates, 6, 37
  tendencies, 34
Cyclical mechanism, 113, 114
  process, 20
  upswing, 3, 6, 95, 230

Deceleration of industrial exports, 11
  agricultural production, 11
  growth, 6, 11
Decentralization, 170, 200, 223
Deficit, 3
  agrarian, 154
  federal, 182
  balance of payments, 70, 71,
    110, 152, 153, 154, 160,
    164, 180, 182, 183, 234
Deflated sales of industry, 150
  of the economy, 122, 150,
    232
Deflation, 150
Deflator, 119, 148
  social product, 136
Demand, 12, 15, 70, 91, 93, 96,

98, 111, 112, 115, 130, 148,
179, 183, 230, 231, 232
  aggregate, 161, 183
  consumption, 149, 161, 233
  export, 149
  intermediate goods, 149,
    233
  internal, 161, 183
  investment, 149, 161, 233
  money, 131
  social, 149
Depression, 38, 40, 50, 94,
  103, 114, 129, 136, 139, 144,
  145, 165, 183, 186, 224, 229,
  233
Destabilizer, 63, 232
Devaluation, 164, 221
Disparity, 138, 141, 142
  prices, 182
Distortion, 32
Distribution according to work,
  88
Divergence of trade, 164
  industrial, 233

Economic
  development, 86, 87
  equilibrium, 24, 153
  organization, 89, 134
  stability, 26, 80
  transaction, 130, 133, 134,
    136
  upswing, 183
Economic balance, 153
  growth, 81, 89, 131, 133,
    187
  process, 107
  regulations, 187
  stabilizer, 94
  stochastic disturbance, 25
  upswing, 95, 129, 178

Economic blockade, 127, 178
Economic theory, 184
Economies of scale, 231
  business activity, 97
Economy
  capitalist, 32, 142, 230
  centrally planned, 92, 114,
    198, 203, 204, 230
  developed, 81
  expansive, 32, 39
  illiquid, 143
  market, 6, 17, 92, 115, 131,
    142, 164, 176, 190, 198,
    204
  national, 93
  planned, 88
  rapidly growing, 6, 143
  readaptation, 130
  semi-administrative, 190
  slow-growing, 6, 81, 93
  socialist, 65
  underdeveloped, 81
  unplanned, 154
  world, 161
  Yugoslav, 1, 4, 6, 34, 35,
    41, 45, 50, 61, 63, 92, 131,
    136, 142, 146, 150, 153,
    181, 190, 193, 199, 202,
    223, 230
Education, 4, 87
Efficiency of investment, 53,
  86, 136
  economic activity, 86, 178,
    231
  utilization of resources, 82,
    89
Electroenergy, 141
  agricultural, 2, 14, 48, 68,
    70, 142, 143, 164, 176,
    200, 229, 236
  capacity, 160

consumer goods, 179
contraction, 154
industrial, 11, 41, 43, 49,
  60, 61, 63, 64, 74, 92, 95,
  97, 103, 115, 141, 155,
  160, 161, 166, 185, 193,
  199, 202, 233
lot, 1, 3, 4
machinery, 42
material, 198
potential, 41, 87
profitability, 142
reduction, 61
unfinished, 96, 97, 98, 111
Employment, 80, 81, 82, 83,
  86, 87, 88
Enterprise, 86, 92, 96, 113,
  114, 116, 130
industrial, 141
Expenditures, 4
  government, 152
  investment, 11
Exports, 9, 11, 81, 133, 149,
  152, 153, 154, 155, 160, 161,
  162, 165, 166, 167, 180, 183,
  200, 220, 221, 233, 236
  agricultural, 165
  expansion, 165, 221
  industrial, 103, 155, 161,
    164, 166, 176, 210, 220,
    221, 233, 236
  invisible, 164

Feedback, 13
Financial instruments, 154
Financial measures, 167
Fixed capital, 83, 86, 114
Fluctuations, 1, 22, 40, 41, 93
  agricultural, 70
  construction, 229
  cyclical, 7, 13, 20, 23, 24,

30, 34, 43, 80, 236
  economic, 2, 4, 7, 24, 41,
    43, 73, 78, 129, 152, 160,
    172, 184, 193, 197, 199,
    203, 227
  exports, 152
  hypertrophied, 198
  imports, 152
  industrial, 70, 127, 198, 210,
    219, 230, 232, 236
  inventories, 230
    industrial, 127
  periodic, 9, 41
  prices, 70
  producers' prices, 149
  residual, 41
  seasonal, 220
  world market, 160, 200
Forecast, 33, 143
Forecasting, 185, 203, 211
  current, 34
  turning of cycle, 184
  upswing, 11, 33
Foreign exchange, 160
Foreign market, 118, 153, 155
Foreign trade, 81, 152, 164,
  168, 181, 232
Foreign trade regulations, 164
  balance, 72
Forestry, 2
Funds, 179
  common consumption, 127

Illiquidity, 117, 118, 129, 131,
  134, 185
Imports, 9, 11, 70, 81, 89, 97,
  102, 106, 111, 149, 152, 153,
  154, 160, 161, 164, 166, 167,
  233
  agricultural, 165, 180
  elasticity, 102

industrial, 103, 155, 160, 161, 180
intermediate goods, 166, 233
raw materials, 166
Income, 2, 26, 87, 143, 152, 161, 178
distribution, 186, 187
economic organizations, 181, 183
net, 180
personal, 10, 87, 90, 138, 140, 143, 147, 150, 180, 182, 231, 235
nominal, 143, 232
social, 152
total, 180
Indebtedness, 129, 130
economy, 129
Indices, 35, 45, 52
agricultural production, 71
chain, 34, 35, 45, 47, 116, 119, 126, 127, 137, 146, 193, 196, 215, 228, 235
employment, 86
exports, 154, 233
foreign trade, 161, 233
fluctuation, 198
growth, 144, 146
imports, 154, 233
income excess, 144, 146, 148
industrial, 23, 44, 145, 155, 180, 187
moving averages, 45
nonagricultural production, 2
prices, 138, 143, 147, 232
producers', 145, 146
retail, 119
wholesale, 4

production, 86, 145
productivity of labor, 86
quarterly, 41, 44, 45, 119
social product, 126, 147, 199
total personal income, 147
turning points, 61
Industrialization, 86
Industrial trade, 165
rate of growth, 189
stability, 198
Industry, 2, 34, 63, 64, 82, 94, 102, 103, 106, 108, 116, 117, 119, 126, 127, 136, 143, 146, 177, 187, 220, 228
basic, 179, 180, 235
durable goods, 97
food processing and tobacco, 70
leather, 70
processing, 180, 235
textile
Inflation, 138, 139, 149, 179, 186
prices, 133
Inflection, 22, 39
Instability, 93, 127, 229
economy, 16, 19, 53, 64, 75, 93, 97, 102, 155, 171, 182, 183, 193, 198, 230, 236
inherent, 17, 24, 27
machinery production, 64
market, 182
material, 229
Institutional factors, 26, 64
Interest rates, 89, 93, 179
Intermediate goods, 103, 106, 110, 113, 154, 167
International division of labor, 87,
trade, 181
Interpolation, 32, 211

Intersectoral links, 130
Intervention, 142
Intracycle of inventories, 102
Inventories, 17, 19, 25, 86, 91,
  92, 93, 96, 98, 102, 103, 106,
  107, 110, 112, 113, 114, 115,
  117, 119, 142, 150, 152, 186,
  225, 230, 234
  accumulation, 3, 10, 93, 94,
    113, 119, 230
  actual, 18
  average, 92
  decumulation, 10, 94, 113,
    114, 117, 230
  final products, 96, 98, 103,
    117
  fluctuations, 93, 115, 119,
    231
  industrial, 92, 96, 98, 110,
    115
  intermediate goods, 96, 98,
    102, 106, 107, 110, 112
  materials, 103
  nonagricultural, 96, 107
  planned, 18
  trade, 107, 110
  unfinished products, 110
Investment, 12, 17, 25, 26, 41,
  61, 63, 95, 114, 116, 148, 149,
  152, 153, 160, 179, 185, 220,
  229, 230, 236
  agricultural, 179
  buildings, 61
  communal, 4
  consumer goods industries,
    179
  economic, 230
  fixed capital, 41, 51, 179,
    182, 230
  industrial, 220, 221, 236
  initial, 83

inventories, 94, 114, 230
  transportation, 179
  uncompleted, 114
Investment balances, 87
  expenditures, 184
  funds, 178
  potential, 160
  programs, 89, 170
Investment funds, 83, 89, 115
Investment goods, 154

Labor force, 81, 83, 86, 88, 89
  marginal, 88
  reserve, 81
Lag, 26, 33, 86, 112, 139, 150,
  160, 165
Linear oscillator, 23, 25
Liquidity, 129, 134, 144, 184,
  233
Livestock raising, 13
Loans, 164, 181
  foreign, 181, 234
Losses, 3, 6, 141
  Yugoslav economy, 6, 60

Machinery production, 61
Market, 17, 70, 95, 97, 106,
  110, 115, 139, 142, 149
  capitalist, 193
  foreign, 153, 183
  internal, 131, 164, 233
  international, 81, 153, 160
  Yugoslav, 160
Market relations, 138, 141, 181
Means of payment, 134
Money, 129, 131, 136, 183
  deposits, 127
  emissions, 131, 133
  restrictions, 134, 142
  supply, 131, 132, 133
  turnover, 131, 134

Movements
  economic, 216
  harmonic, 206, 216
  oscillatory, 40
  periodic — see Fluctuations
  potential, 2
  short-run, 155
  sine curve, 23
  vibratory, 41

National Bank, 117, 119, 134,
  142, 171, 185
NBER technique, 32, 34
Noninvestment goods, 152

Oscillations, 19, 25, 26, 31, 35,
  39, 40, 67, 208, 220
  construction, 49
  IFC production, 49
  social product, 19

Peaks of cycles, 6, 10, 26, 33,
  39, 40, 67, 83, 86, 103, 107,
  161, 210, 215, 228
  business, 114
  exports, 161
  industrial, 110, 161
  inventories, 98
  production, 110, 233
  productivity of labor, 86
Period, 23, 24, 30, 31, 33, 35,
  215, 217
  administrative, 138
  autoregressive, 208
  fluctuations, 19, 210, 216,
  220
  inflationary, 138
  planning, 17
  oscillation, 19, 217, 220
Periodogram, 206, 210, 211,
  215

Phasal shift, 39, 47, 103, 139,
  233
Phase of cycles, 22, 25, 31, 33,
  34, 35, 38, 39
  accelerative, 38, 44, 45, 46,
    48, 114, 115, 136, 225, 230,
    231
  contractive, 40, 45
  depression, 189
  descending, 44, 93, 94
  expansive, 10, 40, 45, 46,
    134
  production, 233
  prosperity, 9
  recession, 231
  retardation, 38, 40, 45, 48,
    117, 136, 160, 161, 179,
    224, 231, 234
  revival, 189, 202
  upswing, 93, 94
Plan, 43, 89
  achievement, 43
  annual, 180
  five-year, 44, 176, 179, 187,
    235
  industrial production, 43
Planning, 34, 43, 44, 198
  administrative-centralized,
    46, 92, 193, 196, 198
  consumption, 20
  global proportions, 178
Points
  downward phase, 40
  economic equilibrium, 39
  inflection, 24, 39, 40
  reference, 33
Policy
  agrarian, 86
  anticyclical, 234
  business, 89
  deflation, 183

economic, 1, 27, 34, 43, 69,
80, 89, 115, 150, 153, 161,
167, 168, 177, 179, 180,
183, 184, 190, 193, 203,
223, 224, 232, 234
export, 168
fiscal, 150
investment, 61, 89
monetary-credit, 127, 134,
150, 182, 185, 235
price, 140, 142
Price Control Bureau, 139, 141
Prices, 3, 9, 13, 89, 118, 119,
129, 131, 132, 133, 136, 138,
139, 140, 141, 142, 147, 168,
231, 232, 233
agricultural, 136, 138, 142,
180
constant, 2, 41, 126, 148
control, 133, 141, 179, 183,
235
current, 184
foreign exchange, 161
industrial, 136, 138, 139,
140, 147, 180
producers', 138, 144, 145,
146, 148, 234
retail, 11, 142, 147, 149,
232
stability, 80, 140
wholesale, 11
Producers, 25, 105, 110, 113,
114, 138, 143
Product
agricultural, 154
industrial, 147, 154
nominal, 133
Production, 1, 2, 4, 6, 7, 25,
41, 60, 64, 73, 80, 81, 86, 89,
91, 95, 97, 98, 103, 107, 110,
112, 114, 117, 126, 130, 131,

133, 138, 144, 153, 166,
177, 187
social, 17, 81, 119
Production chain, 89
Production sector, 92
decision, 13
structure, 161, 166
Productivity
absolute, 81
general social, 88
industry, 89
labor, 80, 81, 82, 83, 86,
136, 139, 143, 145, 149,
150, 178, 181, 185, 232,
233
Profit, 86
Profitability, 140

Rate of exchange, 183
Raw materials, 70
Recession, 38, 40, 47, 94, 110,
114, 117, 130, 134, 142, 189,
202
industrial, 79
Reference cycle, 32
Reform, 3, 40, 126, 130, 134,
138, 144, 146, 150, 164, 180,
181, 200, 223, 224, 225
economic, 182, 186, 187,
190, 235
foreign trade, 164
investment, 186
social, 202
Reproduction materials, 11
coal, 141
current, 95
durable consumer goods, 11
durable producers' goods,
11
flows, 160
IFC, 41, 49

rate, 89
    retardation, 115
    stopping, 95
    structure, 154
Reproductive models, 17
Reserves, 89
    foreign exchange, 152, 181
    internal, 80
    unutilized, 89
Retardation, 27, 44, 46, 95,
    116, 177, 179, 186
    exports, 161, 221, 232
    imports, 155, 232
    production, 47, 64, 69, 79,
        86, 88, 116, 117, 230, 233
Revaluation, 135

Sales, 113, 127, 143
    actual, 18
    expected, 25
    planned, 18
Saving, 152, 153
    rates, 178, 180
Science, 4
Self-management, 64, 87
Serial correlation, 206
Series, 2, 30, 34
    economic, 10, 12, 33
    industrial production, 34
    reference, 34
    social product, 34, 41
    statistical, 9, 30, 41
    time, 32, 200
Services, 11, 198
Servomechanism, 23, 26
Shocks
    exogenous, 25
    stochastic, 24
Simulation, 27
Slutsky effect, 31
Social Accounting Service, 119

Social product, 2, 3, 10, 11, 18,
    19, 24, 60, 61, 74, 82, 91, 92,
    93, 94, 95, 103, 107, 114, 126,
    132, 142, 183, 186, 187, 193,
    198, 199, 200, 201, 204, 225,
    229, 236
    collective agriculture, 91
    industry, 70, 91
    lost, 3
    planned, 18
    potential, 3
    Yugoslav, 48
Stabilization, 11
    economy, 11, 34
    market, 179
Standard of living, 89
Stimulation, 88
Subcycle, 46
Subsidies, 86, 140, 183
Supply, 12, 13, 91, 93, 112, 115,
    149, 179, 183, 231, 232
Systems, 20, 25, 26
    economic, 20, 91, 178, 180,
        186, 187
    financial, 127
    institutional, 139, 142

Tariffs, 181
Taxes, 89, 92, 130, 138, 146,
    185
Transportation, 91
Troughs of cycles, 9, 12, 33,
    40, 83, 98, 127, 136, 182, 215,
    224, 228, 234
    index of divergence, 160
    initial, 33
    final, 33
Turning of cycle, 7, 161
Turning points of cycles, 22,
    33, 40, 61, 113, 117, 143, 162,
    228

chain indices, 47
developed regions, 78
exports, 162
imports, 162
industry, 63, 78, 110, 162, 230
inventories, 99, 102, 110
lower, 40, 117, 118, 225, 236
machinery production, 63, 230
production, 99, 102, 110
underdeveloped regions, 78

upper, 40, 118

Unemployment, 10
Upswing, 86, 165, 189, 190
Urbanization, 89

Variance, 207

Wages, 8, 86
Workers' councils, 89

Yellow Book, 80